The Southern Italian Table

Arthur Schwartz

The Southern Italian Table

Photographs by ALAN RICHARDSON

CLARKSON POTTER / PUBLISHERS
NEW YORK

For Cecilia Baratta, Baronessa Bellelli

Copyright © 2009 by Arthur Schwartz
Photographs copyright © 2008 by Alan Richardson

Published in the United States by Clarkson Potter/Publishers,
an imprint of the Crown Publishing Group, a division of Random House, Inc., New York.
www.crownpublishing.com
www.clarksonpotter.com

CLARKSON POTTER is a trademark and POTTER with
colophon is a registered trademark of Random House, Inc.

Library of Congress Cataloging-in-Publication Data is available upon request.

ISBN 978-0-307-38134-7

Printed in China

Design by Rita Sowins / Sowins Design

10 9 8 7 6 5 4 3 2 1

First Edition

Introduction ... 7

Antipasti Appetizers and Snacks ... 19

Insalate Salads ... 53

Minestra e Zuppe Soups ... 71

Sugo e Ragù Tomato Sauces and Ragù ... 83

Pasta and Risotto ... 97

Formaggio e Uova Cheese and Eggs ... 141

Pesce e Frutti di Mare Fish and Shellfish ... 153

Carne e Pollo Meat and Chicken ... 169

Verdure Vegetables and Side Dishes ... 195

Dolci Sweets ... 225

Acknowledgments ... 251

Index ... 252

My affinity for Southern Italy comes naturally, even though my name is Schwartz. I grew up among Italian Americans in Brooklyn, New York, where, starting in the early 1920s, mostly Jewish, Irish, and Southern Italian immigrants moved from the tenement slums of Manhattan to working-class and middle-class homes and apartments in the city's "outer" boroughs. I was weaned on ziti with ragù by our Neapolitan downstairs neighbors. You might say I was a second-generation Italian-American adoptee. My father also grew up in a two-family house in Brooklyn with a Southern Italian family downstairs. When we visited my grandparents in his childhood home on Sundays, their house was filled with the aroma of Anna Nicotra's "Sunday gravy" and the perfume of her husband Jerry's (Gennaro's) wine in the basement.

It may have been the food of my neighbors that first drew me to the south of Italy, especially to Naples, but I also loved that south of Rome the country often felt like the prewar Europe that was quickly becoming Americanized. You've got to do something between meals, and the south turns out to have more art, beautiful architecture, and important archaeological ruins—gorgeous stuff to see, inspire, and enlighten—than one could absorb in a lifetime.

Southern Italy is a land of drama and contradictions. It has great expanses of unspoiled physical beauty, arid stretches and heroically fertile ones. It has urban slums and hundreds of miles of white sandy beaches. Its people are earthy, often farmers or others who depend on the land for their living, but just as frequently they have advanced educations and live professional, middle-class lives in neat homes and apartments where the kitchen is still the center of life and the table is where everyone meets, even when dressed in Armani and Prada.

There are hillsides and valleys checkerboarded with the matte gray of olive trees and the shiny deep green of citrus. There are high mountains covered with evergreens and deciduous trees that turn red and gold in the fall. On the forest floors grow an amazing number of mushrooms. There are cliffs that end in the sea, cities whose streets are lined with palm trees, ancient hill towns that nearly make you cry with their decrepit beauty, and modern towns built with the lack of zoning and poor construction that new money, old corruption, and the notorious criminals of Southern Italy amply provide.

Travel posters used to call it "Sunny Italy." Italians call it the *Mezzogiorno*, literally meaning "midday," referring to the plentiful, sometimes relentless sun. It is also known as the *Meridionale*. The stereotype of the people—by Northern Italians, other Europeans, and non-Italians in places around the world where Southern Italians have emigrated—is that they are shiftless and carefree, dancing tarantellas under the moonlight, singing love ballads, playing the mandolin on the backs of donkeys. They shout. They argue. They are vulgar. They connive. They are hard-headed, dark-skinned, and dark-eyed.

What you may not hear is that Southern Italians are warm-hearted, welcoming and generous, loyal and kind, with a deep sense of humanity and the conviction that we're all in this together, rich and poor, educated and not. In Southern Italy it is easy to make friends. I had no trouble wheedling my way into other people's lives and kitchens, to peek into their pots and be invited to eat at their tables with their friends and family, which is what food journalists like to do best.

Southern Italians are so proud that the Greeks arrived near Naples as early as 800 BCE, bringing an advanced civilization, that there is a joke about it: "When northerners were still painting themselves blue and hanging from the trees, we were already gay."

The Greeks came to trade with the Iron Age Etruscans, locals whose settlements came as far south as where Naples is today. There were other native Italic peoples on the southern half of the peninsula, too. The Samnites and Oscans were in Campania and Molise. The Brutti and Lucanians were in what is now Basilicata. The Daunii inhabited what is now southern Molise and northern Puglia, and the Messapii were in southern Puglia, in what is now called the Salento Peninsula. Finally, Sicily had the Siculi.

But the Greeks soon had settlements almost everywhere and Hellenized the local populations. Southern Italy became *Magna Grecia*, "Greater Greece." The Greeks built many cities, from Naples down through Calabria, into Puglia, and of course in Sicily, the largest island in the Mediterranean, which was sought after then for its fertile soil, as well as its strategic position. The nearly landlocked and mountainous Basilicata was the only place on which the Greeks did not exert a grip.

Many of the Greeks' temples and the remnants of their cities are still standing, a testament to their astounding construction talents. Among them are three fifth- and sixth-century BCE Doric examples in Paestum, looking very grand along a modern local byway called Via Magna Grecia, on the plain of the Sele River, just south of Salerno and the Amalfi Coast, about a mile down the road from where, for the last decade, I have been conducting cooking classes and culinary-cultural tours with Baronessa Cecilia Bellelli Baratta. Our home base and our kitchen classroom are on her two farms, Azienda Seliano and Masseria Eliseo, which she operates with her two sons, Ettore and Massimino Bellelli. On one, Eliseo, the Bellelli family raise water buffalo, the largest herd in the province of Salerno (about 900 head), while on the other, Seliano, they grow grain and grasses for the buffalo to eat and have guest rooms appointed with vintage furniture, a swimming pool in a garden, and a huge dining room and giant gazebo where guests dine. A staff of local women prepares the guests' meals and caters large parties—weddings, christenings, first communions, and the like. You will meet all my Seliano kitchen friends in this book. I have been cooking with them for twelve years and they have taught me much.

Cecilia is the organizer of our school and the excursions we are always changing, while I am in the kitchen with the students and their tour guide outside it. But Cecilia is a very good cook and her recipes are here, too. And did I mention that she is a walking encyclopedia of Italian food-ways and food products, northern and southern, and that she is fluent in English and French? She has made Azienda Seliano so comfortable, elegant—and quirky!—that it is listed in many guidebooks, including *1,000 Places to Visit Before You Die*.

Together with my spouse, Bob Harned, an archaeologist, and our friend Nicolas Claes, who is Belgian but has been living in his own apartment at Seliano for eighteen years, and frequently Iris Carulli, my former personal assistant, an art historian, and guide who now lives in Rome, and is one of the best cooks I know, I have traveled to every province of every southern region: Campania, Molise, Basilicata, Calabria, Puglia, and Sicily. Most of the recipes in this book have been collected on these trips, then developed and tested with American ingredients in my small apartment kitchen in New York City.

It wasn't until Mussolini drained the swamps of Paestum in the
1920s that the land emerged as the rich vegetable- and fruit-growing zone that it is now, well irrigated by a modern system.

I use Paestum as an example of how, over the millennia, the landscape and the fertility of Southern Italy's soil, for better and for worse, have changed dramatically. Given its strategic situation as the largest land mass in the Mediterranean Sea, the south has always fallen prey to foreign conquests. After the Greeks, the Romans controlled all of Southern Italy. After the fall of Rome, there were invaders from the north, called barbarians by the already high-culture Greco-Roman Italians: the Vandals, the Visigoths, the Ostrogoths, the Lombards, and the Huns. In Sicily, there were the Carthaginians from North Africa. There were Moors from North Africa, called Saracens in Italy. Then there were the Spanish, the French, the Austrians, the French again, the Austrians again, the Spanish again, and finally the powers of Northern Italy, not to mention constant interference by the Roman Catholic popes. They all had their way with the land, the economy, the people—usually abusing all of the above, like renters who don't care about the landlord's property.

In fact, Southern Italy has been abused by so many conquerors and occupiers that, as far as the people are concerned, the rule of law is often a rule to be broken or ignored. There's an old Neapolitan saying: "*O Francia, O Spagna, purche si magna.*" Very roughly translated that means "It doesn't matter who rules us, as long as we get lunch." This culture of lawlessness even extends to menu planning. The same dish can fit into various places in the meal; for example, sautéed clams can be an antipasto, a main dish, or a sauce for pasta. Pasta can be a first course or an only course.

Frequent earthquakes and threatening volcanoes have also shaped the culture and the cuisine. Volcanic soil produces great ingredients. Some of Italy's best fruit- and vegetable-growing areas are around Mount Vesuvius near Naples and Mount Etna on Sicily. San Marzano tomatoes grow around Vesuvius. The famous pistachios of Bronte grown near Etna, as well as great oranges, almonds, and tomatoes.

Living on the edge of a volcano or a seismic fault line also gives Southern Italians a certain fatalism that translates into enjoying each day to its fullest. Naturally, that includes singing, dancing, making love, and appreciating good food and drink while actually not spending that much time in the kitchen. The Southern Italian table is simple, direct, and healthful, each dish prepared with just a few prime ingredients and laden with dishes that can be prepared quickly. What could be more contemporary?

It wouldn't be surprising if the old proverb "Necessity is the mother of invention" was coined in Southern Italy. *La cucina povera*, the food of the impoverished Italian peasant, features dishes with few ingredients used in extremely creative ways, and from this historically poor land come some of the most ingenious and popular foods in the world, including pizza, macaroni, spaghetti, tomato sauce, meatballs, and mozzarella. The food of Southern Italy is still today "the Italian food the whole world knows as Italian," in the words of the late, venerated food writer Waverly Root.

The food of Southern Italy started to become popular internationally in the late 1800s. Within twenty years of the unification of Italy in 1861, when it seemed hopeless to make a good life in the south, the Napolitani, Molisani, Pugliesi, Lucani, Calabresi, and Siciliani tried to escape their miserable poverty by emigrating to Northern Italy, northern Europe, and in great numbers to the English-speaking countries that were seducing immigrants—America, Australia, and Canada. Wherever they went, they opened groceries, pizzerias, bakeries, and restaurants, like the ones in old Hollywood movies, with red-checkered tablecloths and straw-covered wine bottles hanging from the ceiling.

Southern Italian food was pretty much the only Italian food outside of Italy until sometime in the mid-1970s, when so-called Northern Italian food was introduced by restaurants in the big cities of the United States, then London, Toronto, and Australia. However, most of those supposedly Northern Italian menus were cooked by chefs from the south, or the poor central region of Abruzzo, famous for its cooks. All they did was add pasta dishes with butter and cream—fettuccine Alfredo!—and served, instead of veal Parmesan, veal Valdostana, chops stuffed with fontina and ham. Suddenly, macaroni gave way to egg pasta in restaurants.

Then, in the 1990s, the world became aware of the Mediterranean diet, which is heavy in complex carbohydrates, with olive oil as its main fat. The diet was conceived by Missouri-born Ansel Keyes, an expatriate living in the tiny seaside town of Ascea, in the province of Salerno, in southern Campania near the border of Basilicata, where people often live to be more than 100 years old on a diet of pasta, beans, vegetables, small blue-fleshed fish such as sardines and anchovies, and olive oil. Other main protein sources there are eggs and cheese, but very little meat. The International Olive Oil Council learned of Keyes's work, and promoted olive oil as the healthiest fat in the world.

Until thirty years ago, however, much of Southern Italy lived on pork fat, rendered into lard or not. Good olive oil was too expensive for the poor people who produced it. Pork fat, in the form of cured bacon, *pancetta,* and rendered lard, usually called *sugna* in the south, is still used in cooking, but more parsimoniously than it used to be. Still, when you want something to have the same taste and texture that your Calabrian or Neapolitan great-grandma achieved, you have to use the pork fat she did.

Olive oil of both the absolute best and poorest quality is now produced in every region of the south. Puglia, in fact, produces more olive oil than any other region of Italy. The best Pugliese oil has a mild, buttery but very fruity flavor, usually without a strong peppery kick. The worst Pugliese oil is used to lubricate machinery, to make soap and hair products. Like that.

To an amazing extent, Southern Italian cooking is Old World cuisine based on New World ingredients. With influences from the ancient Greeks and Romans, North Africans, the French,

Local cheeses in the market of Siracusa, Sicily.

the Austrians, and the Spanish, much of Southern Italy's cooking is based on produce that comes originally from Mexico and Central and South America. Tomatoes; potatoes; peppers of every kind, color, heat, and sweetness; squash, both hard-shell winter ones and soft-skinned summer ones; corn; chocolate; vanilla; and all beans are from the New World, except for chick-peas, fava beans, and lentils, which are so Old World that they are mentioned in the Bible.

None of these foods existed in Europe until the Spanish brought them back from Mexico and other conquests in the sixteenth century. In the 1520s, Cortés's party returned to Spain from Mexico around the same time as Spain gained control of Southern Italy, the Kingdom of Naples, eventually called the Kingdom of the Two Sicilies.

Originally used by Europeans as ornamental plants, tomatoes didn't catch on as something to eat until the eighteenth century, even though Cortés's party had returned with observations about the mixture of diced raw tomato, onion, chile peppers, and coriander leaves eaten by Mexicans, now known as *pico di gallo*.

Neapolitans love to boast that they were probably the first Europeans to eat tomatoes. The plants thrived in the volcanic soil around Mount Vesuvius, and in and around what are now the towns of San Marzano, Sant' Antonio Abate, and Sarno. Today it's accepted that the incom-parable flavor and acid-sugar balance of these tomatoes is due to that particular soil and climate. Take the seeds and put them in the ground anywhere else and they won't be nearly so special.

Even before tomatoes became an important crop in Southern Italy, the potato was a suste-nance food all over Europe, especially in mountainous areas, where they grow so well. (The potato hailed originally from the high Andes Mountains.) Today, the potatoes from the Sila Grande peaks in Calabria, and those from the hills of Avellino, east of Naples, and from the Cilento, south of Naples, are famously delicious.

About the same time as potatoes, sweet and hot peppers made their way into the Southern Italian kitchen. Soon hot red pepper, whose plants could be grown in a pot on the windowsill,

Calabrians' beloved hot pepper pastes are sold under various suggestive names.

replaced black pepper, which came from Asia through the Austrian port of Trieste, and was therefore much more expensive than something you could grow yourself.

All types of squash are native to the New World, although ironically the American word *zucchini* is Italian, meaning "little squash." They got the vegetable from us, but we got the name from them. Winter squash, such as Hubbard and butternut, and what we call pumpkin and Latinos call *calabaza,* is all *zucca* in Italian. In Southern Italy, squash is used for everything from pickles to dessert.

Beans from the New World, such as cannellini; ruby-mottled *borlotti,* which we call "cranberry beans"; and red beans, *messicani,* meaning "Mexicans," used to be a main source of protein in the poor Southern Italian diet. Today, sophisticated Italians consider pasta and beans part of their patrimony. You might call it Southern Italian soul food.

Corn, originally from Mexico, is also a popular food in Southern Italy. In Naples, it is sold roasted on the cob on the street. Polenta is made mainly in mountainous places where the winters call for such hearty food. In the Cilento and in Basilicata and Calabria, polenta is often seasoned with hot peppers and served in grilled slices.

Need it be said that chocolate and vanilla, both originally from the jungles of South America, are ubiquitous dessert flavors in Southern Italy? And in Sicily, where the Spanish brought cocoa beans and processed them as they had learned from the Aztecs, they even use chocolate in savory dishes, such as Enna's Ground Pork Ragù (page 95).

Garlic is not at all New World. It is mentioned in the Bible. But it is among the chief seasoning ingredients in Southern Italy, used with varying degrees of regularity and abandon in all the southern regions. Neapolitans like to kid themselves that they don't use it as aggressively as, say, the Calabrians, who make prolific use of it. But even Neapolitans, who may well throw out the garlic after it is sautéed in olive oil and given a whiff of itself to the oil, will dress vegetables with raw garlic.

Parsley is a flavor in Southern Italy, not just a garnish, so flat leaves of Italian parsley are often used whole or merely torn into pieces, not chopped, allowing you to taste the herb more. The finer you chop a tender herb such as parsley, the more flavor and aroma you lose. For the same reason, basil is also often used just torn into pieces, or as whole leaves. In general, both are best added at the end of cooking to retain the utmost flavor. Occasionally they are cooked into a dish, usually sautéed in combination with other chopped seasoning ingredients to create a flavor base for a soup, sauce, or stew—a *sofritto* in Italian, which literally means "under fried."

Cooking is so seasonal in Southern Italy that you won't find basil in the market during the winter, but dried oregano can be used all year, obviously. In fact, oregano is never used fresh. Rosemary is the herb most commonly used with chicken and lamb. It also often goes into chickpeas and pasta, other bean dishes, and with sweet winter squash. Sage is also used with chicken, and with beans, but not as much as it is in Central Italy, particularly Tuscany. Italians in general do not put more than one or two herbs in the same dish. They prefer to taste each flavor individually.

Pasta is certainly among the most important foods in Southern Italy, although bread is also a staff of life. Hard, high-protein winter wheat—durum wheat—is grown in Puglia, on Basilicata's border with Puglia, and in the center of Sicily, in the provinces of Enna and Caltanissetta. Italians eat so much pasta and bread, however, that they still must import wheat. The flour of durum wheat is called *semolina* (*semola* when it is not as finely milled), and in the United States today we can buy the absolute best domestic and imported Italian semolina pasta products, from the most industrial to the handmade.

✳ *The Regions* ✳

Italy is divided into twenty regions, much in the way the United States is divided into fifty states. Each region is then divided into provinces, as our states have counties. There are five regions that definitely constitute Southern Italy. Starting from just south of Lazio, the region of Rome, which most Italians would consider the beginning of the south, there's Campania, the region of Naples, Capri, and the Amalfi Coast; Puglia, the region that is the heel and the back of the ankle of the Italian boot; tiny Basilicata, whose people are called Lucanians, after an ancient name for the region, Lucania; Calabria, the foot that kicks Sicily, as some like to say (mainly Calabrians); and Sicily, the largest island in the Mediterranean. Molise, which is on the Adriatic coast and adjacent to Lazio on its west, and to Campania and Puglia on its southern border, is sometimes considered to be Central Italy.

But, at least where food is concerned, Molise has more in common with Puglia and Campania than it does with any other neighboring region, although it was, until 1963, politically lumped together with Abruzzo. Like its neighbor to the north, however, it is sheepherding country. The *transumanza,* the annual migration of sheep from the high ground of Abruzzo to the plain of Puglia, went straight through Molise. Remnants of it are still visible in the *tratturi,* the sheep paths that cut through now otherwise overgrown terrain.

Contributing to its Southern-ness, Molise makes its cheeses using the distinctive Southern Italian process of heating the curd, then stretching it. One of its most particular products is strascinata, a form of mozzarella that is worked in such a way that the cheese breaks into layers. These cheeses—mozzarella, whether made from cow's milk or water buffalo milk, scamorza, provola, caciocavallo, and provolone—are major products and ingredients of Southern Italy. Sheep's milk cheeses are also important, although they are made with a different process.

Molise is still a mostly poor region, without great stretches of agricultural land and with many mountains. Because most of it is undeveloped, although its prosperous coastal city Termoli is very developed and has white sandy resort beaches, its food retains more elements of *la cucina povera,* the poor food of the past. Lamb and full-grown sheep are still the main meat sources. Preserving vegetables "under oil," *sott'olio,* and "under vinegar," *sott'aceto,* is still a much-practiced home art. An antipasto in Molise is sure to feature preserved vegetables.

Campania and Sicily are certainly the most traveled regions of the south. Besides the attraction of Naples, *Bella Napoli,* the third-largest city in Italy and a hotbed of artistic and musical creation, Campania is rich in Greek and Roman archeological sites: Pompeii and Herculaneum, Paestum, and the rich Roman villas of Boscoreale, Stabia, and Oplontis, to name just a few. Of course, the great resorts of Capri and the Amalfi Coast draw tourists from all over the world, and the health spas of Ischia are another enticement. Americans know Neapolitan food the best, too. Pizza was born in Naples, as was spaghetti with tomato sauce. The Campanian diet is based on pasta, vegetables, beans, and fish, with more eggs and cheese than meat or poultry for land-based protein. The two large sea-level plains that flank Naples are where the water buffalo are raised for *mozzarella di bufala,* a cheese that is in high demand all over the world today.

Sicily has become a great tourist destination in the last twenty years, too. It is a fascinating place, seeming like a continent unto itself, with very different culture and food from one

Clockwise from top left: Baronessa Cecilia in her kitchen in Battipaglia; the narrow streets of Siracusa, Sicily; crushing tomatoes; the white beaches of Tropea, Calabria.

end of the large island to the other. The eastern part of the island has Greek influences, and Spanish Baroque, while the west has a North African and Punic (Carthaginian) cast to it. The lusher landscape of the east, from Messina to the southern tip, provides superior citrus fruits and almonds, both of which are used prolifically in savory as well as sweet dishes. The center of the island grows high-quality wheat, perfect for bread and pasta. The west coast is known for its wines, dry white and red table wines, but most famously its Marsala, a fortified wine similar to sherry. Couscous, which is technically a type of semolina pasta, is made up and down the west coast of Sicily, where a large Tunisian immigrant population—fishermen—has made it more popular than ever.

Basilicata has always been the least traveled of the southern regions. Its mountains have, until very recently, been too daunting to traverse. Today, however, astoundingly high bridge-roads connect mountains and make travel and communication easier. The secret about Basilicata is that, although it was once one of the poorest of Italy's twenty regions, it is now relatively rich. When the European Union started plowing money into the economic development of Southern Italy, instead of the money going into the pockets of crooked politicians and organized crime, as it did too often in Campania and Sicily, in Basilicata it actually went to economic development. Except along its border with Puglia, which is a high plateau called the Murge, Basilicata is not very agricultural. That border is wheat country, but otherwise the region is too mountainous and dry for crops other than grapes and olives, or livestock other than goats and white Podolico cattle, an old breed whose cheese is highly prized. The high Pollino mountains do, however, pro-

Left to right: Maratea, in Basilicata, at night; the Bay of Naples and Mount Vesuvius.

vide a very special pepper: Senise peppers are long, sweet horns that are harvested red and then dried on strings. In Basilicata, you see them hanging outside homes and stores. These peppers are flash-fried and eaten crisp, which gives them the dialect name *crushki*. They are now sold as a snack item, like potato chips, but mostly they are eaten as an antipasto or, in contemporary restaurant kitchens, used to garnish almost anything.

Calabrians are famous all over Italy for their devotion to hot red pepper, peperoncino, and garlic. The stereotype is that they are hardheaded and eat hearty. However, Calabria has a gastronomic secret: It is full of mushrooms. Along the roadsides in the Sila mountains, forager-vendors set up their harvest on makeshift tables. The most common are finferli (the name is derived from a German word for chanterelle), but there are tons of porcini and many others. Other special foods and crops include tuna, which comes in cans to the U.S., oil-cured black olives, Tropea's sweet red onions, Rossano's licorice, Pizzo's gelato, and Santa Maria del Cedro's citrons, which, of course, make their way into many desserts and soda, but are also harvested for Jews in America, who use them ritually on Succoth.

Calabria is still a region that few travel, except other Italians. But it has an amazingly diverse and beautiful landscape, including high mountains where you can escape the heat of summer or ski in winter; white sandy beaches across from new, comfortable but simple hotels and condominium developments; and several cities worth exploring. Crotone and nearby Squillace have Greek ruins. One day, it looks like Calabria will be the Florida of Italy. It is still so inexpensive to live here that it attracts many retirees.

Puglia stands out as perhaps the most advanced and organized of the Southern Italian regions. The Pugliese do indeed have the reputation of being precise and cooperative with each other, in a way that other southerners somehow can't manage. The region has a very long coastline, which is why it is sometimes called the California of Italy, and quite varied terrain. The southernmost part of the region, the Salento Peninsula, gets the bulk of tourism. It has the quirky *trulli,* the conically shaped farm buildings that are today being turned into beautiful homes and hotels. Many of its formerly large, self-sustaining estates, *masserie* (*masseria* is singular), have been turned into spas, conference centers, and elegant hotels. If you look at the labels of imported Italian food products at home, you'll also see that more come from Puglia than from other southern regions.

Because it has little groundwater, and therefore little possibility of irrigating the land, Puglia's agriculture is based on three crops that actually thrive on dry land: wheat, wine, and olives. The wheat goes to make extraordinary pasta and bread. The wine, now that it is being made with modern techniques and not being sold up north to fortify thinner wines, is gaining international attention, as are the region's table olives and olive oil.

Gastronomically, the regions have more in common than they have differences, but each certainly has a distinctive cuisine, and every little village has distinctive dishes, although they are sometimes only one ingredient different from the next town's. They all took culinary cues from the big city in Campania, Naples, where the food of the nobility filtered down to the middle class during the nineteenth century, and eventually became part of everyday living in the late twentieth century. Differences come as much from differences in geography and climate—hence agriculture—than they do from human culture. You eat what you have, and as the saying goes, what grows together goes together.

Antipasti
Appetizers and Snacks

Antipasti

can be anything from a few slices of salami to the fourteen-course extravaganza that I was once served at a wedding in the Matese Mountains, on the border of Campania and Molise. The first antipasto of that evening was called La Fantasia dello Chef, which means "The Imagination of the Chef." This chef had *some* imagination. His "fantasia" consisted of a dozen showy seafood antipasti, including lobster, crayfish, cuttlefish, and several kinds of shrimp. Then came thirteen more "antipasti."

Technically, we hadn't even started the feast. The word *antipasto* means "before the meal," *pasto* meaning "meal" in Italian. The dish that comes *after* the antipasto, which is most often pasta in the south, is the official beginning of an Italian meal, the *primo*.

At home, before the meal, until the pasta is on the table, Italians may nibble on nothing more than olives or that aforementioned slice of salami. However, in the forty years that I have been traveling in Italy, the antipasto course in Southern Italian restaurants has often become a multidish showcase for local products and specialties. As at that wedding in the Matese Mountains, it sometimes makes any course beyond a *primo* seem unnecessary, irrelevant, impossible.

In contemporary colloquial use, the word *antipasto* is usually used for a dish that you eat at the table, probably with a fork and knife. Italians didn't, until fairly recently, eat many things with their fingers. Now, antipasti are passed around and eaten standing up while wine is served, American style, and in that case they are often called *aperitivi*, the same as the beverage that goes with them.

Antipasti and *aperitivi* can also be called *sfizzi*, which means "whimsies," but is these days also used to mean "snacks." *Sfizzi* could include pizza or deep-fried items (pages 22 to 51), and local specialties such as *Panini Napoletani*, rolled bread dough filled with bits of cured pork sold on the streets of Naples and in New York City pizzerias; *Focaccia di Patate* of Lecce, from Puglia (page 40); and big, stuffed rice balls, *Arancini Siciliani al Ragù* (page 24), sold on nearly every city corner in Sicily.

Because almost any dish in the seafood chapter (page 153) or the vegetable chapter (page 195) can serve as antipasti or *sfizzi*, this chapter presents just the recipes that don't neatly fit those other categories and would only be served "before the meal" or as a snack.

Fritti: Fried Items

No one in Southern Italy seems to be willing to give up deep-fried foods. An array of fried vegetables and fried cheese continues to be a popular, standard appetizer before a pizza, and sometimes as the opening to an elaborate meal in a formal restaurant. *Un fritto misto di verdure*, a mixed vegetable fry, is most Italians' idea of bliss, no matter what region they live in.

In Neapolitan dialect, there's an expression about fried foods: *frijenno magnanno*. It means "frying and eating," conveying the urgency of getting oil-crisped foods into your mouth while they are still crunchy, before surface oil seeps into the center and makes the whole thing soggy. Well-fried foods are not nearly as oil-laden as we imagine because when the oil is at the correctly high temperature, the surface seals instantly and doesn't allow penetration.

On the following pages is a selection of some of the most typical fried items in the vast Southern Italian repertoire.

Olive Fritte
Fried Olives

Crumb-crusted fried green olives have lately become a trendy antipasto in pizzerias all through Southern Italy. Sometimes the olives are stuffed with seasoned meat. If they are, they are called *Olive Ascolane*, referring to Ascoli Piceno, in the Marche region. Empty or tediously stuffed, they are the perfect pickup food for a party. They even maintain their appeal at room temperature, although hot-out-of-the-fryer is always best.

Large pitted, green olives from Sicily and Spain are not hard to find these days. Do not use California-grown canned olives; they don't have enough flavor to make this recipe worthwhile. If all you can buy are good pitted olives with a stuffing—pimiento, almond, or cheese—those work well, too. To some tastes, the additional stuffing will make them even better.

1 egg
¾ cup all-purpose flour
¾ cup fine dry bread crumbs
30 pitted large green olives
Vegetable oil for frying

Break the egg into a small bowl. Beat until well blended.

Place the flour on a plate. Place the bread crumbs on a plate.

Roll the olives first in the flour, then in the egg, and finally in the bread crumbs, making sure they are well coated with crumbs. Place the olives on a large plate as they are breaded. Refrigerate for at least 30 minutes, uncovered, to set the breading.

Pour about ¼ inch of oil into a skillet. Place over high heat. When the oil is hot enough for an olive to sizzle immediately, but not furiously, adjust the heat to medium and fry as many olives as the pan will hold comfortably without crowding it. Fry on all sides until well browned, 2 or 3 minutes. Drain on absorbent paper.

Serve immediately.

Arancini Siciliani al Ragù
Sicilian Rice Balls Filled with Ragù

All over Sicily, but particularly in Palermo, one cannot escape the call of *arancini*. These balls of deep-fried, crumb-crusted rice are displayed and sold everywhere, in every snack shop, pizzeria, and fast-food joint, on what seems like every street in the city. They can be great or awful, but it's hard to tell until you bite in, a good excuse for eating too many. They are usually filled with a ground meat and pea ragù called *arancini al ragù* (see page 93), as in this recipe, but they can also be filled with molten white sauce and cooked ham, with only ham and cheese, or with ham and cheese in white sauce. The euphemism for these is *al burro*, "with butter," even though butter is the least of it, or *al bianco*, meaning "in white" as opposed to with red meat sauce.

5 cups water or light chicken broth

1½ teaspoons salt (if using water)

½ teaspoon saffron thread (0.008-ounce packet)

2 cups (just under 1 pound) arborio or other Italian rice

½ cup grated cheese, preferably well-aged caciocavallo Ragusano, but also pecorino and Parmigiano combined, or all pecorino or all Parmigiano

3 large eggs, separated (yolks for rice, whites for bread-crumb coating)

⅓ recipe Sicilian Ground Meat Ragù with Peas (page 93)

10 to 12 ½-inch cubes young caciocavallo Ragusano cheese (also called *tuma* or *primosale*), young provolone, or mozzarella (optional)

2 cups fine dry bread crumbs

Oil for frying

In a 3-quart saucepan, over high heat, bring the water or broth to a rolling boil. If using water, add the salt. Add the saffron. Simmer for 1 minute. Add the rice. Stir well. When the liquid returns to a simmer, adjust the heat so it simmers briskly for about 18 minutes, until the rice is tender but slightly al dente. The water should be entirely absorbed. Pour the rice into a bowl and let it cool slightly.

Stir the grated cheese and 3 egg yolks into the rice. Using a ½ cup measure, scoop out a scant ½ cup of rice and turn it out onto the palm of your hand. Flatten the rice and place a heaping table-spoon of meat filling in the center of the rice. If desired, place a cube of cheese in the center of the filling. Put another scant ½ cup of rice on top of the filling, then form the rice into a ball. Place the ball on a platter. Make all the rice balls.

In a pie plate or other shallow but rimmed dish, beat the egg whites with a fork until they are foamy. Roll the formed *arancini* in the egg whites, then roll them in the bread crumbs. Refrigerate for at least 30 minutes, uncovered, to let the breading set.

Heat at least 1 inch of oil in a pan that is deep enough to fry the *arancini* half submerged in oil. Remember that once you put several *arancini* in the pan, the oil's depth will increase.

When the oil sizzles on contact with the handle of a wooden spoon, add the *arancini*. They should fry instantly, but not so fast that they will become brown before the center has heated through and the cheese has melted. On a thermometer the oil should be between 350 and 375°F. Drain on absorbent paper.

Serve immediately.

NEONATI

NEWBORN FISH

Newborn fish go by many different names, depending on which region is talking about them. All over the south, they are either *neonati* or *bianchetti*, the most proper Italian names for them. In Campania, however, they may be called *cicianielli*, their Neapolitan dialect name. In Calabria, they are *rosamarina* or *sardella*. In eastern Sicily, they are called *muccu*, and undoubtedly there are even more obscure names for these translucent spawn of anchovies and sardines, one of the great delicacies of Southern Italy.

In Naples and Sicily, you'll find them simply sautéed with garlic and oil, or turned into a batter and fried as *frittelle*, little pancakes or fritters. Both would be served as an antipasto. In Calabria, they are also preserved in hot pepper paste and sold in jars or by the gram at the supermarket delicatessen counter. It's for spreading on *bruschetta* and *crostini*, to season spaghetti or macaroni, or to season a tomato sauce for pasta.

Cecilia's Paestum artichoke hearts "under oil."

Sott'olio e Sott'aceti

OIL-PRESERVED AND PICKLED VEGETABLES

Everywhere in the world, people preserve the bounty of their growing season, if they have any. In Southern Italy, pork is cured with salt to make salamis and hams. The abundance of tomatoes is dried, made into tomato paste, and canned. Fruits are turned into jams and marmalade. And vegetables are often preserved in oil with seasonings, called *sott'olio*, literally "under oil," or boiled in and packed in vinegar, *sott'aceti*, "under vinegar." A plate of these preserved vegetables, humble as it sounds, makes a fine antipasto, and the fixings can be kept on hand for months in the refrigerator. Add some cheese, salami or prosciutto, and a few olives, and you have the classic Southern Italian antipasto.

In the days before there was plenty of food to eat and refrigeration became universal, it was a matter of survival to have preserved vegetables on hand. Today, while preserving foods in seasoned oil or vinegar is no longer a necessity, the taste for them lives on. When you see "Antipasto Molisano" on a menu, it means an array of *sott'aceti* and *sott'olio*. In Naples, the smallest grocery and most meager home pantry is stocked with, at least, marinated eggplant and pickled peppers. In Calabria, whose woods are full of mushrooms, porcini and golden chanterelles go "under oil." The marinated artichoke hearts of Paestum are famous. They're now available on the Internet. Zucchini, winter squash, onions, cauliflower, carrots, green beans, even grape hyacinth bulbs—in Southern Italy, there is hardly a vegetable that is not pickled. And when many pickled vegetables are combined, the mixture is called *giardiniera*.

Everywhere you go in the south, these convenient preserved foods—we can even say convenience foods—appear on the antipasto table. Those who don't preserve any foods, as their grandmothers and great-grandmothers did, still may put up a few jars of something to satisfy their appetites, as well as their southern sensibility. It's a connection to times past. In Italy, the supermarket shelves are lined with them. In the United States, you can find many *sott'olio* and *sott'aceti* on supermarket shelves and specialty food shops.

Panelle
Chickpea Fritters

MAKES ABOUT 36 PERFECT ONES, PLUS SCRAPS;
ENOUGH FOR 6 TO 8

Panelle are rectangles of fried chickpea batter, and they vie with *arancini* as Palermo's most favored street snack. Sicilians eat *panelle* as a sandwich filling on a big roll. To me, *panelle* are too good to be buried in bread. They are perfect as a pickup item to serve with wine and cocktails. With a salad and cheese, they make a very good lunch. You can also serve them as a garnish or side dish to many main courses. In the United States, chefs, following the lead of Jean-Georges Vongerichten, who introduced chickpea sticks at JoJo in New York City more than twenty years ago, have been cutting the firmed batter like thick French fries and selling them as "chickpea fries."

2 cups chickpea flour

3½ cups cold tap water

1 teaspoon salt, plus more for sprinkling

¼ teaspoon freshly ground black pepper

Oil for frying

Salt to taste

Prepare a baking sheet by rinsing off its underside and leaving it wet.

Pour the flour into a 2-quart saucepan. Add the cold tap water, then, with a whisk, blend together until smooth. Stir in the salt and pepper. Place the mixture over medium heat and stir constantly with a wooden spoon or whisk, continuously scraping the bottom and sides of the pot, for 10 to 15 minutes.

Recipe continues

In La Pescheria, Catania, Sicily's outdoor market.

Chickpea Fritters continued . . .

Eventually the mixture will become a thick dough, and you will be able to see the bottom of the pot when the paste is stirred. If the mixture gets lumpy at any time, beat more vigorously with the whisk.

When the dough has formed, immediately scrape the hot mixture onto the back of the moistened baking sheet. An offset spatula is a helpful tool for this; moisten the blade so it won't stick as much. Working quickly, spread the paste out to no more than ¼ inch thick. If the paste gets too difficult to spread with a spatula, place a sheet of plastic wrap over it and gingerly press it out with the palm of your hand. There won't be enough paste to entirely fill the bottom of the pan, but almost. Don't worry about the rough edges. In fact, although they are not as attractive as the neatly cut pieces, their ragged edges and thinness fry up particularly crisp.

Let the paste cool for at least 1 hour, until it is firm.

Cut the sheet of paste into 1 by 3-inch rectangles. (Remember: don't discard those edges.)

In a 9-inch skillet (I prefer black cast-iron), heat about ¾ inch of oil over medium-high heat. When the oil sizzles around the handle of a wooden spoon, the oil is hot enough to fry. The *panelle* should sizzle vigorously when they hit the oil. Fry as many as will fit loosely in the pan. Fry for about 2 minutes on each side. Drain on absorbent paper and sprinkle with salt.

Serve immediately.

OLIVES

Olive trees like to grow in poor soil and need very little water, which is why in the last thirty years large arid stretches of Southern Italy have been planted densely with olive trees. With subsidies and grants, and in the name of economic development, the European Union has encouraged olive oil and table olive production, not only in Italy but also in other southern European countries. Table olives and oil olives are not necessarily one and the same, however, and most areas of Southern Italy specialize in one or the other.

Campania produces some great olive oil, particularly on the slopes of the Cilento and in the province of Avellino, but its basic table olive is from Gaeta, the big port in Lazio, just up the coast from Naples. Until 1861, when Garibaldi finally defeated the Bourbon army in Gaeta (it is sometimes called the kingdom's Alamo), it was, indeed, part of the Kingdom of Naples. Gaeta is not a type of olive, but the place from where they are distributed and shipped. The Gaeta olive is small and green-brown to purple. The ones you see in Italy are usually mottled with both colors. The ones that are sold in the United States are usually dark purple. Besides their vivid flavor, what makes Gaeta such a good cooking olive is that they are freestone, which means they can be pitted very easily. Just squeeze the olive and the pit pops out; well, most of the time. They are used extensively as a condiment or ingredient, seasoning all kinds of dishes from antipasti to main courses.

Sicily's large green, meaty, and mild table olives are a favorite table olive everywhere in Italy. And although Puglia produces more olive oil than any other region in Italy—some of it the highest food quality, some for industrial use—the region also grows one very famous table olive, Cerignola, named for the town where they are grown. Cerignola appear to be the largest table olives in the world, with meaty texture and a very mild flavor. They are now sold in American supermarket delicatessen departments. They have eye-catching colors—deep red, bright green, and dark black—because they are dyed.

Both Calabria and Sicily grow plenty of oil olives, and Sicilian oil is finding good distribution in the United States The oils of the Monti Iblei, in the southeast corner of the island, are particularly fruity without having a strong peppery bite. Both regions also cultivate and process black, oil-cured olives that are used in cooking, as well as at the table. With an oily surface and wrinkled from their drying treatment, they are a flavor connection to North Africa.

Olives are a popular antipasto or *aperitivo,* enhanced or not. To add flavor, let them marinate at least several hours with orange or lemon zest, lightly crushed fennel seeds, minced garlic and/or hot pepper, and enough olive oil to carry the flavors and coat the olives.

Polpette o Palle di Melanzane
Eggplant Balls or Patties

Eggplant balls, one of Southern Italy's most typical fried antipasti, are often made with already fried eggplant and moistened stale bread, but in this lightened version I use boiled eggplant, dry bread to absorb its moisture, and chopped oil-cured black olives for additional flavor, a Calabrian touch. The garlic and mint–flavored tomato sauce, on the other hand, is typical of the Sicilian island of Lipari.

2 pounds eggplant, peeled, cut into quarters or eighths, depending on the size of the eggplant(s)

3 cups cubes of firm bread dough (*mollica;* see page 34)

¼ cup chopped fresh mint

2 garlic cloves, finely minced

12 oil-cured black olives, pitted and coarsely chopped

½ cup grated pecorino cheese

2 large eggs, lightly beaten

1½ teaspoons salt

½ teaspoon freshly ground black pepper

1 cup fine dry bread crumbs

Vegetable oil for frying

3 cups Tomato Sauce (optional; page 86, prepared with mint instead of basil or parsley)

Bring a large pot of water to a rolling boil with a tablespoon of salt. Add the eggplant and let it boil for 12 to 15 minutes, depending on the size of the pieces. They should become soft, but not fall apart.

Drain the eggplant well in a colander. While it's still in the colander, put a plate over the top and then a weight—a large can of tomatoes, for instance. Let it stand to drain until cool enough to handle, about 30 minutes.

Put the cooked and drained eggplant in a large bowl with all of the bread cubes. With your hands, break apart the eggplant and bread and mix them together until they are well amalgamated. Add the remaining ingredients, except the bread crumbs, oil, and optional tomato sauce. Work the mixture together again with your hands.

Put the bread crumbs on a plate in front of you, along with a plate to place the formed balls or patties. With your hands, form balls about the size of walnuts. Either leave them as balls or flatten them slightly to make patties. Dredge each ball or patty thoroughly in bread crumbs to coat well. (The balls or patties can be made ahead to this point. Freeze them on a baking sheet, then pack them into a plastic bag.)

In a medium to large skillet (I prefer black cast-iron), over medium-high heat, heat about ½ inch of oil until the handle of a wooden spoon collects bubbles around it. A thermometer should read 350 to 375°F. Fry the patties, without crowding the pan, for about 2 minutes a side. As soon as the first balls or patties are in the oil and begin frying, lower the heat slightly so they don't brown *too* fast. When they are well browned, remove with a slotted spatula and drain on absorbent paper.

Serve hot, salted without tomato sauce, or unsalted but with tomato sauce.

Crostini di Salsicce
Sausage Canapés

This is Cecilia's invention, combining crumbled pork sausage with rosemary, sage, and a little butter to make a sort of pâté to top baked *crostini*. The pâté gives up some of its fat to the bread that it's baked on, and it makes a divine cocktail snack or, with a salad, a lunch main course. In our Cook at Seliano classes, we always make these on our final day, when we have the wood-burning oven ablaze for baking pizza. The *crostini* are our 11 A.M. *aperitivo*, with a glass of the sparkling, dry red Gragnano wine from the Sorrento coast that is our favorite wine with pizza.

½ pound sweet Italian sausage (with or without fennel), removed from casings

2 teaspoons finely chopped fresh rosemary

2 teaspoons finely chopped fresh sage

2 tablespoons unsalted butter

10 (½-inch-thick) slices of bread, each about 2 by 3 inches

Preheat the oven to 375°F.

In a small bowl, combine all the ingredients except the bread. With a fork, work them together until well blended.

Spread each slice of bread with an approximately ⅛-inch layer of sausage. Cover to the very edge. Place the *crostini* on a baking sheet. They can be prepared ahead and kept covered with plastic wrap.

Bake for 10 minutes. Run under the broiler for 30 seconds or so to brown the tops. Serve hot.

BREAD

It's said that the farther south you go in Italy, the better the bread. With some notable northern exceptions, it's true. Italian bread gets better as you go south from Rome. It gets denser, moisture, and more yeasty, with a chewier, thicker crust. Sometimes it is called *pane casereccia,* "homemade bread," even if it comes from a commercial bakery. It can be made with white flour, or semolina with its yellow cast, or with whole wheat, or a combination, but it is always a satisfying bread.

BREAD IN COOKING

If you asked a Southern Italian to name the most important food on his table he would surely say "pasta." But if you asked a Southern Italian *cook,* he would know the true answer is "bread." Fresh bread is essential on the Southern Italian table, but its afterlife is even more critical, and there is even a vocabulary for the various stages and parts of the loaf.

Day- or two-day-old bread is called *pane raffermo,* which could be translated as "firmed bread." It is the most frequent base for stuffings. It is essential to add to ground meat for meatballs (page 172) and meatloaf (page 176). It's a binder and, yes, it extends the meat. But it also makes the meatballs soft and light. One old Southern Italian recipe using stale bread, one made nowadays mainly out of nostalgia for the miserable old days, is fake meatballs made of bread. They are called *polpette di pane,* "little bread balls." They are seasoned just like meatballs, with cheese and garlic and parsley, and you cook them, fried first or not, in tomato sauce.

The inside of the bread has a name in Italian, too: *mollica di pane. Mollica* can be fresh or from *pane raffermo,* but in Sicily they also sometimes use the word *mollica* for bread crumbs, which are more properly *pangrattato* in Italian.

BREAD CRUMBS

As I cook Southern Italian food, I sometimes think this is actually a bread-crumb cuisine. Bread crumbs add crunch—textural interest—to innumerable baked dishes, they form crusts on fried foods, they can line a baking pan or a cake pan so the contents don't stick. They are moistened for fillings, used as a thickener, and fried or toasted for toppings. They can be seasoned in more ways than one can record, but typical are additions of minced garlic, minced parsley or basil or mint, dried oregano, crushed fennel seed, grated cheese, and anchovies melted into olive oil. Let's not forget olive oil, salt, and pepper.

While some commercial bread crumbs you can buy in an American supermarket are just fine, please do not buy flavored ones. Flavor them yourself. And beware of products that contain corn syrup. They will brown more readily than bread crumbs made from bread with no sugar or sweetener. I make my own bread crumbs with Italian bakery bread that I save in a paper bag until it gets hard and has few other uses.

TOASTED BREAD CRUMBS

Crunchy toasted bread crumbs are as basic a pasta topping as there is, and one of the most satisfying. Throughout Southern Italy, but especially in Puglia, Basilicata, and Calabria, they're eaten on humble dishes like spaghetti with garlic and oil (page 125), harkening to *la cucina povera,* and on pastas based on seafood (page 127). In western Sicily, where fish is eaten much more than meat, toasted bread crumbs are put on the table instead of or along with grated cheese.

To "toast" bread crumbs, put them in a small skillet and toss them over medium heat until they brown lightly. Be careful: if your bread was baked with sugar, the crumbs may burn quickly.

HARD BREAD

Really dry bread, not just day- or two-day-old bread, can go beyond bread crumbs. It can be cooked with liquid and possibly vegetables, even a bit of meat, to make *pancotto,* "cooked bread" (page 74), a gruel or pap. It's the Southern Italian version of the famous Florentine dish *pappa al pomodoro,* which is old bread blended with tomato sauce. By the way, *pancotto* can also be bread and tomato sauce. Remember that it's Southern Italians who perfected tomato sauce.

Some bread is intentionally hardened to preserve it. After it is baked, it is sliced and baked slowly again to dry it out. This is called, generically, *pane biscottato*—literally "twice-baked bread." (The word *biscotti,* meaning the cookies, means twice-baked, too. It's where we get the word *biscuit* in English.) *Pane biscottato* comes in several shapes. Small crusts, no more than 1½ to 2 inches square, are sometimes actually called *crostini.* Quickly dip them in saltwater to soften them slightly, drizzle with olive oil, season with a pinch of oregano and maybe a tiny bit of salt, and you have a beautiful snack. They are also meant to be put on the bottom of a bowl of *zuppa,* to sop up the liquid.

There are larger shapes for that purpose, too. Freselle are rings of twice-baked bread, formed by slicing a ring-shaped roll in half. The cut side absorbs more quickly than the crust side, so put them flat side up in a bowl. The same can be said of the rectangular form of the bread, which is more common. These types of hardtack, to use an old-fashioned English word, are also used for *Caponata Napoletano* (page 61), which is also called *Acquasale,* "saltwater," because one dips the *pane biscottato* into saltwater to soften it, as fishermen at sea used to.

Bread is so treasured, and so extensively used in every stage of its life, that even the crusts can be featured. I'll never forget asking about the unusually robust texture and taste of some stuffed tiny green peppers I ate in Maratea, in Basilicata. "Oh," said our host, surprised we noticed some difference, "the filling is made only with crumbs from the crust." Even dried heels of bread, *tozzetti,* are salvaged by putting them in broth or flavored boiling water (page 74).

Stuzzico
Eggplant, Red Pepper, and Onion Spread

Corigliano Calabro, Calabria

Azienda Favella is a large agricultural estate in Corigliano Calabro, in the province of Catanzaro in northern Calabria. Although the farm has recently begun breeding water buffalo to produce milk for mozzarella and ricotta, and it supports a variety of other livestock, Favella's main business is growing vegetables for its own processing plant. There, right by the fields, the vivid flavors of this rich agricultural land are preserved in oil or vinegar and shipped in jars all over the world.

The product Favella calls *Stuzzico* is meant to be a spread for *crostini* or crackers. The word comes from the verb *stuzzicare,* "to tease" or "to whet," but it is used to mean "snack." Cecilia and I loved Favella's *Stuzzico* so much that we bought a few jars and figured out the recipe. With the help of her kitchen staff, Cecilia now makes it in grand batches to keep in the pantry and serve as an antipasto or *aperitivo* to her guests at Azienda Seliano. I make it in more modest amounts at the end of the summer, when eggplant and peppers are at their height.

1 large eggplant (or several small ones, about 2 pounds), cut into ½-inch-thick slices

5 medium red bell peppers (about 1¾ pounds), seeded and cut into big pieces

2 medium onions (about 12 ounces), cut into wedges

4 medium garlic cloves, cut in half

1½ cups white wine vinegar

2 teaspoons salt

¼ cup fresh mint leaves

1 well-packed cup wild fennel fronds, or 1 teaspoon fennel seed, ground in a mortar and pestle

1 teaspoon red pepper flakes, or even more to taste

1½ tablespoons dried oregano

2 cups extra-virgin olive oil

Preheat the oven to 375° F.

Combine and toss together the eggplant, peppers, onions, and garlic in a roasting pan. Roast for 30 minutes, stirring once or twice. While the vegetables are still hot, pour the vinegar over the vegetables and add the salt, mint, fennel, red pepper, and oregano. Allow to cool slightly.

In a food processor, using the pulse function, process the vegetables in two or three batches until very finely chopped, almost a puree. Scrape the mixture into a large bowl.

In a small saucepan, heat the olive oil to approximately 200°F. You will have to use a thermometer. Stir all but about ½ cup of the oil into the vegetables. Pack the spread into five 1-pint jars that have first been sterilized by dipping them into boiling water, then handled with tongs that have also been sterilized. Leave about ½ inch headroom in each jar. Top off each jar with about ¼ inch of olive oil.

Store in the refrigerator and return to room temperature before serving, unless the spread is going on hot toast, in which case it softens quickly enough.

Pappucelle con Tonno e Giardiniera
Pickled Cherry Peppers Stuffed with Tuna and *Giardiniera*

Cecilia grows her own hot cherry peppers, which come into season in great abundance—overabundance, even—at the end of the summer. That's why this has become a frequent antipasto for her *agriturismo* guests. Hot, sweet, acidic, savory, creamy, and crunchy all at once, they are irresistible. (She also puts the peppers up under oil, after they are boiled in vinegar and water, stuffed with pinches of tuna, bits of anchovy, a few capers, and pieces of green olive.)

It is quite a project to make these from fresh peppers, however. You'd need Cecilia's staff to make them in any quantity. September afternoons, when the pepper crop is at its peak, Cecilia's kitchen staff sits at the long tables outside the kitchen, cleaning them and boiling them. When it is communal work like that, and there is gossip to share, the time passes quickly. In some supermarkets and in Italian markets, you can buy very good, already cleaned and pickled cherry peppers, as well as whole cherry peppers in jars or loose. Instead of those, I like to use the tiny pickled peppadew peppers now available in the United States. They are from South Africa and both slightly sweet and slightly hot.

1 (6-ounce) can solid light tuna packed in olive oil, drained

¾ cup *giardiniera* (pickled mixed vegetables), very finely chopped (see Note)

⅓ cup mayonnaise (homemade or commercial)

36 pickled hot cherry peppers, or other small peppers (see Note)

In a small bowl, combine the tuna, chopped *giardiniera*, and mayonnaise. With a fork, break up the tuna and work the ingredients together until very well blended.

If the peppers have not had their tops cut off and been seeded, do this yourself. Using a small spoon, stuff each pepper with the tuna mixture.

Arrange on a platter and serve.

NOTE: You can buy *giardiniera* in jars in the supermarket or loose at a good Italian market. Try to find one that is not mostly cauliflower. For this recipe, be sure to include some carrot slices, red pepper, and green celery. If you care to include a few olives, any kind, chopped, would make a good addition.

If you want to start from scratch with fresh cherry peppers, cut off the stem ends and seed them—a teaspoon works well. Bring a pot of half white wine vinegar (or distilled white vinegar) and half water to a rolling boil. Put in the peppers—not many more than can float on the surface. When the liquid returns to a boil, boil them for 2 minutes. Scoop them out with a strainer or slotted spoon, then drain them, placing them upside down on a clean kitchen towel to dry.

Focaccia di Patate
Filled Potato "Pizza"

Puglia   SERVES AT LEAST 8

Strolling and window-shopping along Lecce's main street, I can never resist going into a snack shop for a slice of this pizza substitute. It is not a flat bread, as the name *focaccia* usually implies, but thin layers of mashed potatoes encasing a tomato filling with olives, capers, onions, and anchovies. Outside, a crisp shell of bread crumbs holds it together and frames the creamy, salty interior. It's a strictly local specialty, sometimes also called *pizza di patate* or *pitta di patate*. It's an inexpensive, filling, and deeply delicious snack, but it is also perfect party finger food when cut into small, square "*crostini*" that are manageable with a glass of something in the other hand.

3 pounds russet potatoes, peeled and cut into large pieces

1½ teaspoons salt

8 tablespoons extra-virgin olive oil

1 medium onion, very thinly sliced (about 1 cup)

1 (14-ounce) can peeled Italian tomatoes

½ cup pitted oil-cured black olives (about 30, or 3 ounces), quartered or very coarsely chopped

1 rounded tablespoon salted capers, rinsed well

2 salted anchovies, filleted, or 4 oil-packed anchovy fillets, cut into ½-inch pieces

1 tablespoon butter

¾ cup fine dry bread crumbs

In a large pot, cover the potatoes with cold water. Bring to a boil over high heat and cook until the potatoes are tender. Drain well.

While still hot, puree the potatoes in a food mill or with a ricer. You can puree them back into the empty pot they were boiled in. Stir in the salt and 4 tablespoons of the olive oil. Set aside. You should have 4 cups.

In an 8- to 10-inch skillet, combine 2 tablespoons of the olive oil, 3 tablespoons of water, and the sliced onion. Place over medium heat and simmer together for 5 minutes, adding additional water by the tablespoon if it boils out.

After 5 minutes with water, sauté the onion with only the oil for 5 minutes longer, until the onion is very tender but only slightly golden. Add the tomatoes to the pan. Break them up with the side of a wooden spoon. Simmer gently for 15 minutes, until the mixture has reduced to a very thick sauce. Add the olives, capers, and anchovy pieces. Stir to mix well.

With the butter, grease the bottom and halfway up the sides of a 9 by 13-inch Pyrex pan. Coat with half of the bread crumbs by shifting them around the bottom and sides. Leave the excess bread crumbs in the pan.

Using about half of the mashed potatoes (about 2 cups), drop spoonfuls of potato on the bottom of the dish. Being careful not to upset the bread crumbs on the bottom, gently pat the potatoes into a thin layer that covers the bottom of the pan. Spread the tomato filling evenly over the potatoes. Build a top layer of potato the same way you did the bottom: drop the potatoes by spoonfuls, then pat them into a thin layer.

Combine the remaining 2 tablespoons of oil with the remaining bread crumbs and sprinkle the mixture over the potatoes. Gently pat the crumbs into the potato surface. The focaccia can be made ahead to this point.

Place a rack in the top third of the oven. Preheat the oven to 400°F. Bake for 30 minutes, until the bottom has browned and you can see the focaccia slightly pulling away from the sides of the pan. Cool thoroughly before cutting.

Serve in slabs as a plated antipasto or afternoon snack, or cut into small squares for a pass-around *aperitivo* or *sfizzo*.

BOTTARGA

Bottarga is salted and compressed fish roe, either tuna eggs or silver (sometimes called gray) mullet eggs. Tuna roe is the most common in Sicily and Calabria. Sardinia is the source of most mullet bottarga.

Both types of *bottarga* come in two forms. It can either be a firm cake of roe, usually still contained in the fish's egg sac, sometimes waxed to preserve its moisture; or it can be granulated, in which case it is sold in jars and in small plastic bags that hold a portion or two. The cake type is more expensive, and the most extravagant way to serve *bottarga* is to shave a cake into paper-thin slices and dress them with a little olive oil and lemon juice. Bread is essential. To make a little *bottarga* go a long way, use it to dress pasta or to top *crostini* rubbed with garlic and dressed with oil.

Excellent-quality *bottarga* is now available from Internet sources. It pays to buy a whole jar or a whole egg sac. *Bottarga* is, after all, a preserved product, and a jar of *bottarga*, tightly closed, will keep in a cool pantry for at least six months. The cake type will last several months in the refrigerator if wrapped snugly in plastic.

CROSTINI DI BOTTARGA

To make *Crostini di Bottarga*, grill small toasted slices of dense bread, rub them with a cut clove of garlic, drizzle with extra-virgin olive oil, then top with shaved or granulated *bottarga*. *Bottarga* can be sliced very thinly with a sharp knife, or, if you have one, with a truffle slicer.

Vincenzo Imperatore, the pizza master at
Europeo di Mattozzi in Naples.

Pizza Napolitana

Pizza varies wherever you go in Italy. In the south, the Neapolitan style reigns supreme—individual pies with a thin but soft crust and a puffy "frame" or edge. On the other hand, every little locality likes to claim its own special variance on the Neapolitan model. For instance, in Salerno, which is only sixty miles south of Naples, they'll tell you that their crust is crisper, their frame less puffy and narrower, hence their pizza is superior. In Puglia, you see more sheet-pan pizza than round, individual pies. In Sicily, they have many more kinds of pizza than Neapolitan-style, sold in snack shops and bakeries all over the island.

Over the many years I have been making and teaching pizza, I have used less and less yeast and given the dough more and more time to rise. If you make dough that rises quickly because it has a large dose of yeast and rests in a warm place, the pizza crust is likely to taste like white bread. Not bad, mind you, but not with the developed wheat and yeast flavor of a long-risen dough. For that you need to think ahead and prepare the dough a day ahead and use the refrigerator for its rising and flavor development. Salt also retards the yeasts' work, so I use a greater amount than most cookbook recipes call for, which also adds to the savor of the dough, highlighting its wheaten flavor. Following the strictest Neapolitan recipe, you would not put olive oil in the dough, but some people do. It offers a little tenderness, some flavor, and can make the bottom of the pie a tad crisper. If you choose to use oil—I don't—add no more than 2 tablespoons of oil to the following formula, incorporating it with the second dose of water.

1 teaspoon active dry yeast (not fast-rising)

1½ cups warm water (between 100 and 110°F)

3½ to 4 cups unbleached all-purpose flour

2 teaspoons salt

At least 30 minutes before mixing the dough, in a minimum 2-cup liquid measuring cup, sprinkle the yeast on ½ cup of the water. Wait a minute, then stir with a fork until the yeast is dissolved. Stir in ½ cup of the flour. Set aside at room temperature and let the mixture increase to at least double, about 1½ cups.

Combine 3 cups of the flour with the yeast mixture and the remaining 1 cup of warm water in the bowl of a stand mixer fitted with the dough hook. Mix on low speed until the dough just begins to mass together. Add the salt, and continue to knead the dough with the dough hook until it looks smooth and the machine struggles a little.

Stop the machine. Gather the dough into a ball and turn it out onto a lightly floured work

Recipe continues

surface. Knead the dough for another 5 minutes, folding and turning it onto itself, then pushing it away from you with the heel of your hand(s), adding just enough flour to keep the dough from sticking. Be careful not to add too much flour or too much at one time. When you have finished, the dough should not stick to the board—it should be smooth, silken, slightly damp on the surface, and very elastic.

Dust the dough lightly all over with flour and place in a bowl to rise, covered with a clean dish towel. Place in the refrigerator overnight, or at least for 6 hours. It will have risen slightly, but not nearly doubled.

Remove from the refrigerator. When the dough warms to room temperature (time depends on the temperature of your kitchen, but at least 1 hour), it will continue to rise. Let rise until doubled.

Deflate the dough by pressing it down, then divide it into four parts. Each part makes a 9- to 10-inch pizza. Knead each piece of dough into a ball, then let it rise, a couple of inches apart, covered with a clean towel, on a floured board, until doubled. Alternatively, if you intend to use only a portion of the dough, divide the dough into fourths and refrigerate or freeze the pieces not to be used immediately.

If desired, to further develop the flavor of the dough, knock down the dough one more time and let it rise one more time before forming pizzas.

Preheat the oven to 500 to 550°F—as hot as your oven will go. If you are using a pizza stone, which will give extra lift to the pizza, place it on the bottom rack of the oven before you begin preheating, and let the oven preheat longer than usual—at least 30 minutes, so the stone is preheated as well. With or without a pizza stone, I bake pizza on a thin aluminum baking sheet. It's easier than using a wooden peel.

To form the dough into a pizza, flatten a ball of dough into a thick disk. On a lightly floured board, rotating the disk as you go, flatten the center of the pizza with your fingertips or the heel of your hand. When a ridge of dough starts appearing on the perimeter of the disk, lift the dough up with both hands and, holding onto the ridge, let gravity and the weight of the dough stretch the circle. Keep turning the dough to get a relatively even 9- to 10-inch circle. Keep pulling the ridge slightly so the circle gets larger. Be careful not to make the center too thin or the ridge more than a ½ inch deep. At some point the pizza will become too flimsy to handle. Spread the formed pizza dough onto a large baking sheet that has been lightly dusted with flour.

Alternatively, you can use a rolling pin to form the pizza, but it's not as much fun and it's harder to make a puffy edge.

Top as desired. See the many choices listed on pages 46–47.

Bake for 6 to 8 minutes depending on your oven and the topping—a simple herb and oil topping requires less cooking time than tomato or other heavier/moister toppings—and on how well baked you like pizza. I like the border tinged with brown, even speckled with black. The bottom should be golden brown.

In Naples, strips of pizza dough, when rolled and baked around various fillings, are called *panini napoletani*, a popular street food.

Focaccia and Pizza Toppings

Before tomatoes were eaten in Europe, flat breads were topped with herbs, oil, salt, onions, and garlic. Today this is usually called *focaccia*, although it is not like the high-rise and well-oiled *focaccia* with which Americans are most familiar.

To make a flat *focaccia*, roll out the pizza dough to a rough rectangle or round, then drizzle with olive oil and sprinkle with either rosemary or torn sage, and some coarse salt. You could also add very thinly sliced onion broken into rings, or very finely sliced or slivered garlic. In that case, drizzle the oil on last, over the onion or garlic. Bake as you would pizza, on the bottom of your oven on the hottest temperature it will reach. It should be done in less than 5 minutes.

PIZZA TOPPINGS

- **Pizza Marinara:** This was the first tomato pizza, topped with just crushed tomatoes, chopped or slivered garlic, and dried oregano. It is still the second-most popular pizza, after pizza Margherita. Outside Naples, marinara often has anchovies, too. In the city of Naples, that's called *napoletana*.

- **Pizza Margherita:** Scatter crushed tomato sparingly over the dough, then add a few dots of cow's milk mozzarella (*fior di latte*) and a couple of torn leaves of fresh basil. This is the most popular pizza in the world.

- **Tomato and Smoked Cheese:** Place shredded or chopped smoked mozzarella or scamorza on top of crushed tomatoes. Sprinkle with red pepper flakes.

- **Prosciutto and Argula:** This is a very fashionable pizza. Place slices of prosciutto and leaves of arugula, preferably the tiny, so-called wild type (see page 55), on a tomato and mozzarella-topped pie as soon as it comes from the oven. Both the ham and greens wilt ever so slightly on their way to the table.

- **Patate, Cipolle, e Rosmarino** (Potato, Onion, and Rosemary): Arrange paper-thin slices of precooked potato over the raw dough. Dress with salt, rosemary leaves, and a few rings of raw onion, and drizzle with olive oil.

- **Bianca** (White): Smear a thin layer of ricotta on the raw dough. Dot with small cubes of mozzarella. Dress with salt, freshly ground black pepper, and olive oil.

- **Quatro Formaggi** (Four Cheeses): Divide the pizza into quadrants and put a different cheese in each; for instance, mozzarella, gorgonzola, smoked scamorza, and Swiss Gruyère or Emmentaler.

- **Quatro Stagione** (Four Seasons): This is a vegetable pizza, each quarter of the pie topped with a different vegetable. This usually includes mushrooms, artichokes (marinated artichoke hearts, sliced), a cooked green such as broccoli rabe, and roasted peppers.

- **Patate Schiaccite e Porcini** (Mashed Potatoes and Porcini): Smear the unbaked dough with mashed potatoes flavored and enriched with olive oil, then top with reconstituted dry porcini that have been sautéed with garlic and parsley.

- **Uove e Cippole** (Egg and Onion): Sauté onion in olive oil, then stir it into raw beaten egg with some chopped parsley. Spread this mixture on top of the raw dough and sprinkle with grated cheese, preferably pecorino, or beat the grated cheese into the egg and onion mixture.

- **Patate e Salsicce** (Potato and Sausage): On top of a tomato and mozzarella pie, add cubes of precooked (boiled or roasted) potato, crumbled and cooked sweet or hot sausage (out of the casing), and rosemary leaves.

- **Capricciosa:** This word can mean almost any topping—it's the chef's caprice or whim. Most usually, however, a *capricciosa* is a pizza piled high with many different toppings. For instance, on a tomato and mozzarella pie, put sautéed mushrooms, peas, diced or slivered prosciutto, pitted olives, and oregano. On top of this, you can add a hard-cooked egg after baking, or a whole raw egg broken onto the center and baked with the other topping ingredients.

- **Tonno e Cippole** (Canned Tuna and Sliced Onion): On top of dough with crushed tomatoes, or tomatoes and mozzarella, flake a half-can of tuna, arrange rings of raw onion, and sprinkle with dried oregano.

- **Speck, Arugula, e Scale di Parmigiano** (Speck, Arugula, and Parmigiano Scales): Straight from the oven, after baking a pizza topped sparingly with crushed tomatoes, mozzarella, and dried oregano, place paper-thin slices of *speck* (a smoked meat from Lombardia, readily available in the United States), a few leaves of arugula, and large shavings of Parmigiano cheese cut with a vegetable peeler.

- **Valdostana:** Bake a pizza topped with crushed tomato, shredded fontina, and thinly sliced domestic mushrooms. While hot from the oven, dress with scales of Parmigiano cheese and a slice or two of prosciutto.

- **Pugliese:** Bake a pizza with halved cherry tomatoes, olive oil, and oregano. When it comes from the oven, garnish with wild arugula, a green frequently used in Puglia.

Pizza Rustica
Savory Cheese Pie with Salami or Prosciutto

Pizza rustica is sometimes called *torta rustica* or by Italian Americans, *pizza gain*, an old dialect name that comes from the Italian *pizza ripiena*, meaning "stuffed pie." *Ripiena* is also pronounced, in some dialects, *chiena* (key-enna), which is how Italian Americans arrived at *pizza gain*. Whatever the name, the word *rustica* does not mean "rustic." It means "savory," or the opposite of "sweet," *dolce*.

    Pizza rustica can have many different fillings. Although *pizza rustica* is often served as an antipasto, it can also be a snack or light meal, or a hospitality offering, for when someone drops by and you give them a glass of wine. On Easter Monday, it is traditional to take a *pizza rustica* like this, filled with ricotta, cubed cheese, and cured pork products, on a picnic. It is great traveling food and tastes delicious at room temperature—or, I should say, picnic temperature.

FOR THE PASTRY

2¾ cups all-purpose flour

1 egg

1¼ teaspoons salt

1¼ teaspoons sugar

⅔ cup dry white wine

½ cup extra-virgin olive oil

FOR THE FILLING

3 large eggs

1 (15-ounce) container whole milk ricotta (1¾ cups)

½ cup ¼-inch diced sopressata or salami (about 3 ounces)

½ cup ½-inch diced mozzarella (about 3 ounces)

½ cup ½-inch diced sharp provolone or caciocavallo cheese (about 3 ounces)

½ cup freshly grated Parmigiano or pecorino cheese

½ teaspoon salt, or more to taste

¼ teaspoon freshly ground black pepper, or more to taste

To make the pastry: Combine the flour, egg, salt, sugar, wine, and oil in the bowl of a stand mixer fitted with the paddle attachment. Mix on medium speed until well blended and coming together into a sticky ball on the paddle. Divide the pastry into two pieces, about one-third and two-thirds of the pastry. Form each piece into a disk, wrap separately in plastic, and refrigerate for several hours.

    To make the filling: Beat the eggs in a large mixing bowl until well mixed. Remove about a tablespoon of beaten egg and set aside in a cup to use later as an egg wash. Stir the ricotta into the beaten eggs until well mixed. Add the remaining ingredients and mix well again.

    To form and bake the pie: Set a rack in the lower third of the oven. Preheat the oven to 375°F. Have ready a 10-inch springform pan—there's no need to grease or flour it.

    Place the larger disk of pastry on a floured surface, then roll it into a very thin 16-inch circle. Line the springform pan with pastry, letting the pastry drape over the rim so it stays in place.

Refrigerate the lined pan for 15 minutes to make the pastry easier to work with.

Spread the filling evenly into the pastry-lined pan.

Roll out the smaller disk of pastry into a thin, approximately 12-inch circle. Set aside for the moment.

Using scissors or a very sharp, small knife, cut the bottom pastry so that it comes no more than 1 inch above the top of the pie filling. Fold this extra edge of the bottom pastry over the filling. Brush the edge with a little of the reserved egg wash. Lay the second circle over the filling. Push down on the edges, to seal them together. No crimping is necessary.

Brush the top with the remaining beaten egg. Cut a small slit on the top of the pastry. Bake for 45 minutes. Let cool for a few minutes, then remove from the pan and place on a cake rack to finish cooling.

Serve warm.

NOTE: To store, keep the pizza on the base of the springform, and when cooled to room temperature, wrap in plastic and refrigerate. Return to room temperature before reheating in a 350°F oven. Place the pie in the cold oven and let it heat while the oven is preheating. Bake for about 5 minutes once the oven is hot. It should be warmed through. A whole pie will, of course, take longer to reheat than if the pie is cut into pieces.

Variation

Pizza Rustica dell'Orto (Pizza Rustica with Summer Vegetables): Use the same pastry for a double-crusted pie filled with the stars of the summer garden—eggplant, zucchini, and sweet peppers.

La Tasca
"The Pocket," Egg and Cheese Pie

La Tasca is a very rich form of *pizza rustica*—a buttery, sweetened, almost cakey pastry filled with eggs and cheese. The recipe is from Padula, a town in the Cilento that is famous for the Certosa di San Lorenzo, a former monastery, now a museum, that once housed monks from Naples' richest families. These men lived in splendor, not monastic simplicity. Perhaps *La Tasca* was created by the rich monks. This version comes from Paula Romanzi, who lives in Padula. Originally, *La Tasca* was made with young pecorino cheese, but Paula prefers young caciocavallo. I use Swiss Gruyère to great effect.

FOR THE PASTRY

3 cups all-purpose flour

¾ cup sugar

¼ teaspoon salt

10 tablespoons cold butter, cut into cubes

3 whole eggs, lightly beaten, plus 1 egg for a glaze

FOR THE FILLING

10 large eggs

1 cup finely cubed prosciutto or salami (4 to 5 ounces)

8 ounces (without rind) young caciocavallo or Gruyère cheese, shredded

To make the pastry: Combine the flour, sugar, and salt in the bowl of a stand mixer fitted with the paddle attachment. Stir together on low speed. Add the butter and continue mixing on low speed until the butter is broken into pea-size pieces. Add the whole eggs and mix until the dough comes together. Wrap the dough in plastic and chill in the refrigerator for at least 30 minutes.

Place a rack in the center of the oven. Preheat the oven to 375°F.

To make the filling: Whisk the eggs together in a large mixing bowl. Whisk in the salt, prosciutto or salami, and cheese.

To form and bake the pie: On a lightly floured board, roll out two-thirds of the dough into a slightly larger than 13-inch circle. Line a 9-inch-diameter, 2-inch-deep cake pan with the rolled dough, leaving the excess for now. Pour in the filling. Brush some egg on the edge of the bottom crust.

Roll out the second piece of dough to fit the pan, then place it over the pie. Crimp the top crust and bottom edges together. Brush the top with egg.

Bake for 35 to 40 minutes, until the top crust is golden.

Let cool for about 15 minutes before serving. It's best served hot or warm but it reheats very well.

BRUSCHETTA

"No other food can compete with a slice of bread hot from the oven with a drizzle of oil poured over it. It is a simple food, ancient and wise, to be eaten slowly, meditating all the while, since each mouthful is full of history." I quote a brochure called "Sicilia, A Thousand Delights: Sicilian Cooking, Its History and Legends" that I once found in a hotel room. I haven't been able to trace the author. I wish I'd written it. It describes what I always felt was the primal appeal of *bruschetta* at its simplest—bread and oil, the bread toasted, the oil from the olive.

The word is pronounced brew-SKET-ah, and it means "toast," not the topping of diced tomato salad with which the toast is almost always dressed in the United States. Still, American companies are selling jarred diced tomatoes as *"bruschetta."*

It is the Neapolitan-style *bruschetta* topped with tomatoes tossed with garlic, parsley or basil, and olive oil that has, like pizza, almost become an American food, it is so popular here, not that Italians from the Alps to Pantelleria don't dote on it, too. It's irresistible, especially in August and September, when the tomatoes are ripest, the basil most fragrant, and the temperature and humidity so stifling that a slice of oiled bread and a glass of cold wine are all you think you want to eat. Then, mysteriously, this snack you intended to satisfy your appetite has ended up piquing it instead. What's next? This makes *bruschetta* a perfect antipasto.

Southern Italians have lately taken to making a whole meal of various *bruschette*. The Neapolitan tomato salad topping remains the most popular, just as pizza Margherita (tomato, mozzarella, basil) is still the most popular pie. But as has happened with pizza, there are now long lists of *bruschetta* possibilities. Sometimes, in fact, the pizzeria is also the place to go for *bruschetta*.

The most basic *bruschetta* is toasted bread rubbed with a cut clove of garlic, then drizzled with olive oil. Salt and pepper are optional. Another simple *bruschetta* is toast spread with reheated, leftover tomato sauce. Good-quality tomato paste, right out of the can or the tube, is a great spread, too. Instead of tomato salad, a sliced tomato is easier. If you've rubbed the bread with garlic and moistened it with oil, that's enough. Or put on an anchovy, a dusting of dried oregano, and a small slice of mozzarella for *finta* (fake) pizza.

The very first meal I ever ate at Seliano started with a slice of toasted bread topped with buffalo-milk ricotta, some freshly ground black pepper, and Cecilia's own very fragrant and fruity olive oil. This is a great antipasto (or lunch) with American supermarket ricotta, too. In the southeast corner of Sicily, they'd top their ricotta with chopped toasted almonds or pistachios.

Boiled beans or chickpeas dressed with minced garlic and olive oil also make a great topping for toast. And try boiled leafy vegetables, dragged around a hot skillet with olive oil, garlic, and hot pepper. Truly, almost anything you can think of eating with bread can be eaten on top of toasted bread and be called *bruschetta*.

Insalate
Salads

Insalate.

Eating salad is a relatively recent development in Southern Italy. There are very few old, traditional salad recipes, in the broad meaning of dishes eaten cold and/or prepared with raw vegetables. Still, given a climate conducive to salad eating, an agriculture that produces so many vegetables, and a tourist trade that demands international-style food with a local twist, Southern Italians have taken to eating salads as happily as Southern Californians.

Salads of cooked vegetables, mushrooms, legumes, seafood, and even meat and poultry are considered stylish, and they appear on restaurant and celebratory antipasto tables, are eaten more as main courses, and are featured at fashionable resorts. To name two internationally famous resorts and their salads, there's Capri and its delicious cliché of mozzarella, tomatoes, and basil, *Insalata Caprese*, and the Aeolian Islands and Pantelleria with their *Insalata Eoliana* (page 58) and *pantesca*, respectively, both of which feature capers and tuna from a can or jar.

Green salads made from fine lettuces, however, were not common in Southern Italy until twenty years ago. Now, the Sele Plain, south of Salerno, is one of the largest growers, in greenhouses, of mixed salad greens sold already washed in plastic boxes. Still, all but the youngest and older sophisticated Southern Italians prefer well-cooked vegetables and dark leafy greens, albeit they are sometimes served at room temperature with oil and lemon juice, like a salad. That said, these days a tossed green salad is a frequent accompaniment to grilled or roasted meat or fried fish, and it can come after a main course, possibly with cheese, at an elegant dinner.

Pale green, broad and buttery head lettuce, what we call Boston, is the lettuce I see most in Southern Italian markets. There is plenty of iceberg, too, which I've even seen labeled as *iceberga* (pronounced itch-ay-*bear*-ga), and romaine. Curly-edged loose-leaf lettuces, both red and green, are rarer, but they are often included in the prewashed bags of greens now in Italian supermarkets. The waxy purple, somewhat tough and bitter radicchio that has taken over the world is also usually included in those mixes.

ARUGULA

The Italian-American word for this peppery green, *arugula*, which is popular all over Southern Italy because it grows wild everywhere, is fossilized Southern Italian dialect, meaning it is a dialect word no longer in use in the homeland. I have seen the word *rugala* used in Sicilian markets, but in proper Italian the word for this green is *rucola*. (The word for it in English, still used in Great Britain, is *rocket*.)

The type we see most in the United States exists in smaller form in Italy, although those smaller leaves are now beginning to be available here as well. There is yet an even smaller and more peppery arugula, called *ruchetta*. This leaf is usually no more than 3 inches long, very narrow, and unlike its rounded-edge larger cousin, it is very deeply toothed, like a miniature dandelion leaf. In Italy it is usually called "wild rocket," *ruchetta selvatica*, but it is actually cultivated. (Not to say it won't run amok in your garden if you plant a few seeds.) This "wild" type is also beginning to appear in our supermarkets.

Arugula is a much more important green in Southern Italy than the sweet lettuces, and the so-called wild variety is used extensively in Puglia in particular, where it was commonly foraged before it became available in stores. In Puglia, and to a lesser extent, over the border in Basilicata, arugula is often used as an herb, finely chopped and added to a dish just as you would parsley. *Rucola selvatica* has also become a trendy green, added nowadays to many a salad (along with radicchio), but also used as a pizza topping or tossed into pasta.

Insalata di Pomodori
Tomato Salad

SERVES 4 TO 6

As my exuberant Neapolitan friends love to say, tomato salad is a dish on which to work your imagination. For a start, you can use cherry or grape tomatoes that have been cut in half, the better to be seasoned with dressing. Or you can use round salad tomatoes cut into wedges or cubes or chunks or slices.

You can add chopped garlic, or you can smash it lightly or cut it in half and tuck it into the salad bowl so it subtly imparts its aroma. Before you eat the salad, you toss out the stinking lily. That would be the Neapolitan way.

Red onion makes for a pretty salad, and if you let it stand long enough in the tomato juice it adds to the salad's piquancy overall. Or, you can sweeten onion to be put in the salad and eaten raw by soaking it for a few minutes in cold water. Or just start out with a sweet onion! The long, tapered red onions of Tropea, in Calabria, are famous all over Italy for their sweetness—like a Vidalia but red.

As for herbs, basil, of course, is classic, but so is dried oregano, never fresh. In a pinch, there's always parsley, even curly parsley. It's not Italian, but it works, and well. In Sicily, and particularly in the Aeolian Islands, they use as much mint as basil with tomatoes. You can use a combination of oregano and basil, or mint and parsley, but don't overdo the herbs, or the number of herbs in one salad.

Capers are a great addition to tomato salad, too; and bits of purple or green olive, or chopped anchovies, or cubes of mozzarella cut the same size as the tomatoes, whatever size that is. Or serve the salad plated, garnished with olives, anchovies, and/or canned tuna or cooked shrimp.

The following recipe is the most basic salad. Use, as it is, on ziti or penne, as a *bruschetta* topping (see page 51), or in Bread and Tomato Salad (page 61).

About 2 pounds ripe salad
  tomatoes, cut into ½- to 1-inch
  chunks (about 4 cups)

1 garlic clove, slightly smashed or
  cut in half lengthwise, or minced
  or sliced

6 to 8 leaves fresh basil or mint,
  torn or coarsely chopped, or
  1 teaspoon dried oregano

½ teaspoon salt, or more to taste

Several twists of the peppermill

3 tablespoons extra-virgin olive oil,
  or slightly more

Put the tomatoes in a serving bowl. Add the garlic, herb, salt, pepper, and olive oil. Toss well.

Let stand a few minutes before serving.

Insalata Eoliana
Aeolian Salad

Aeolian Islands, Sicily

SERVES 2

This could just as easily be called *insalata pantesca*, referring to Pantelleria, another Sicilian island that, like Salina in the Aeolian archipelago, grows some of the world's best capers, and also attracts some of the world's wealthiest vacationers.

The second-home and summer people of Pantelleria and the Aeolian Islands seem to like nothing better than sitting at outdoor restaurants (or on their own terraces overlooking the sea), eating composed salads with chilled white wine. Add green beans to this recipe and it could be called *salade niçoise*. Capers and caper berries (*cucunci*) are, however, the essential ingredients here. To serve it as they do at the island's cafes, arrange the ingredients on individual plates. With crusty bread it's the perfect summer lunch—pretty and light.

2 medium potatoes, boiled, peeled, and cut into thick slices or large cubes

½ large sweet red or white onion, sliced or diced

12 to 16 small cherry or grape tomatoes, cut in half if desired

2 (5-ounce) cans light tuna packed in olive oil

8 slices cucumber

Lettuce or arugula leaves

2 tablespoons salted capers (preferably large), well rinsed

6 caper berries

Lemon wedges

Extra-virgin olive oil

Red wine vinegar

On individual dinner plates, arrange the potatoes, onion, tomatoes, tuna, and cucumber, along with a few leaves of lettuce or arugula. Scatter the capers over it all. Garnish with caper berries and lemon wedges.

Pass the extra-virgin olive oil and wine vinegar at the table.

Insalata di Arance, Cipolle, e Olive
Orange and Onion Salad with Olives

SERVES 4

In Sicily, salads based on the island's amazingly sweet yet refreshingly astringent oranges are very popular, and this one may be the most popular of all. The salads are mostly made with sweet orange-colored oranges, but sometimes the red, sour blood oranges are sliced or cubed and put on the plate, especially when the oranges are combined with seafood. Sicilian blood oranges are exported to the United States, but they are crazy expensive and not nearly as good as they are in Sicily. I have found U.S.-grown blood oranges, which are only slightly less expensive than the imports, to be altogether unacceptable. But I am ready and waiting to be proved wrong. This is the most basic of orange salads, but there are many variations. To this I often add fresh crab meat or small cooked shrimp. Tiny red shrimp, eaten raw, are what Sicilians use, and these are sometimes available in the United States from Maine and Iceland in the winter months. Another popular orange salad combines the sliced fruit with very thin slices of fennel bulb. Whatever the salad combination, use the best-quality extra-virgin olive oil to dress it.

3 large navel oranges

4 scallions, cut crosswise into thin slices, using all the white and just the palest green of the stem, or about ¼ cup diced red onion or sweet onion, such as Vidalia or Maui

2 to 3 tablespoons extra-virgin olive oil

Freshly ground black pepper

At least 8 oil-cured black olives

Peel the oranges the Sicilian way: score the rind with the tip of a small sharp knife, cutting from pole to pole and all the way down, but just to the pulp. Then, peel down each segment of the rind.

Cut the peeled oranges crosswise into ¼- to ½-inch slices, or into cubes. Arrange the slices or cubes on a serving platter. Scatter the sliced scallions on the oranges. Drizzle with olive oil. Season with several grinds of the peppermill. Garnish with the olives.

Serve within an hour or two, chilled (in the refrigerator) or at room temperature.

Caponata Napoletana o Acquasale
Bread and Tomato Salad

In Naples and Salerno, *acquasale*, although it means "saltwater," refers to a bread and tomato salad made with *pane biscottato* (see page 35). This "twice-baked" bread is dipped briefly into saltwater to soften it—hence the name. The name *caponata* refers to the bread itself, *capone* being the rusks that fishermen used to dip in the sea to make them manageable to eat. Although tomatoes are the essential base topping for the bread, almost any other ingredient can be added. Fish and seafood are traditional because of *caponata*'s fisherman origins, and in the late eighteenth century, aristocrats took the dish to Rococo heights, making huge set pieces for banquets of piles of bread and expensive seafood and vegetables. *Pane biscottato* is made in some Italian-American bakeries, often in a ring shape called *freselle*, which is the shape preferred for a layered as opposed to tossed salad. In fact, in Calabria, this salad is often called *insalata freselle*. Both *pane biscottato* and *freselle* are also imported from Italy, available packed in bags and boxes in Italian specialty markets. I much prefer the whole wheat (*integrale*) to the white.

1 teaspoon salt

2 cups water

4 to 6 whole-grain *freselle* or *pane biscottato* or oven-dried whole-grain country-style bread

1 tablespoon red or white wine vinegar

1 recipe Tomato Salad (page 56), the tomatoes sliced or diced

Fresh basil or flat-leaf parsley leaves, torn or shredded

In a medium bowl, make a saltwater bath by dissolving the salt in the water. Dip the *pane biscottato* or *freselle* very briefly—just a few seconds—into the salted water, to soften just the surface. The bread will continue to soften as it stands. In addition, you will be adding moisture with vinegar, and you will be topping it with juicy tomatoes. It should not end up mushy.

Depending on whether you are making a composed salad or a tossed one, either arrange the *freselle* or dried bread slices on a platter or break them up into approximately 1½- to 2-inch chunks and place them in a serving bowl. Sprinkle the vinegar over the bread.

If using sliced tomatoes, arrange them over the whole bread on the platter, then pour on their juices and oil. For a tossed salad, put the tomato salad in the bowl with the broken bread. Garnish or toss well with some additional fresh basil or parsley leaves.

Serve immediately.

Recipe continues

NOTE: Once refrigerated, the salad loses its appeal, although you may still find it quite acceptable. It can, however, be turned into a delicious version of *pancotto* (see Variation, page 74), "cooked bread"; a *minestra*, which should be served hot with extra-virgin olive oil drizzled over the top; or better yet with *olio santo* (see page 73). Put the soggy salad into a saucepan and place it over medium heat. With a wooden spoon, beat the mixture, adding a little water as necessary, to form a thick gruel. It should not be perfectly smooth—rather, more like the consistency of oatmeal. Serve very hot.

Variations

Crumble 1 can of solid light tuna in olive oil, drained, onto or into the salad. And/or add a handful of Gaeta or other olives, as much as a heaping tablespoon of rinsed salted capers, and/or a few anchovy fillets. Sweet or hot pickled red peppers, cut into strips, are a good addition or garnish, as is pickled eggplant, marinated mushrooms, or artichoke hearts.

CAPERS

All around the Mediterranean Sea, the ground-hugging caper bush (*Capparis spinosa*) grows wild, rooting itself in the cracks of stone walls. What we call capers, the treasured seasoning ingredient, are the plant's flower buds preserved in either salt or vinegar. After the buds bloom, the flowers turn into the olive-shaped fruits that are called caper berries, *cucunci,* that are nowadays a fashionable cocktail garnish in the United States. The bush's leaves are also edible. In Greece, they are pre-served in vinegar, just like the flower buds, and used in salads.

The best capers, ones with a strong flowery scent and not a trace of bitterness, no matter the size, may well be the carefully cultivated and salt-cured varieties grown on two Sicilian islands. Pantelleria is between Sicily and Tunisia, and besides being famous for its capers, it has unique whitewashed dome-shaped houses, produces Passito di Pantelleria, a sweet wine made from dried grapes, and grows small brown lentils that are, in Italy, as renowned as the capers. Salina is the largest island of the Aeolian archipelago, which also includes Lipari, the most developed of the islands. The Aeolians are nestled between Sicily and Calabria, and like Pantelleria, all of them are either active or dead volcanoes. Apparently, capers taste best and smell the most fragrant when grown in volcanic soil surrounded by the salty sea. (The best Greek capers are from Santorini, an island that is a dormant volcano.)

In small amounts, capers enliven pasta dishes and salads, add interest to sauces and vegetable dishes, and are frequently used in antipasti. Folk wisdom says they stimulate the appetite.

One reason they are expensive is that capers must be harvested by hand, usually from May to July, and it takes many passes through the fields to gather them. Not all buds appear at the same time. Then the capers must be sorted by hand. Small capers can be sold for more than large and are often labled "nonpareil," a French word used in both English and Italian to mean "without peer." They don't really have better flavor than large capers, but they distribute well throughout a dish. An equal amount of large capers must be chopped to do the same.

After harvest, the capers are separated from their leaves and twigs, then buried in salt, which extracts moisture and bitterness from the capers and preserves them. Like olives, capers are too bitter to eat before they have been salted. I know. I've tried.

The capers sit for about a week in their own brine—the liquid the salt extracts from them—before they are drained. They are then sun-dried for a day or so, then salted again. The best capers stay dry after their final salting.

The highest quality capers from both Pantelleria and Salina are readily available in the United States, if not from a store near you, then on the Internet.

Insalatina Sott'aceto
Pickled Carrot and Celery Root

MAKES ABOUT 4 CUPS

This vegetable slaw, handy to have on hand in the refrigerator, can be bought in a jar in any Sicilian supermarket. It is also ubiquitous in the seafood salads of the west coast of Sicily, in the province of Trapani. No matter what seafood is in the salad, you can count on these threadlike strands of pickled carrot and celery root. I find the salad also comes in handy to add crunch and a little acidity to chicken salad, with or without mayonnaise, and to tuna and egg salad with mayonnaise. I've used it to good effect to garnish fish, especially fatty ones such as salmon and mackerel, and I like it on a ham and cheese sandwich. It will keep for months in a jar or plastic container in the refrigerator.

1 small celery root (about ½ pound), trimmed and julienned on a mandoline (about 2 cups)

3 medium carrots, peeled and julienned on a mandoline (about 2 cups)

2 cups white wine or distilled white vinegar

2 cups cold water

½ teaspoon salt

Combine the julienned vegetables in a heat-resistant bowl—stainless steel, ceramic, or glass.

In a small saucepan, combine the vinegar, water, and salt. Bring to a rolling boil. Immediately pour the hot liquid over the vegetables. Let stand until cooled to room temperature.

Pack the vegetables in their brine in glass jars or tightly closed plastic containers. Store in the refrigerator for up to 3 months.

Insalata di Mare Trapanese
Seafood Salad, Trapani Style

Trapani, Sicily

SERVES 6 TO 8 AS AN ANTIPASTO,
4 TO 6 AS A MAIN COURSE

Shrimp, squid, and octopus are the typical base for seafood salads in the province of Trapani, on the west coast of Sicily. I haven't seen clams or mussels, but there's no reason you can't add them to the mix that follows. No matter the seafood base, however, the salads almost always feature *insalatina sott'aceto* (opposite), filaments of celery root and carrot that Sicilians can buy in jars in the supermarket, already pickled. It's a very different salad than the Neapolitan version (page 66), and much easier to prepare if you have insalatina in your refrigerator.

1 pound fresh, cleaned squid, the sacs cut into ¼-inch-wide rings, the tentacles cut in half lengthwise, if large

1 pound smallest available shrimp in their shells

1 cup Pickled Carrot and Celery Root (opposite), drained

3 tablespoons minced sweet or hot pickled peppers

¼ cup finely shredded flat-leaf parsley

Juice of 1 lemon

2 to 3 tablespoons extra-virgin olive oil

Pinch of red pepper flakes, or more to taste

In well-salted boiling water, cook the squid for barely 1 minute, until it just turns opaque. Remove the squid with a slotted spoon and transfer to a bowl.

Add the shrimp to the boiling water in which the squid was cooked. Boil the shrimp for 1 to 3 minutes, depending on the size of the shrimp, until they've turned pink and are cooked through. Taste one to judge. Drain well.

When cool enough to handle, shell the shrimp. If they are not tiny shrimp, cut them crosswise in halves or thirds. Add to the bowl with the squid. Add all the other ingredients and toss well.

Serve chilled on the same day it is prepared.

Insalata di Mare Napoletana
Neapolitan Seafood Salad

Trapani, Sicily

SERVES 6 TO 8

Insalata di mare is made all over Italy, but the traditional Neapolitan version is somewhat different from others. The seafood combination is whole mussels and clams, small shrimp, and either rings of calamari or cut-up octopus. The dressing is extra-virgin olive oil, lemon juice, and an "abundant" amount, as Italian recipes always say, of finely cut parsley. It never contains onion or celery, as so many other seafood salads do. The other typically Neapolitan aspect of this recipe is the way the seafood is cooked. First, the bivalves are steamed open in a dry pan; then the broth they exude is used to cook first the shrimp, then the calamari and/or octopus. Keep the final broth in the freezer. It's a good base for fish soup or stew.

2 pounds mussels (1½ cups cooked shelled mussels)

1 pound Manila clams (½ cup cooked shelled clams)

1 pound octopus, without the head (2 cups cooked)

1 pound small shrimp (2 cups cooked and shelled)

¼ cup extra-virgin olive oil

Juice of 4 lemons (½ cup plus 2 tablespoons)

½ cup parsley, coarsely chopped

1 teaspoon Dijon mustard (optional)

2 large garlic cloves, finely chopped

1 teaspoon salt

1 teaspoon freshly ground black pepper

Scrub the mussels under cold running water, pulling out any black "beards" that stick out of the shells. Place the mussels in a bowl of cold water to soak for about 20 minutes. Change the water after 10 minutes. Scrub the clams under cold running water and let them soak for 20 minutes, too, changing the water after 10 minutes. Drain both mussels and clams, rinsing them very well under cold water.

In a large sauté pan, place the shellfish together in one layer, cover, and let the shells steam open over high heat for 3 to 5 minutes. Drain the mussels and clams, reserving the liquid they have exuded. When they are just cool enough to handle, remove the shells, discard them, and place the meat in a covered container in the refrigerator. Add any extra liquid to the reserved liquid; strain into a clean 2½-quart saucepan.

Rinse the octopus well, place it in the shellfish liquid, and let it cook, covered, over medium-low heat until tender, for 30 minutes to 1 hour. Remove the octopus from the cooking broth and set it on a plate to cool.

Rinse the shrimp well in cold water and place them in the cooking broth over medium-high heat. Cover the pan and bring to a slow boil. Make sure to remove the shrimp with a small strainer as soon as they turn pink, in about 3 minutes. Set them aside to cool slightly.

Slice the octopus in ¼-inch rounds and place them in a salad bowl. Add the cooked mussels and clams. Shell the shrimp and add them.

In a small bowl, whisk together the olive oil, lemon juice, parsley, mustard, garlic, salt, and pepper. Pour the dressing over the seafood and toss gently, adjusting the seasonings to your taste. Cover tightly and place in the refrigerator to marinate for at least 1 hour. If you leave the salad in for longer be sure to toss it from time to time to evenly coat the seafood with the dressing.

Remove the salad from the refrigerator about a half hour before serving.

Insalata di Pollo alla Enrica
Enrica's Chicken Salad

Salerno, Campania

SERVES AT LEAST 6 AS AN ANTIPASTO,
AT LEAST 4 AS A MAIN COURSE

When the ingredients are finely cut and dressed lightly, as Cecilia's sister Enrica Cunzulo Baratta does so well, this is a very elegant salad. In fact, Enrica is often asked to bring it to parties and Cecilia has incorporated it into her catering menus. What makes it taste special is the potatoes cooked in vinegar, plus additions of ham and cheese. Think of it as the Southern Italian version of chef's salad. Enrica and Cecilia serve it as an antipasto, but it is also a great lunch or dinner main course.

1 cup white wine vinegar, rice vinegar, or distilled white vinegar

2 medium potatoes (10 ounces), cut into ⅛-inch strips like French fries (about 3 cups)

3 tablespoons mayonnaise

3 tablespoons heavy cream

1 cup julienne strips of cooked chicken breast (less than 1 breast)

¼ cup julienne strips of white celery heart

¼ cup (about 1 ounce) julienne strips of Emmentaler (Swiss) or Gruyère cheese

½ cup julienne strips of boiled ham (about 2 ounces), or half ham and half tongue, or all tongue (you could also use speck)

1 tablespoon chopped parsley (optional)

1 tablespoon minced or julienned pickled red pepper (optional)

1 tablespoon minced pickled carrot (from *giardiniera*; optional)

Salt and pepper to taste

Lettuce leaves

Cherry tomatoes or mixed pickled vegetables (*giardiniera*; for garnish)

In a medium saucepan, over high heat, combine the vinegar with 1 cup of water and bring to a boil. Add the potato strips and boil until barely tender, about 12 minutes. Drain well, then let cool, or cool quickly in an ice-water bath.

In a large mixing bowl, whisk together the mayonnaise and cream. Add the cooled potato strips, the chicken, celery, cheese, ham, optional parsley, pickled pepper, and carrot. Toss well, seasoning with salt and pepper.

Line a platter with lettuce leaves, then pile on the salad. Garnish with cherry tomatoes or pickled vegetables. Serve lightly chilled.

Minestre
e Zuppe
Soups

Minestra e Zuppa.

The easiest translation of *minestra* would be "soup." But it is much more than that. It is often a meal in a bowl and sometimes, even today, the only dish for supper—a big bowl of vegetables and the seasoned broth that results from their cooking poured over or eaten with a slice of stale or toasted bread drizzled with olive oil. If it sounds humble and primitive, that's because it is. *Minestre* (the plural) predate pasta as the everyday food of the peasantry. Before pasta was dried to feed the masses, in the seventeenth century, the poor cuisine of rural Italians—*la cucina povera*—was largely based on boiled greens and vegetables. In fact, northerners derogatorily called southerners *mangiafoglie*, "leaf eaters."

Most *minestre* are vegetable soups, and a big, thick, multivegetable soup is called *minestrone*; the *one* suffix, pronounced "Oh-nay," means "big." But pasta and bean dishes, and hearty bean, lentil, and chickpea soups, are *minestre*, too, even when they are dry dishes, not liquid, such as the Baked Pasta and Beans of Salerno (page 106).

Zuppa is another category of minestra. In English, we'd translate *zuppa* as "sop" because it is not merely a broth or brothy soup but a brothy mixture, actually sometimes not even that brothy—could be animal, vegetable, or fish—poured over bread so that the bread sops up the liquid and flavors. These days, sometimes the starch in a zuppa is potatoes instead of bread. Or it could be pasta soaking up the flavors.

Broth, *brodo*—particularly broth made from meat or poultry—is not an especially Southern food. In order to make broth you need precious protein—meat or poultry. Southern Italians would prefer to put those in their sauces, their ragùs (see pages 83–95). With the grand exception of *minestra maritata*, the ancient soup of gelatinous pork broth with greens, most Southern Italian soups have water as their base. They rely on their solid ingredients and olive oil for flavor. The only true broth that most people would make, outside of celebration meals, is vegetable broth. Truth be told, bouillon cubes have made their way into the Italian kitchen, too, and cooks all over Italy think nothing of adding a bouillon cube to boost the flavor of almost anything. These are largely salt, as they are in the United States, so I do not use them.

OLIO SANTO

HOT PEPPER OIL

In Southern Italy, hot pepper oil is considered so sacred it is called *olio santo*, or "sainted" or "holy" oil. A jar, cruet, or bowl of it is always on the sideboard, waiting to be drizzled or dropped off the tines of a fork on a thick soup, especially a bean soup, pasta and beans, or pasta and vegetables.

I made the mistake once of trying to prepare hot pepper oil with fresh red chiles. Cecilia came into my New York kitchen and immediately threw it away. "You can die from this," she said, referring not to the heat strength of the oil but to the white fungus that had begun to grow on the peppers. At Seliano, they string the hot peppers at the end of the summer, hanging them from the beams of the outdoor kitchen and drying them to the rubbery point, although not to the totally desiccated, crisp stage. Only then do they put them under oil—heated oil.

I go an even safer route: I use the red pepper flakes that I buy in the supermarket or the totally dried whole red chiles that are now available in almost every American supermarket. Against the instinct to make the best pepper oil using extra-virgin olive oil, I find the oil tastes better and lasts longer if you infuse vegetable oil—peanut oil, corn oil, grapeseed oil—not olive oil.

Put 3 heaping tablespoons red pepper flakes or several whole dried chilies in a small jar. Top with ½ cup of warmed vegetable oil. Let stand at least one day before using.

Acquacotta

The name literally means "cooked water," and at its most basic, *acquacotta* is the most meager of *cucina povera* dishes—at its most primitive, nothing more than stale bread reconstituted with boiled water and seasoned with garlic, parsley, hot pepper, and a little olive oil. You could also add a few beans or chickpeas, or as an American chef-friend suggested, some shrimp—not exactly *cucina povera*, but good.

1 medium onion, thinly sliced

1 large garlic clove, thinly sliced

1 cup flat-leaf parsley, finely shredded

1 small hot red pepper, or ¼ teaspoon red pepper flakes, or more or less to taste

4 tablespoons extra-virgin olive oil

1 cup canned peeled Italian tomatoes, with some of the juice from the can, or 1 cup tomato puree, or 1 cup crushed canned tomatoes

¾ teaspoon salt

3 cups water

4 slices firm or hard (at least several days old) crusty dense bread or bread heels, broken into chunks

In a medium saucepan, combine the onion, garlic, parsley, red pepper, and olive oil. Place over medium heat and cook, stirring often, until the onion is very tender, 8 to 10 minutes.

Add the tomatoes and break them up with the side of a wooden spoon. Add the salt. Let the tomatoes simmer for 10 minutes. Add the water and return to a simmer. Simmer 5 minutes longer, then turn off the heat. (You can make the broth ahead, even refrigerate it, but it should be simmering when the bread is added. And once the bread has been added, you won't want to let the soup stand or be reheated, unless, that is, you want to turn *acquacotta* into *pancotto*, "cooked bread" (see variation).

Break up the bread into large chunks and add it to the liquid, softening it before serving it in shallow bowls with the broth. Or, place the bread in individual soup bowls, then ladle on the hot broth. Serve immediately.

Variation

Pancotto is made exactly as above, but the bread is cooked in the broth until it falls apart and forms a sort of porridge. In Puglia, at a wine estate, I was rather ceremoniously served a local version. The bread was moistened with chopped broccoli rabe and its cooking water, which had been seasoned with olive oil, garlic, and hot pepper. The mixture was then packed into the crust of the huge loaf from which the bread had been scooped out. Our hostess then instructed us to pour her own gorgeous, recently pressed olive oil over it all—liberally, she said. Here's another case where *cucina povera* has been made elegant.

Zuppa di Fagioli e Funghi alla I Corti
I Corti's Bean and Mushroom Soup

SERVES 6 TO 8

I corti means "the little people," and this very traditional Neapolitan restaurant is called that because it was opened by two brothers who were midgets. They developed a recipe for Nocino, a green walnut and spice liqueur that is famous throughout the south. The restaurant is now run by the thirty-something great-niece and -nephew of the little people, while their mother is in the kitchen with their aunt, the brothers' last remaining sibling, a full-sized woman. Sant' Anastasia is one of the horribly congested and shabby suburbs of Naples, but people come from all over to eat at I Corti. Not all the food is as traditional as this soup. One of the restaurant's original creations has gained wide fame not only for its deliciousness but also for its name, Garbage Pail Thick Spaghetti (page 112). I use shiitake mushrooms for this soup because they are flavorful and readily available in the United States. At the restaurant, they use a type of chanterelle. Any flavorful fresh mushroom does just fine.

1 pound cannellini or small white beans, soaked for at least 8 hours in 2 quarts cold water

1 large celery rib, diced (about ½ cup)

1 small onion, diced (about ¾ cup)

1 large garlic clove, coarsely chopped, plus 2 more cloves, lightly smashed

2 teaspoons salt, or more to taste

3 tablespoons extra-virgin olive oil

10 to 12 ounces shiitake mushrooms, tough stems trimmed off and discarded (or used to make vegetable broth), the caps sliced thinly or very coarsely chopped

2 rounded tablespoons coarsely chopped flat-leaf parsley

Freshly ground black pepper to taste

In a minimum 5-quart pot, combine the beans and their soaking water, adding 6 cups fresh water, the celery, onion, and chopped garlic. Bring to a boil over high heat, then partially cover the pot and adjust the heat so the soup simmers for 45 minutes to an hour, until the beans are tender. Add salt after about 30 minutes.

Meanwhile, combine the oil and the 2 lightly smashed garlic cloves in a 10-inch or slightly larger skillet, over low heat. When the garlic starts sizzling, turn it once or twice, squishing it down as it softens with the back of a wooden spoon to release its juice into the oil. Cook until the garlic is very tender but still white.

Add the mushrooms and parsley. Increase the heat to medium and sauté, tossing the mushrooms frequently for 3 to 4 minutes, until tender. Remove the whole garlic, if you can find it and you care to.

Add a little more than a cup of the beans' cooking water to the mushrooms in the skillet. Simmer for 5 minutes. Pour the mushroom mixture into the beans and simmer together for 5 minutes. Adjust the salt, and season with freshly ground black pepper.

Serve very hot.

Maccu di San Giuseppe
Bean and Greens Soup for the Feast of Saint Joseph

All Regions

SERVES AT LEAST 8

It's not so much that this soup is made to honor Saint Joseph, but like many dishes made for feast days, it's all about seasonality. Saint Joseph's Day is March 19, the beginning of spring. The point of this soup is to use up all the odds and ends of dried beans, peas and lentils, even some grain and dried chestnuts, that were stored for winter, adding some of the tonic spring greens that can be foraged for at that early time in the new growing season. These days, in both Italy and the United States, all year long you can buy a mix of beans for making a soup like this. You don't need a saint's feast day as an excuse to make it. As for the greens, spinach is fine. Dandelions, chicory, borage, and fennel fronds are traditional because they are among the first spring greens.

1 pound mixed beans (such as Goya's 16-Bean Soup Mix)

4 ounces lentils, preferably small brown European lentils

4 ounces dried peeled yellow fava beans

4 ounces red kidney beans

2 ounces large lima beans or other large beans

2 ounces cannellini or other large white beans

4 ounces any other bean

8 ounces dried chestnuts

1 cup finely chopped carrots

1 cup finely chopped celery

1 cup finely chopped onion

2 teaspoons fennel seeds, lightly crushed, or several sprigs of wild fennel greens

1 tablespoon salt

2 pounds fresh spinach, well washed, left as whole leaves, or 2 pounds mixed spring greens, such as dandelions, chicory, borage

Extra-virgin olive oil or *olio santo* (see page 73)

Rinse the beans and chestnuts. Place them all in a very large pot with cold water to cover by several inches, about 4 quarts of water. Let the mixture soak overnight, at least 8 hours.

Do not change the water, but add enough to come at least 3 inches above the beans. Add the chopped vegetables and the crushed fennel seeds (but not the fennel greens, if using). Over medium heat, bring to a simmer and cook, uncovered, for about 2 hours, or until the largest beans are tender. After 1 hour, add the salt.

Add the well-washed spinach or other greens, and the fennel greens, if using. Simmer another 10 minutes, or slightly longer, until the greens are well cooked and tender.

Serve with extra-virgin olive oil or *olio santo* to drizzle on top of each portion.

Zuppa di Lenticchie con Salsicce e Broccoli di Rapa
Lentil Soup with Sausage and Broccoli Rabe

It's said that "what grows together, goes together," and legumes (beans, lentils, chickpeas), sausage, and broccoli rabe are all grown or produced in Southern Italy. It's natural that they'd be used together in various combinations, as in this thick soup, a hearty meal in a bowl. Follow it with a piece of cheese and some fruit. During Cook at Seliano sessions, I make it for my classes on the day we have our buffet of local cheeses and *salumi*. Cheeses, cold cuts, bread, and this soup are, in fact, a wonderful menu for an informal party.

1 pound lentils (about 2¼ cups), rinsed

½ pound sweet Italian sausage (preferably without fennel), removed from casings

2 tablespoons extra-virgin olive oil

2 garlic cloves, finely chopped

3 tablespoons tomato paste

1 teaspoon salt, or more to taste

¼ teaspoon red pepper flakes

1 bunch broccoli rabe, heavy stems peeled, leaves washed, all cut into 2-inch pieces

Extra-virgin olive oil or *olio santo* (see page 73; optional)

In a 4- to 5-quart pot, combine the lentils and 2 quarts of water. Bring to a boil, uncovered, over high heat. Lower the heat and simmer for 20 minutes, or until the lentils are almost tender.

Meanwhile, combine the sausage, oil, and garlic in a small skillet over medium heat, breaking up the sausage with a wooden spoon, until the bits of meat have lost their raw color. Set aside.

When the lentils are almost cooked, stir in the cooked sausage, tomato paste, salt, and red pepper flakes. Simmer another 10 minutes. Set aside until ready to serve.

Bring at least 4 quarts of water with 1 heaping tablespoon of salt to a rolling boil. Add the broccoli rabe and let the water return to a boil. Cook the broccoli for 5 minutes. Remove with a strainer, draining well. Reserve the broccoli cooking water in the pot.

Add the brocooli rabe to the lentils with enough of the broccoli-cooking water—at least 2 cups—to give the soup a thick but spoonable consistency. Taste and adjust the salt. (If making the soup ahead, reserve about a quart of the broccoli water. The soup will thicken as it stands and you will want to add more liquid when reheating it. You can also use plain tap water.)

Serve with either a cruet of condiment-quality olive oil or *olio santo* for diners to drizzle over their soup to taste.

Brodo di Agnello or Cutturiddu
Lamb Broth

Accetura, Basilicata

SERVES 6

Cecilia and I once took a group of Italian Americans back to the southern provinces from which their families had emigrated. We called it our Italian American Roots Tour. Among our group were five family members headed by 90-year-old Aunt Aggie, her daughter and son-in-law, and nephew and niece-in-law. That's how we ended up in Accetura, in the province of Matera, high on a mountain in southern Basilicata, where, as it turned out, half the town was related to Aunt Aggie. The family name was Filardi, and they were prominent builders who devised a stone-and-brick construction that has withstood many earthquakes. The current town priest was a Filardi, and the town historian was married to a Filardi, Domenica Filardi Labbate, who gave me this recipe. It's a simple but flavorful broth that is eaten as a *zuppa*, poured over stale bread, or served with broken spaghetti or small macaroni. In the old days, it would have been made only with bones. Still, the meat can be shredded and served in the bowl with the soup. If you like, you can make the broth stingingly hot with red pepper. As Lucanians have an abiding taste for *peperoncino*, that's what they do.

3 pounds boney lamb shoulder, cut into large pieces

1 whole head of garlic, separated and each clove lightly smashed and peeled

2 tablespoons dried oregano

1 tablespoon salt, or more to taste

½ teaspoon red pepper flakes, or 1 fresh hot red pepper

Stale bread or 6 ounces broken spaghetti (see page 81) or small pasta, such as ditalini

Combine all the ingredients except the bread or pasta in a 4- to 5-quart pot with 3 quarts of cold water.

Bring to a boil, uncovered, over high heat, then lower the heat and simmer briskly, partially covered, for about 2 hours. Add more water if necessary to keep the lamb well covered. Let the soup cool somewhat, then refrigerate overnight. The next day, peel off the hardened fat on the surface. The soup will be quite gelatinous.

In a large pot, over high heat, bring the soup to a simmer, then remove the meat with a slotted spoon. Strip the meat off the bones and discard the bones. Shred the meat and put it back in the broth or serve it in larger pieces, separately, with a cooked vegetable, such as broccoli rabe.

Serve the broth very hot, poured over stale bread or with broken spaghetti or small macaroni. The pasta can be cooked separately and added to the broth, or cooked directly in the broth, which is what I prefer.

Brodo di Aragosto con Spaghetti Ruoti
Lobster Broth with Broken Spaghetti

SERVES 4

This tastes like so much more than it is, which is merely lobster cooked in tomato broth prepared with tomato puree, onion, and a bay leaf. It is an old-time, standard dish on the west coast of Sicily. Broken spaghetti—*ruoti* is the preferred local word for "broken"—is the standard addition, but you could use other pasta. Some recipes have you flavor the broth with garlic, as well as onion, and some use *peperoncino*, hot red pepper, instead of black. You decide. Torn leaves of basil can be added just before serving.

3 tablespoons extra-virgin olive oil

1 medium onion, finely minced (about 1 cup)

3 cups tomato puree

1 bay leaf

1 teaspoon salt

¼ teaspoon freshly ground black pepper

1 (2½-pound) live lobster

4 to 6 ounces spaghetti, broken into lengths no longer than 3 inches (see opposite), cooked very al dente

Several torn basil leaves (optional)

In a pot that will accommodate the disjointed lobster, heat the olive oil over medium heat and sauté the onion until tender and golden, about 8 minutes. Add the tomato puree and 3 cups of water, using some of the water to rinse the can or bottle in which the puree was packed. Add the bay leaf, salt, and pepper. Bring to a simmer and let cook gently for 5 minutes.

Meanwhile, with a very sharp knife, kill the lobster by putting the point of the knife into the head between the eyes. Use the knife to chop off the claws.

Increase the heat so the soup boils. Add the lobster. Cook for about 12 minutes from the time it is added. It should be just cooked through. Remove it from the soup with tongs, letting it drain into the soup.

Once the lobster is cool enough to handle, crack it open and remove all the meat from the body and claws. Cut it into pieces no bigger than you would want to spoon up. Discard the shells and innards. If preparing ahead, put the lobster in a bowl and cover with plastic wrap. Refrigerate the soup and the lobster meat.

At serving time, reheat the broth and boil the spaghetti in plenty of well-salted water. When the pasta is almost cooked but still a little too firm to eat, drain it well.

Add the separately cooked and drained broken spaghetti and the lobster pieces to the simmering soup. Turn down the heat and simmer very gently until the pasta is tender enough to eat, or even a little softer than you'd eat a sauced pasta dish.

Serve very hot, garnished with torn basil, if desired.

SPAGHETTI SPEZZATI

BROKEN SPAGHETTI

Just the sound of the words *spaghetti spezzati,* "broken spaghetti"—never mind the actual food—has nostalgic sentiment for Southern Italians. Then, there is the music made by pasta being popped into pieces in a clean dish towel. It's enough to make almost any Italian over 30 launch into memories of *mamma* or *nona* (grandma) or a lovely old aunt whose kitchen always smelled of ragù or *minestra.*

Broken spaghetti was a food of necessity in the Southern Italians' impoverished past, when nothing was wasted, not even a few millimeters of macaroni. In the old days, it might have been gleaned from the bottom of a barrel. The grocer could not charge the same for bottom-of-the-barrel broken pieces as he did for whole strands. And even today, the pasta factories of Gragnano (and I suppose elsewhere) are happy to sell, at a serious cut rate, what remains after they've neatly cut the pasta to fit into modern boxes. Some pasta factories also donate these remains to nursing homes and hospitals.

Mother or Grandmother herself may have broken the spaghetti to serve it in broth (see pages 79 and 80), with beans or lentils (see page 106 and 109), or with any of the vegetables frequently prepared with pasta, such as squash (see page 120) and potatoes (see page 114). Combined with other pasta shapes, broken spaghetti is also featured today in packages of *pasta mista,* "mixed shapes."

Breaking spaghetti is fun, too: Wrap the pasta in a clean dish towel so it doesn't pop all over the kitchen. Holding one end of the pasta down on the work surface, break it by pressing down every couple of inches.

Sugo e Ragù
Tomato Sauce and Ragù

Tomato Sauce.

Nothing symbolizes the Southern Italian kitchen more than tomato sauce, and so it is often disparaged as "red sauce cuisine." Of course, it is so much more. But even if it were, what's so bad about that? The nutritionists now tell us that cooked tomatoes are one of the healthiest foods—not raw, cooked.

Tomatoes were introduced to Europe in about 1520, when the explorer Cortés returned to Spain from Mexico, where he had found the Aztecs eating them. Tomatoes were not actually eaten in Europe until sometime in the early eighteenth century, however. They were used as ornamental plants but were said to cause "humors"—some might translate that to mean indigestion, *agita*, in Italian. Neapolitans like to claim that they were the first Europeans to dare eat tomatoes because indigestion is better than starvation.

Naples and its environs turned out to be one of the best places on earth to grow tomatoes. At the base of Mount Vesuvius, near the Roman cities of Pompeii and Herculaneum that were so swiftly buried by the volcano in AD 79, the soil of San Marzano and towns near it, plus the intense sun and summer heat, provide the perfect environment to grow "the golden apple"—*pomo* ("apple") *d'oro* ("of gold").

It's not possible to reproduce the flavor of tomato sauce as it is in Italy without a good tomato, preferably Italian; and even Southern Italians, who have some of the best tomatoes in the world, use canned peeled tomatoes, commercially jarred tomato puree, and tomato paste. It's not only for their convenience, but also because they are generally better than fresh. The tomatoes are canned, jarred, or concentrated when they are at their peak of ripeness.

The genuine San Marzano–type tomato is no longer canned, however. The Roma tomato is the variety grown and canned in and around San Marzano today. These are the same "plum" tomatoes that we grow in the United States, mainly in California. But Romas grown near Vesuvius have more acidity than American tomatoes, have richer flavor, and are less pulpy. Truth be told, many Italian canned plum tomatoes are now coming from Basilicata, from in and around the town of Gaudiano, where Italy's second-largest canning factory is. San Marzano tomatoes, however, have a DOP designation from the Italian government—*denominazione di origine protetta*—guaranteeing their origin, which is some indication of quality. Next best, but hardly a hardship, are other Italian canned tomatoes, and many California tomatoes. There are also "imported" tomatoes from countries other than Italy, but I am wary of them. They can be acidic or bitter or both.

Sugo di Pomodoro *Pummarulo* (Neapolitan dialect)
Tomato Sauce

MAKES ABOUT 2 CUPS; ENOUGH FOR 10 TO 12 OUNCES
OF PASTA, SERVING 4

Tomato sauce is unquestionably Southern Italy's greatest contribution to world cuisine. Spaghetti with tomato sauce, with or without meatballs, could easily be the world's most popular dish. Contrary to popular belief, a small batch of basic tomato sauce can be cooked in less than 20 minutes, including chopping and sautéing garlic or onion. Whether you use fresh plum tomatoes, canned plum tomatoes, cherry tomatoes, or tomato puree from a bottle, can, or box, the whole point is to cook it briefly so the tomatoes retain their sweetness. In Southern Italy, when a tomato sauce is to go with fish or seafood, it is generally seasoned with garlic and parsley or oregano. For other purposes, including dressing pasta, it is usually seasoned with onion and basil, which makes for a sweeter sauce.

Old-fashioned home cooks in Southern Italy often hand-crush canned peeled tomatoes, and I love to do it myself. If it is just a few tomatoes, crush each in your fist as you lift it from the can and put it in the pot. If you are crushing many tomatoes, put them in a bowl and tackle the job with both hands.

2 rounded tablespoons finely minced onion, or 1 large garlic clove, lightly crushed or cut in half, or minced or sliced

2 tablespoons extra-virgin olive oil

2 tablespoons water, or more as needed

1 (28-ounce) can Italian peeled tomatoes with their juice, or 1½ pounds very ripe fresh plum tomatoes, peeled and seeded

½ teaspoon salt, or more to taste

Pinch of red pepper flakes or a few turns of freshly ground black peppercorns

2 or 3 fresh basil leaves, roughly torn, or ½ teaspoon dried oregano

To make the sauce with onion, combine the onion and oil in an 8- to 9-inch skillet. Place over medium heat. As soon as the onion begins to sizzle, reduce the heat and cook the onion, tossing often, for about 3 minutes. Add the water and continue cooking until the water has evaporated and the onion is tender but still white, about another 5 minutes. You can add more water, a tiny bit at a time, if the onion begins to color before it is tender.

To make the sauce with garlic, put the garlic and oil in a small skillet. Place over low heat and cook the garlic until it is tender and, at most, lightly colored. If using a slightly crushed or halved clove, you can remove it. A Neapolitan cook would; a Calabrian cook probably would not.

Add the tomatoes. Puree them directly into the pan through a food mill, or use your hand to crush them into the pan, or pour them whole into the pan and break them up with the side of a wooden spoon. Increase the heat so the tomatoes come to a simmer. Season with salt and pepper flakes or black pepper.

Recipe continues

Stirring frequently, simmer briskly for about 12 minutes, until the sauce is thick. Add the basil for the last minute, or add the oregano for the last 5 minutes.

Serve very hot. The sauce reheats beautifully, but don't recook it.

NOTE: This recipe is easily multiplied. When multiplying, however, you will not need to increase the oil nearly as much as the other ingredients, and you will certainly have to cook the sauce longer. The more sauce, the longer it takes to cook. One can of tomatoes takes no more than 12 to 15 minutes of steady simmering in an open skillet. For two, three, or more cans of tomatoes, use a deep skillet or sauté pan, wide saucepan, or stove-top casserole (I love enameled cast-iron) to encourage quick evaporation. A two- or three-can sauce will take about 30 minutes of steady simmering to cook down to the right consistency.

TOMATO PASTE

CONCENTRATO, ESTRATTO, STRATTU

Tomato paste is an underrated, undervalued product in the United States, although old-fashioned Italian-American cooks use it extensively. Their first-generation ancestors made their rich ragùs with it, so they do, too. In Italy, there are cooks who also disdain tomato paste as an old-fashioned product, although in the south, particularly in Sicily, it is often used to boost the flavor of soups and sauces, or perhaps just add some needed color to a dish. I've heard Southern Italian cooks say that tomato paste "carries flavor," a bit of folk wisdom that is backed by science. Tomatoes and, even more so, tomato paste are natural sources of MSG.

There are several levels of paste. What is called *concentrato* is about the same as American tomato paste, a soft, high-moisture product. *Estratto* ("extract") or, as they call it in Sicily, *strattu,* is a very dense, sun-dried product. The genuine article is sometimes available in the United States, but it is hard to find and it is generally expensive and sold by weight. American-canned tomato paste works fine, though, and the recipes in this book are formulated using it. Unfortunately, our paste, because of its high moisture content, spoils easily. When using just a small portion of a can, transfer the remainder to a freezer container and freeze for future use. If you do find genuine Italian tomato extract, keep it refrigerated in a tightly closed jar. It actually improves with age, even when the color darkens. It's like good wine.

Sugo di Maiale
Pork Sauce or Ragù

MAKES ENOUGH FOR 1½ POUNDS OF PASTA,
SERVING AT LEAST 8

The "Sunday gravy" of my youth—the sauce simmered for what my Italian-American childhood friends all bragged and exaggerated was dozens of hours—was usually based on pork. Their mamas may have added meatballs and/or sausage, or *bracciole* (stuffed beef or pork rolls), or hunks of beef or lamb that could be served as a second course after the sauce itself went on pasta, but it was pork and its fat that gave the ragù its velvety richness. Fatty pork ribs were popular, although today I use pork shoulder or butt with the skin still attached, which is the way it is sold in most American supermarkets. Pork shoulder and butt provide more meat than ribs, and the gelatin-rich skin, the *cotica*, adds luxurious texture. That said, using the same directions that follow, I often make a more Neapolitan-style, but no less gorgeous ragù with only flavorful, fat-marbled beef, such as what is these days called tri-cut or Porterhouse tail, both terms for short loin trimmings, a relatively inexpensive cut. Chuck works well, too.

1 tablespoon extra-virgin olive oil

2½ teaspoons salt, or more to taste

2 pounds pork shoulder, cut into approximately 3-inch pieces, with skin and bone, but a good part lean

1 medium onion, finely chopped (about 1 cup)

½ cup dry red wine

3 (28-ounce) cans Italian peeled plum tomatoes

2 large bay leaves

¼ teaspoon red pepper flakes

Heat the oil in a 4- to 5-quart pot over medium-high heat until a piece of meat will sizzle immediately. Season each piece of meat all over with salt, using about 1 teaspoon. Add the meat and onion together to the pot. Turn the meat often to lightly brown it on all sides, about 10 minutes.

Add the wine and continue to cook, turning the meat in the wine, until all the wine has evaporated. Purée the tomatoes directly into the pot through the medium blade of a food mill, or use your hand to crush them in. Stir well and season with the remaining salt, bay leaves, and red pepper flakes.

Bring to a gentle but steady simmer over medium heat, then adjust the heat so the sauce continues to simmer very gently for about 2½ hours. Stir well every 15 to 20 minutes, making sure nothing sticks to the bottom of the pot and stirring down the concentrated residue that collects on the side, just above the surface of the sauce.

Use the sauce on any pasta. Although the meat will be rather cooked out, it can be served as a second course with a vegetable side dish. The skin is considered a delicacy.

Sugo Gratinato
Baked Tomato Sauce

Campania

MAKES ENOUGH FOR 8 TO 10 OUNCES
OF PASTA, SERVING 3 OR 4

At Azienda Seliano, Baronessa Cecilia's *agriturismo*, the staff often makes tomato sauce this way—just pouring everything into a roasting pan and putting it in the oven. It is a great method when you have a vast number of people to feed, as they often do—you don't have to mind a pot on top of the stove. And the flavor, what with capers, fresh basil, parsley, *and* dried oregano, is deep and complex. Canned cherry tomatoes, which are now available in some American specialty markets, are the perfect product to use in this sauce, but canned plum tomatoes work well, too. If you use fresh cherry tomatoes that have been cut in half, they won't exude much juice, but they still make a good pasta dressing, as well as a vegetable antipasto or a side dish.

1 (28-ounce) can peeled Italian plum tomatoes; or 2 (15-ounce) cans *pomodorini collini,* Italian cherry tomatoes; or 1 pint grape or cherry tomatoes, each cut in half or quarters, depending on size; or 1 pound small round, salad-type tomatoes, each cut into quarters or wedges

¼ cup loosely packed fresh basil or flat-leaf parsley

1 rounded tablespoon salted capers, well rinsed

1 or 2 garlic cloves

½ teaspoon salt

¾ to 1 teaspoon dried oregano

3 tablespoons extra-virgin olive oil

3 tablespoons fine dry bread crumbs

Put a rack in the lower third of the oven. Preheat the oven to 350° F.

Put the tomatoes in a shallow baking dish—a 10-inch round pie plate is perfect. If using canned plum tomatoes, drain each one by cutting it in half over the can, then cut it into large pieces directly into the baking dish. The tomatoes should not be totally dry, but the juices should not come more than about halfway up the tomatoes. If using canned cherry tomatoes, use the entire contents of the can, including the juice.

Place the basil or parsley, capers, and garlic on a cutting board and finely chop them together. Season the tomatoes with salt, then add the chopped mixture, sprinkle with oregano, then drizzle with oil. Toss well to mix. Sprinkle the bread crumbs evenly over the top.

Bake for 30 to 45 minutes, until the tomatoes are bubbling and the bread crumbs have lightly browned. The crumbs will not be very crunchy. Rather, they thicken the sauce.

Serve immediately, tossing with any pasta or as a topping for *bruschetta.* If using fresh cherry tomatoes or salad tomatoes, it's a good side dish, served hot or at room temperature.

Salsicce al Ragù con Patate
Sausage in Sauce with Potatoes

My friend Michelangelo Arezzo is a lawyer who lives in Catania. But his noble family home, now his weekend home, is on the countryside near Modica. With all that, he swears by the sausage of nearby Ragusa, which is flavored with fennel seed and made with meat that is hand-chopped and a little coarser than other sausage. In the United States, I also try to buy a more coarsely ground sausage, not just for this recipe but everything else. Any good, plain Italian sausage will make a fine sauce. However, don't use sausage with cheese, parsley, or any ingredient except fennel seed. Save flavored sausage for grilling, roasting, or frying (see pages 187–190). Lean poultry sausage will not work well here, either. But if you like a fiery sauce, you can use sausage seasoned with hot red pepper.

3 tablespoons extra-virgin olive oil, plus ¼ cup each extra-virgin olive oil and vegetable oil to fry the potatoes

1 cup finely chopped scallions (green onions), white part only

1 heaping tablespoon tomato paste

6 cups tomato puree

3 pounds sweet Italian sausage, preferably with fennel

1 cup Nero d'Avola wine, or other hearty dry red wine

2 pounds all-purpose potatoes, peeled and cut into wedges

Combine 3 tablespoons of the oil and the chopped scallions in a 4- to 5-quart pot over medium heat. Sauté, tossing frequently, until the scallions are wilted but not browned, about 5 minutes.

Add the tomato paste and half of the tomato puree. Stir to dissolve the tomato paste, then add the remaining tomato puree. Bring to a simmer. Add the sausage, return to the simmer, then adjust the heat so the tomatoes simmer gently for 1½ hours, stirring every 15 to 20 minutes.

Add the red wine and stir well. Continue to simmer 1 hour longer.

Heat the remaining oil in a heavy skillet until hot enough to form bubbles around the handle of a wooden spoon, 350 to 375°F. Fry the potato wedges until lightly browned but not quite tender enough to eat. Add the potatoes to the sauce with the sausage and simmer for about 20 minutes, until the potatoes are fully cooked.

Serve the sausage and potatoes together, with bread to mop up the sauce.

Variation

Leave out the potatoes, serve the sauce on pasta, and serve the sausage as a separate course with a green vegetable, such as broccoli or broccoli rabe.

Ragù Siciliano con Piselli
Sicilian Ground Meat Ragù with Peas

MAKES 7 CUPS, ENOUGH FOR ABOUT 2½ POUNDS PASTA

This is the quick meat sauce that is used to fill *arancini*, the rice balls (see page 24) that are, in Sicily, sold everywhere from snack stands to fine restaurants. It is also the sauce that is mixed with pasta rings—anneli or anneletti—and cheese, then baked with a bread-crumb crust (see page 132). Spooned up, cut into blocks, or served as individual timbales (*timballi*, in Italian), the combination is sold, generically named *pasta al forno* (as if there were no others), at every level of Sicilian eatery. The sauce is also excellent on macaroni or spaghetti, even if not baked. This recipe makes a good quantity, more than you may need at once, but it freezes perfectly. I pack it in 2-cup containers, each enough to dress 12 ounces of pasta, feeding four as a first course. For the *arancini* recipe in this book, make the sauce with ½ pound of ground beef and one-third of everything else.

3 tablespoons extra-virgin olive oil

1 medium onion, finely minced (about 1 cup)

1 large carrot, finely minced (about 1 cup)

1 small celery rib, finely minced (about ½ cup)

1½ pounds ground beef chuck

2 teaspoons salt, or more to taste

½ teaspoon freshly ground black pepper

½ cup dry red wine

3 cups tomato puree

1 (10-ounce) box frozen green peas (not baby peas)

Heat the oil in a 3-quart saucepan or stovetop casserole over medium heat and sauté the onion, carrot, and celery for 15 minutes, stirring frequently, until the vegetables are very tender and just beginning to brown.

Add the meat and break it up with a wooden spoon as you mix it with the vegetables. Add the salt and pepper. Raise the heat slightly and cook, continually breaking up the meat until it has lost its raw color. Add the wine and let it evaporate, stirring frequently. After about 5 minutes, you will see there is mainly fat at the bottom of the pot.

Add the tomato puree. Rinse out the puree bottle, box, or can with 1 cup of water and add to the pot. (If using the sauce to fill *arancini*, use only ¼ cup water for rinsing the container.) Adjust the heat so the sauce simmers steadily but gently for 20 minutes.

Add the frozen peas. Stir well, return to the simmer, and cook 5 minutes longer, until the peas are tender but still green.

Serve hot, if using directly on pasta. Reheat if using in a baked pasta. It can be cold for filling *arancini*.

Ragù Barese, Ragù di Macelleria
Multi-Meat Ragù from Bari, Butcher's Ragù

Bari, Puglia

MAKES ENOUGH TO SAUCE 1½ POUNDS PASTA, SERVING 8 TO 10

The Barese have a reputation for wanting it all. That's how they happen to have the remains of Santa Claus in their big basilica. In 1087, when a city wasn't on the map, so to speak, unless it had the relics of a saint, the Barese crossed the Adriatic and stole Saint Nicholas's bones from Myra, in Asia Minor (now Turkey), where he was born. Now his bones are enshrined in a stunningly decorated crypt under the big church. You can see how this wanting-it-all attitude extends to the city's favored ragù, which is sometimes simply called *ragù barese*, but also *ragù di macelleria*, "butcher's ragù," because it contains every meat the Barese butchers sell—lamb, beef, and pork, all diced into tiny cubes—and crumbled sausage. The sauce is designed to go on orecchiette, the city and region's favorite pasta, with which it mixes beautifully. But I've served it on rigatoni and no one complained.

¼ cup extra-virgin olive oil

2 large garlic cloves

¾ pound sweet Italian sausage (can be with fennel), cut out of its casing and broken up

¾ pound boneless pork shoulder, cut into ⅓-inch pieces (see Note)

¾ pound well-trimmed boneless lamb shoulder, cut into ⅓-inch cubes (see Note)

¾ pound boneless beef chuck, cut into ⅓-inch cubes

1 medium onion, minced (about 1 cup)

1 cup dry white wine

1½ quarts tomato puree

1 (6-ounce) can tomato paste

¼ teaspoon red pepper flakes, or more to taste

2 teaspoons salt, or more to taste

Grated pecorino cheese, for serving

Combine the olive oil and garlic in a minimum 4-quart pot over low heat. Cook the whole garlic cloves until soft, but still white, pressing them into the oil a few times and turning them as they cook. Discard the garlic.

Add the sausage, increase the heat to medium-high, and break up the sausage further with the edge of a wooden spoon. Add the pork, lamb, beef, and onion. Cook the meats together, stirring often, until the juices that collect in the pot have all evaporated, leaving the meat cooking only in fat.

Add the wine, stir well, and when the wine has almost evaporated, add the tomato puree, tomato paste, 2 cups of water, and the red pepper flakes. Stir well, add salt as needed, and bring to a simmer. Cover and let the sauce simmer gently for about 2 hours, stirring about every 20 minutes.

Serve very hot. Pass grated pecorino at the table.

NOTE: The meats can be bought as chops or slices in most supermarkets, but be sure to buy more than a pound of both the pork and lamb if it comes on the bone. You will have to trim the meat and fat off these bones, reducing the weight significantly.

Ragù Ennese
Enna's Ground Pork Ragù with Chocolate

Enna, Sicily

MAKES 7 CUPS, ENOUGH TO SAUCE 2 TO 2½ POUNDS PASTA

The province of Enna is smack in the middle of Sicily. The ancient Greeks called it the *umbellicum*, the navel of Sicily. At more than 3,000 feet above sea level, the old city of Enna is the highest provincial capital in Italy. My subcompact car barely made it up the winding road to the historic center where I had traveled to get a taste of Chef Michele Bonaccorso's *ragù Ennese* and other local specialties at his Antica Hostaria. Chocolate and a trace of cinnamon are what make this ragù special. They are the legacy of the Spanish, who brought both from Mexico to Sicily in the early sixteenth century. A few Sicilian towns still hold on to their Mexican-via-the-Spanish chocolate heritage. The classic pasta for this is thick-ish tagliatelle, wide egg noodles. Very wide egg noodles, such as papardelle, are perfect. I also like large tubes, such as paccheri or rigatoni.

1 medium onion, finely chopped (about 1 cup)

2 tablespoons extra-virgin olive oil

1 pound ground pork (not too lean)

½ cup dry red wine

1 (12-ounce) can tomato paste

2½ teaspoons salt

¼ teaspoon freshly ground black pepper, or more to taste

⅛ teaspoon ground cinnamon

1 ounce unsweetened chocolate

1 teaspoon sugar

Grated cheese, for serving

Combine the onion and oil in a 3- to 4-quart saucepan or stovetop casserole over medium heat. Sauté the onion for 5 minutes, until wilted.

Add the ground pork to the pan, and still over medium heat, break it up with a wooden spoon and cook until the raw color is almost all gone. Add the wine, increase the heat slightly, and simmer 2 minutes.

Add the tomato paste and 1 quart of water (you can use some of the water to rinse out the can(s) of tomato paste). Stir until well mixed. Bring to a simmer. Add the salt, pepper, cinnamon, chocolate, and sugar. Stir until the chocolate melts. Reduce the heat, partially cover, and simmer gently for 30 minutes. Taste for salt and pepper. I like it a little peppery.

Serve very hot on pasta. Pass grated Parmigiano, pecorino, or for a very exotic but not really authentic touch, serve it with shredded piacentino cheese, which is spotted with peppercorns and colored and subtly flavored with saffron. It is another specialty of Enna, and available now in the United States.

Variation

One old Ennese recipe has you spreading lasagne with ricotta, arranging the pasta on a platter, then topping it with sauce. It's messy to serve and eat, but extremely rich and delicious.

Pasta and Risotto

Pasta and Risotto.

Many years ago, when Ettore Bellelli, Cecilia's older son, came to New York for the first time, I thought that on his last night here I would treat him and his future wife, Veronica, his brother Massimino, and his future sister-in-law Barbara to the best steak in the city. But as we were leaving for the restaurant, Ettore asked, "Do we really have to eat steak tonight? You know, you can eat American food two, maybe even three days in a row, but then you have to have pasta."

Instead of going to Peter Luger, Veronica and Barbara washed and filleted salt-packed anchovies that we ate on buttered crackers. Massimino ran downstairs and bought fresh salad greens and bread. I put out the pickled and marinated vegetables I always have on hand, and we indulged in big bowls of spaghetti with ragù from my freezer, quickly defrosted in the microwave.

Italians may eat pasta daily, but they eat smaller portions than Americans do. They usually follow it with a small portion of protein and at least one vegetable. The two-ounce serving specified by federal regulation on the back of American pasta packages may be considered puny to many of us, but it is, in fact, more like the usual Italian portion. While Americans are apt to pile every food group into one pasta bowl and eat it as a main course, Italians like to spread the wealth into separate courses.

Dried pasta is every Southerner's everyday pasta, but the south also has an ancient tradition of fresh pastas. At least a millennium before Marco Polo ate noodles in China, the Romans made fresh pasta, a flat cut called *lagane*, a word still used in some places in Southern Italy and a shape also known by other names. In Molise, it is *taccozze* or *pettole*, and it is the most popular pasta shape.

Unlike Northern Italian fresh pastas, however, which are often rich with eggs, Southern Italian pastas are traditionally made with only water and semolina—the flour of hard, high-protein durum wheat—or a combination of flours that includes semolina. These are the *pasta fatt' a casa,* literally "homemade pasta," that people still talk about with reverence, and it is this pasta, made by mothers and grandmothers with loving care and from long tradition, that are the most distinctive pasta products of the south. Fortunately, they are all nowadays also available dried and packaged and sold in the United States at specialty stores, on the Internet, and perhaps even in your local supermarket.

There are three main methods of making fresh pasta in Southern Italy. One is to form the pasta shape on an iron wire or rod. These pastas are known as *fusilli,* from the same root as the English word "fuselage," referring to the long metal rod that is used in the barrel of a gun. They are also generically called *pasta al ferreto,* or "pasta on iron." This method produces several shapes and many local names, not just fusilli. In Calabria, they are called *filei* or *fileja.* Near Palermo and in western Sicily, the coil formed this way is called *busiati.* It is the prototype for the long factory-made fusilli so familiar in the United States. Fusilli can also be called *maccheruni, maccheroni,* or *matriciana.*

Another Southern Italian handmade pasta technique results in *orecchiette,* "little ears," and several other similar shapes, all made by pressing and stretching a small ball of pasta dough.

Cavatelli—little dumplings cut from a rope of dough and rolled into a cupped oval dumpling—are the most familiar shape made by the third technique. The cavatelli we know in the United States are what some southerners would refer to as "one-finger cavatelli," but there are two-, three- and four-finger versions all made essentially the same way, just longer and each with its own local name.

Fresh semolina and water pasta dough is also rolled and cut to make ribbons, squares, and other flat shapes. *Lagane* are rectangles or ribbons paired with chickpeas. *Tagliatelle* are thicker, shorter, and chewier than the egg pasta by the same name in the north. They are usually served with beans or ragù. *Trie* is the famous Pugliese version of ribbon pasta; its name comes from the Arab word for pasta.

All of these pastas are still made at home in Southern Italy. In Calabria, it used to be said that a girl couldn't get married until she knew fifteen ways to form pasta. Today, however, working women have little time for making pasta, so the fresh pasta tradition is mainly kept alive in small pasta workshops where you can see women sitting around floured wooden tables, hand-making dinner for their whole town.

....

COLATURA
....

Sometimes called anchovy syrup or essence of anchovy, which I always think—funky smelling as it is—makes it sound like perfume, *colatura* is the liquid that results when anchovies are preserved in salt. *Colatura* is made every fall in Cetara on the Amalfi Coast, and in Pisciotta, on the Bay of Salerno. After the fish heads are snapped off, one flick of a finger removes what it can from the insides, then the fish are layered with sea salt and packed into barrels.

For about the first six weeks in salt, the reddest, most blood-soaked juices are allowed to drip out through a hole in the bottom of the barrel. The barrel's bung is then secured in place and the remaining liquid, the best portion, is dripped out closer to Christmas. The word *colatura* is from the word *colare*, "to drip."

Colatura plays a starring role in Naples and Salerno at Christmas Eve dinner (see page 103), and a few drops adds some edgy flavor to spaghetti with clams and other seafood dishes. I also love it on broccoli and broccoli rabe.

Colatura is sold in some American specialty food stores, and it is readily available on the Internet. Upscale Italian restaurants in the United States are using it, and Italian chefs all over Italy now play with it.

Pasta e Ricotta
Pasta with Ricotta

Few things are simpler or more comforting than this creamy dish—just boiled pasta blended with ricotta and grated cheese, salt, and pepper. It's the Italian equivalent of the noodles and pot cheese from my Eastern European Jewish heritage. You can add a chopped herb, such as parsley, basil, or mint, but you don't really need to.

In southeastern Sicily, near Siracusa, where so many nuts are grown on the slopes of the Monti Iblei behind the city, they add chopped hazelnuts, toasted almonds, or pistachios. With the nuts sprinkled on top, it looks good, too; and they provide crunch against the creamy ricotta.

FOR EACH PORTION

2 to 3 ounces spaghetti, or any pasta you like

¼ cup ricotta

1 heaping tablespoon grated pecorino or Parmigiano cheese

Salt and freshly ground pepper to taste

Boil the pasta in at least 1 quart of water with 2 teaspoons of salt. (Increase the water and salt in proportion to the number of servings you are making.)

Spoon the ricotta into a pasta bowl. Blend in the grated cheese.

Just before the pasta is cooked to taste, scoop out about 2 tablespoons of the pasta cooking water and, with a table fork, mix it into the ricotta so the ricotta is a little runny.

Drain the pasta well, then toss with the ricotta. Season to taste with salt and pepper.

Eat immediately.

Variation

In Campania, a very popular summer dish is cow- or buffalo-milk ricotta blended with grated Parmigiano or pecorino cheese, plenty of torn basil, and enough tomato sauce "to pink it up," as I've heard Neapolitan friends say. The traditional pastas for this are paccheri, the giant tubes, and perciatelli (bucatini), the thick spaghetti-length pasta with a tiny hole. Use about ½ cup of simple tomato sauce for each 1 cup of ricotta and several tablespoons of grated cheese. At the last minute, tear several basil leaves into the tomato-ricotta sauce.

Linguine con Noce e Colatura
Linguine with Walnuts and Colatura

Amalfi Coast and Salerno, Campania

The most elaborate form of *aglio olio*, although it is hardly elaborate at all, is this special Christmas Eve dish from the Amalfi Coast, Sorrento, Naples, and all through the province of Salerno. It is at the end of the year that *colatura* is bottled, and at the same time, the particularly well-flavored sweet walnuts of Sorrento are ready for eating. Most important, Catholics are not supposed to eat meat until after midnight on Christmas Eve, so that night's feast, La Vigilia, or The Vigil, is an all-fish meal. Besides this pasta, the menu usually includes stewed eel, *capitone,* and a salt cod, *baccalà,* dish—perhaps just shredded boiled cod dressed with parsley, chopped raw garlic, olive oil, and lemon juice, perhaps with the addition of pickled sweet red peppers.

½ pound linguine

3 tablespoons extra-virgin olive oil

3 large garlic cloves, lightly smashed

⅛ teaspoon red pepper flakes

⅓ cup walnut halves, coarsely chopped

1 tablespoon *colatura* (see page 100), or to taste

Cook the linguine in at least 2 quarts of boiling water with 1 tablespoon of salt.

Meanwhile, combine the oil, garlic, and red pepper flakes in a deep 9- to 10-inch skillet over low heat. As the garlic softens, smash it with the back of a wooden spoon to release its flavor into the oil. Do not let it brown. Remove the garlic.

Add the chopped nuts. Continue frying the walnuts and pepper another minute or so, raising the heat to medium. Be careful not to burn the nuts.

Drain the pasta, reserving about ½ cup of pasta cooking water.

Add the pasta to the pan with the oil and nuts. Toss well over medium heat, adding a bit of pasta cooking water if you want the sauce juicier, or adding an additional drizzle of olive oil, if desired. Drizzle on the *colatura* and toss one more time.

Serve immediately.

Variation

Salted or oil-packed anchovies can substitute for the *colatura.* Use 4 whole salted anchovies, thoroughly rinsed and filleted, or 8 oil-packed anchovy fillets, rinsed. Add them to the pan with the walnuts. Mash them with a fork so they melt into the oil.

Lagane e Ceci
Flat Pasta and Chickpeas

Chickpeas and pasta, seasoned in various ways, is a true dish of *la cucina povera*, the poor peasant's kitchen, but it is nowadays a fashionable retro dish, a homey evening meal for cosmopolitan people who ache to keep in touch with their rural pasts.

Lagane, a short, wide ribbon or rectangular fresh semolina-and-water pasta, is the traditional pasta used in this dish. However, factory-made pasta with chickpeas is the norm in Italy today. Prepared with chickpeas from a can or jar, seasoned with nothing more than garlic, either parsley or rosemary, and fragrant olive oil, it's the best kind of convenience food.

2 large garlic cloves, finely chopped

3 tablespoons extra-virgin olive oil

⅛ to ¼ teaspoon red pepper flakes, or ½ to 1 fresh or dried hot red pepper

2 tablespoons fresh rosemary leaves, coarsely chopped

2 (15–16-ounce) cans chickpeas

8 ounces dried small pasta, such as lagane, ditali, pennette, or broken lasagne

In a small saucepan, combine the garlic, oil, red pepper flakes, and rosemary. Over low heat, let the garlic sizzle until it barely begins to brown.

Add the chickpeas with all of their liquid. Simmer gently, uncovered, for 5 minutes.

Boil the pasta in at least 3 quarts of water with 1 heaping tablespoon of salt.

Just before the pasta is done, with a potato masher or the bottom of a tumbler (or more carefully with an immersion blender), mash about half the chickpeas, right in the pot.

When the pasta is done, drain well, but scoop out a cup of pasta cooking water first, in case you want to loosen the sauce.

Combine the pasta with the chickpeas in a large serving bowl. Toss well. Add a little of the reserved pasta cooking water if the pasta is too dry. (It should not be soupy, however.)

Serve very hot with either *olio santo* (see page 73) or condiment-quality extra-virgin olive oil to drizzle over the top.

Variation

Ciceri e Trie is a famous Pugliese form of this dish. Use a fresh ribbon pasta—the thickish supermarket brands work perfectly in this case—and fry some of it in olive oil without boiling it first. Fry until crisp. Dress the mixed boiled pasta and chickpeas with strips of the fried pasta.

Pasta e Fagioli al Forno
Baked Pasta and Beans

Salerno, Campania   SERVES 4 TO 6

Pizzeria Vicola della Neve is on one of the narrow medieval shopping streets of Salerno's historic center. The street is called Vicola della Neve, "Alley of the Snow," because under it there are caves where, in the seventeenth through early twentieth centuries, ice was stored in summer to make frozen desserts and cooled drinks. In spring, donkeys would haul ice down from Campania's snow-capped mountains, and it would be kept insulated in straw in such underground freezers.

The pizzeria is about eighty years old, filled with local people and paintings by local artists, and cooperatively owned by the waiters. Cecilia and I always take our cooking classes here for the atmosphere, but also because they make great Neapolitan-style pizza and this unusual local version of pasta and beans—a baked dish, not a soup. Pig skin—*cotica* (*cotenne* in proper Italian), cut into tiny pieces and cooked into a tomato sauce—gives the dish its richness and an elusive background porky flavor, not unlike American baked beans with salt pork. But in this case, there's pasta, too. I prefer *pasta mista* for this dish, but at Pizzeria Vicolo della Neve they use 4- to 5-inch lengths of ziti—broken spaghetti-length tubes of ziti.

2 ounces pig skin (*cotica*), cut no larger than in ¼-inch dice (see Note)

2 tablespoons extra-virgin olive oil

2 large garlic cloves, coarsely chopped

¾ cup canned Italian plum tomatoes, with some juice, finely chopped

1 cup water, or more as needed

Big pinch of red pepper flakes

2 (15.5-ounce) cans or 1 (30-ounce) can cannellini beans

Salt to taste

4 ounces rigatoni, ziti, penne, or *pasta mista*

Olio santo (see page 73) or olive oil

Combine the pig skin, olive oil, and garlic in a 3-quart saucepan over low heat, and cook gently for 10 minutes, until the pig skin begins to render some fat and the garlic is tender, but still white.

Add the tomatoes, 1 cup of water, and red pepper flakes. Increase the heat to high and bring to a boil. Lower the heat so the liquid simmers gently for 30 minutes, adding water as needed to keep the mixture liquid. When the bits of *cotica* are tender, stop adding water and let the sauce become dense.

Add half of the beans, along with all the liquid from the cans. Increase the heat to bring the mixture to a simmer. With a wooden spoon, smash the beans against the side of the pot. Crush them into a rough puree. Continue to simmer the beans for several minutes, stirring in a few spoons of water so they remain a thick but pourable puree.

Add the remaining whole beans and again bring to a simmer. Let simmer 2 or 3 minutes, stirring frequently so the beans don't stick to the bottom of the pan. Remove from the heat and set aside.

Place a rack in the top third of the oven. Preheat the oven to 500°F.

Boil the pasta in at least 1 quart of water with 2 teaspoons of salt. When still slightly undercooked, scoop the pasta out of the water with a strainer and transfer to the bean pot. Do not discard the pasta cooking water.

Stir the pasta into the beans, then if necessary stir in a few spoons of the pasta cooking water to get a thick but pourable consistency. Pour the mixture into a shallow 2-quart baking dish. (The dish can be made ahead to this point. Refrigerate it until about 2 hours before you are ready to serve it, so the beans are at room temperature when they go in the oven.)

Bake for 20 minutes, or until the top is well crusted.

Serve hot with *olio santo* and/or olive oil to drizzle on top.

NOTE: Pig skin, *cotica*, is generally still attached to pork shoulder, pork butt, and fresh ham hocks when these meats are sold in U.S. supermarkets. You can trim some off to make this recipe, or to use in long-cooked sauces, such as *Sugo di Maiale* (Pork Sauce or Ragù, page 89).

Variation

....

Before putting the casserole in the oven, top with 3 tablespoons of fine dry bread crumbs tossed with 1 tablespoon of oil.

Pasta e Lenticchie alla Siciliana
Pasta and Lentils, Sicilian Style

There are dozens of ways to combine lentils and macaroni. What makes this particular version Sicilian is the *sofritto*, the base flavoring of slowly cooked minced vegetables, pancetta, and tomato. Although this recipe calls for tomato puree, you can use leftover tomato sauce, some hand-crushed canned tomatoes, or to be very Sicilian, tomato paste diluted with wine or water. The Sicilians have a special tomato paste, *strattu*, dialect for "extract," and it is an extra-dense, mahogany-hued, sun-dried tomato paste with a particularly heady aroma and deep flavor (see page 88). American tomato paste works perfectly, too.

1 medium onion, finely minced (about 1 cup)

2 outside celery ribs, finely minced (about 1 cup)

2½ teaspoons salt

1 pound lentils, preferably from small European brown lentils

¼ cup extra-virgin olive oil

2 tablespoons finely minced pancetta (about 1 ounce)

1 small carrot, finely minced (about ½ cup)

1 large garlic clove, minced

½ cup finely shredded flat-leaf parsley

1½ cups tomato puree, or 1 (14-ounce) can peeled plum tomatoes, crushed

1 tablespoon tomato paste (optional)

¼ teaspoon freshly ground black pepper or red pepper flakes, or more to taste

8 ounces broken spaghetti (see page 81), *pasta mista*, pennette, or other small tubular pasta

Extra-virgin olive oil or *olio santo* (see page 73)

In a 4- to 5-quart pot, over high heat, bring 3 quarts of water to a rolling boil with half the minced onion, half the minced celery, and 2 teaspoons of the salt. Let boil for a minute or so. Add the lentils and boil them for about 20 minutes, until they are almost, but not quite tender.

Meanwhile, combine the olive oil and pancetta in an 8- to 9-inch skillet over medium heat. When the pancetta starts sizzling, add the remaining onion, remaining celery, the carrot, garlic, and parsley. Cook until the vegetables are tender, stirring often, about 8 minutes. Add the tomato puree or tomatoes, the tomato paste if using, the remaining ½ teaspoon of salt, and the black pepper or red pepper flakes. Simmer gently for 10 minutes, stirring often.

When the lentils are tender, pour the tomato sauce into them, stir well, then reduce the heat and simmer the sauce and lentils together for 10 minutes.

Recipe continues

Add the pasta, increase the heat so the mixture boils, and continue boiling until the pasta is done to taste, stirring frequently so the pasta does not stick to the bottom of the pot. The pasta can be firm or soft, and the dish can be soupy or dry. Add more water, as necessary, a little at a time so the soup doesn't stop boiling, to bring it to the consistency you like and cook the pasta to the degree you like. Remove from the heat and let stand for 5 minutes before serving.

Serve with condiment-quality olive oil or *olio santo*. Grated cheese is not usually served with this, but if you like a sharp pecorino or well-aged caciocavallo, Ragusano would be good.

Variations

To further embellish the dish, you can stir in blanched and chopped Swiss chard, spinach, or other greens at the very end—with or without pasta.

This *sofritto* can be used to flavor precooked beans and chickpeas, as well as lentils. A mix of beans cooked like this—simmered in the *sofritto* for a few minutes, without the addition of a liquid beyond the bean cooking liquid—would be called *fagiolata*, "a mess of beans." Serve it as a side dish or an antipasto.

Orecchiette con Cime di Rapa
Orecchiette with Broccoli Rabe

If any dish is emblematic of Puglia, it is this humble but noble plate of orecchiette, "little ears," tossed with broccoli rabe that has been "dragged" around the pan, *strascinato*, in olive oil with garlic and hot red pepper. There are now wonderful dried, but handmade orecchiette available in American supermarkets, and this dish has become popular in the United States.

2 bunches broccoli rabe, washed, heavy stems peeled

4 tablespoons extra-virgin olive oil

3 or 4 large garlic cloves, coarsely chopped or thinly sliced (about 1 heaping tablespoon)

½ teaspoon red pepper flakes, or 1 small fresh hot red pepper, split lengthwise, or more or less to taste

1 teaspoon salt, or more to taste, plus 2 tablespoons

12 ounces orecchiette

Freshly grated pecorino cheese

See page 150 for directions to initially cook the broccoli rabe. Drain the rabe. If you would like to cook the pasta in the same water as the rabe, scoop the greens out of the water with a strainer. Otherwise, use a colander as usual.

Combine the oil, garlic, and hot pepper in a 10- to 12-inch skillet or sauté pan, place over low heat, and sauté until the garlic is tender but still white.

Add the boiled broccoli rabe to the pan, season it with 1 teaspoon of salt, and toss it to coat with oil. Cover the pan and cook for 15 minutes, turning it occasionally, until the rabe is falling apart.

Boil the orecchiette in the rabe cooking water or 4 quarts of water with 2 tablespoons of salt, until done to taste. Just before the pasta is done, scoop out and reserve a cup of the pasta cooking water. Drain the pasta well. Add it to the pan with the broccoli rabe.

Toss the pasta with the broccoli rabe over medium heat for a minute or so, adding a little pasta cooking water if you feel it is too dry, and adjusting the salt.

Serve with grated pecorino cheese.

Variation

Instead of broccoli rabe, use regular broccoli, including the stems cut into small pieces. With either broccoli rabe or broccoli, as a final extra fillip, just before adding the vegetable add 2 to 4 anchovy fillets to the pan and mash them into the oil until dissolved. See Sausage with Broccoli Rabe (page 188) for another variation.

Spaghettoni all' Setaccio dell' Immondizia
Garbage Pail Thick Spaghetti

"Garbage pail," in this case, is like saying "everything but the kitchen sink," referring to the unusual number of condiments dressing the pasta—three kinds of nuts, plus raisins, capers, diced tomato, oregano, parsley, and olives. But despite the number of ingredients, this is a very simple dish. It's a signature dish of the famous I Corti restaurant just outside Naples, although the fame of the place is due more to its unusual heritage—it was founded by two midget brothers (*I Corti* means "the little people" in Italian)—and to its house-made green walnut liqueur, which is gift-boxed and sold all over Italy. Thick spaghetti is not very popular in the United States, but Barilla, the most popular brand in Italy, does market spaghettoni here. In fact, it's made in Iowa.

3 tablespoons extra-virgin olive oil

1 tablespoon finely chopped walnuts

1 tablespoon finely chopped hazelnuts

1 rounded tablespoon pine nuts

2 tablespoons raisins, preferably golden

1 rounded tablespoon salted capers, rinsed and coarsely chopped if very large

¼ cup diced cherry or grape tomatoes

½ teaspoon dried oregano

1 tablespoon finely chopped flat-leaf parsley

6 Gaeta, Alfonso (Greek), or Kalamata olives, pitted and coarsely chopped

8 ounces thick spaghetti (spaghettoni) or regular spaghetti

Salt to taste

Grated pecorino cheese (optional)

In a 9- to 10-inch skillet, heat the oil over medium heat. When hot, add the walnuts, hazelnuts, and pine nuts. Sauté them until the pine nuts become lightly browned. Be careful not to burn them.

Add the raisins, capers, and tomatoes. Cook, stirring frequently, for about 5 minutes. Add the oregano, parsley, and olives. Stir well. Cook 1 minute longer. Set aside until you are ready to dress the pasta.

Boil the spaghetti in at least 3 quarts of water with a heaping tablespoon of salt. Drain well.

Add the pasta to the pan with the sautéed ingredients. Over medium heat, toss the pasta until well amalgamated with the seasonings, about 1 minute. Taste and correct the salt as necessary.

Serve with grated pecorino, if desired.

Pasta e Patate all'Europeo di Mattozzi
Europeo di Mattozzi's Pasta Mista and Potatoes

SERVES 6 TO 8

Pasta *and* potatoes in the same bowl? It may seem peculiar, but to Southern Italians this calming coincidence of starches is comfort food. To many Italian Americans the mere mention of *pasta e patate* brings back memories of Grandma.

Depending on the region, province, and household, pasta is combined with potatoes in many different ways. But the potatoes are usually cut into cubes and are almost always flavored with some sort of pork fat: *sugna*, rendered lard; *guanciale*, preserved pork cheek (it's called hog jowl in the American South); pancetta, preserved bacon; or the fat from the *gambuccio*, the shank of a prosciutto. Butter is not an option, but all olive oil is. The other ingredients are variable: celery, onion (scallion, in the case of this recipe), sometimes carrot, usually a little tomato, but not enough to make it red or even pink, and herbs, either parsley or basil. In Puglia, they might use chopped arugula instead of an herb. In Enna, in the middle of Sicily, I ate pasta and potatoes with capers. In Palermo, I ate it with peas. This particular recipe is from Europeo di Mattozzi in Naples, where Alfonso Mattozzi and his daughter, Fabiana, are famous for serving *pasta e patate* as you'd get it at home, if only there was someone at home who still made it.

4 ounces *guanciale*, *gambuccio*, or pancetta, cut into tiny cubes

¼ cup finely minced (green) celery outer rib (less than ½ rib)

¼ cup finely minced scallion, white and very light green parts

2 tablespoons extra-virgin olive oil

1 heaping tablespoon finely shredded flat-leaf parsley

1 heaping tablespoon finely shredded fresh basil

2 tablespoons tomato puree, or 1 canned peeled tomatoes, crushed (in your hand and into the pot) or finely chopped

1½ pounds (approximately) all-purpose potatoes, peeled and cut into ½-inch cubes

1½ teaspoons salt

¼ teaspoon red pepper flakes

12 ounces *pasta mista* or any small fanciful shape (tiny shells are particularly good)

⅔ cup grated Parmigiano cheese

4 to 6 ounces smoked scamorza, or other smoked cheese that melts easily (see Note), cut into ¼-inch cubes

Combine the minced *guanciale, gambuccio,* or pancetta, celery, scallion, olive oil, parsley, and basil in a 3-quart saucepan. Over medium heat, let the ingredients cook together very gently, uncovered, stirring occasionally, for about 10 minutes, until some of the fat has rendered and the vegetables are tender.

Add the tomato puree or tomatoes, the potatoes, salt, red pepper flakes, and 3 cups of water. Stir well. Cover and simmer very gently for about 15 minutes, until the potatoes are very tender. (The potato base can be prepared ahead.)

Boil the pasta in at least 4 quarts of water with 2 tablespoons of salt. Cook only until half done. Check package directions; timing varies depending on the form of the pasta and the manufacturer. When the pasta is half cooked, scoop it out of the pot with a strainer and put it into the potato base. Don't worry about adding a little of the pasta water in the process.

Stirring frequently, cook the pasta with the potatoes and their liquid. The pasta will probably not be covered with liquid at first. Eventually, it will cook fully and most of the liquid will have been absorbed. At this point, remove it from the heat.

Add the grated and cubed cheeses. Stir well, until the cubed cheese has melted and mostly melded with the pasta and potatoes into a creamy, dry (not soupy) dish.

Serve immediately.

NOTE: If smoked scamorza is not available, smoked Gouda is a good substitute, or any smoked mild cheese that melts well. Smoked mozzarella is good, too, but it becomes stringy when heated, not creamy. You could also make the dish without smoked cheese, and use any combination of cheeses you have on hand, either diced or grated. That's what a Neapolitan home cook would do.

Alfonso Mattozzi and his restaurant in Naples, Europeo di Mattozzi.

Pasta e Cavolfiore
Macaroni with Cauliflower

Sicily   SERVES 8

Cauliflower is not known, even in Italy north of Rome, as a particularly Southern Italian vegetable. In fact, I understand that most of the cauliflower grown in Campania and Sicily, to name the two southern regions that grow it in abundance, is shipped to Northern Italy and Europe. Still, Southern Italians love it, and they eat it fried, pickled, braised, boiled, and dressed with oil and lemon, and, of course, added to pasta. This Sicilian treatment, with strong seasoning, pine nuts, and raisins, makes it irresistible.

1 medium head cauliflower (about 2 pounds), broken into small florets, washed

¼ cup extra-virgin olive oil

1 medium onion, minced (about 1 cup)

⅓ cup pine nuts

2 or 3 anchovy fillets, rinsed well if packed in salt

⅓ cup currants or raisins

1 tablespoon tomato paste

Big pinch of powdered saffron (optional)

Salt and pepper to taste

1 pound any tubular macaroni, such as penne, ziti, or ditali, or orecchiette

Toasted bread crumbs (see page 35) or grated pecorino cheese

In a large pot of boiling, well-salted water, cook the cauliflower until quite tender, about 10 minutes. Drain well, reserving 1½ cups of the cauliflower cooking water.

In a 10-inch skillet or sauté pan, heat the oil over medium heat and sauté the onion for about 4 minutes. Add the pine nuts and sauté them until they have browned lightly and the onion is golden, about 5 minutes. Add the anchovies and mash them into the oil with a fork or the back of a wooden spoon. When dissolved, add the raisins and the cauliflower. Toss well, reduce the heat to low, and heat together a couple of minutes.

Meanwhile, dissolve the tomato paste in ½ cup of the cauliflower cooking water and add the saffron.

Stir the dissolved tomato paste into the cauliflower, adding a bit more of its cooking water if a moister sauce is desired. Simmer gently for 2 or 3 minutes, tossing the cauliflower in the liquid. Taste for seasoning and add salt and freshly ground black pepper as necessary.

Boil the pasta in 4 to 5 quarts of water with 2 heaping tablespoons of salt. Drain well.

Toss the cooked pasta with the sauce, again adding a bit more cauliflower cooking water as needed. Stir and toss together for 1 minute, so the pasta absorbs some of the flavor from the sauce.

Serve immediately, preferably with toasted bread crumbs or grated pecorino cheese.

ANCHOVIES

There are two words for anchovy in Italian. *Acciughe* are anchovies that have been preserved in salt; *alici* are the fresh fish, although sometimes salted anchovies are also called *alici salate*.

Whatever the name, baked, fried, cooked in sauce, or marinated raw, they are said to be one of the foods that account for the longevity of Southern Italians. They are rich in antioxidants, and because they are at the bottom of the food chain, relatively free of the mercury and other metals that larger fish collect. Unfortunately, in the United States, preserved anchovies have the reputation of being painfully salty and having an offensively fishy taste and smell. Those, however, are low-quality anchovies. Anchovies from the Mediterranean or North Atlantic are plump, mild, and not at all stinky. They are sold packed in oil in cans and small jars, just like lesser anchovies, but they also come packed in salt or brine. Anchovies packed in dry salt are sometimes sold loose, by weight, or in 500-gram cans, in specialty stores. These usually come from Sciacca, on the south coast of Sicily. In the refrigerator, tightly closed (some cans come with plastic lids), they last for months before becoming too dry.

SERVING SALTED ANCHOVIES

In Salerno, they put fillets of salted anchovy on cold toast that has been slathered with sweet butter. Melba toast is perfect for this. A plate arrayed with anchovy fillets needs no more garnish than a wedge of lemon. Serve on *crostini* topped with melted mozzarella and/or a slice of tomato.

FILLETING SALTED ANCHOVIES

The anchovies that are preserved in salt or brine are generally whole. Although they have been otherwise cleaned, they need to be filleted.

Work at the sink with your hands under cold running water. Remove any stringy material on the split side of the fish. Under the running water, rub the salt off the surface. Some silvery skin will come off, too. Leave what's left. With your thumbs and forefingers, gently pry open the fish at the end where the head was. The spine will stick to one side. Gently pull it off. Drain the anchovies on absorbent paper. Discard the tail if it is still attached to one of the fillets.

Maccheroni con Zucchine e Ricotta
Macaroni with Zucchini and Ricotta

Paestum, Campania   SERVES 6

I learned this dish from Gerardina Costanza, one of Cecilia's amazing cooks and one of the women who assist me in my Cook at Seliano classes. This is a dish of few ingredients and very much about technique. The zucchini is cut two ways, into batons and finely chopped in a food processor. I especially like this sauce on *elicone*, "helicopters," whose large spirals catch the zucchini strips like no other pasta does.

4 medium zucchini (about 1½ pounds)

1 small onion

¼ cup extra-virgin olive oil

¼ cup finely shredded flat-leaf parsley

1 teaspoon salt

½ teaspoon freshly ground black pepper

1 pound large macaroni, such as elicone, paccheri, or rigatoni

1 cup ricotta, at room temperature

Grated Parmigiano or pecorino cheese

Cut 3 of the zucchini into fine strips, about 3 inches long by ¼ inch. Chop the fourth very finely in a food processor. Slice the onion in half from root to stem end, then cut into fine strips in the same direction.

Heat the oil in a large skillet over medium-high heat. Fry the zucchini strips until a few are just beginning to brown, about 5 minutes. Add the onion and fry another 3 or 4 minutes, until the onion is wilted but still a little bit crunchy.

Add the grated zucchini and toss well with the already fried vegetables. Toss in the parsley. Fry only 1 minute, seasoning with salt and pepper. Transfer the vegetables to a large serving bowl.

Cook the pasta in at least 4 quarts of boiling water with 2 tablespoons of salt. Drain well and pour the pasta into the bowl with the vegetables. Add the ricotta and toss well.

Serve immediately, passing grated cheese at the table.

Paccheri con Zucca e Salsicce
Giant Pasta Tubes with Butternut Squash and Sausage

Salerno, Campania

SERVES 6

Paccheri (also called schiaffoni) are the largest of all pasta tubes and a favorite shape in Naples and Campania. They are often combined with seafood sauces, and a classic dish is paccheri with ricotta, tomato sauce, and basil (see Variation, page 101). This sauce of winter squash and sausage is original with Anna D'Amato, head cook at Cecilia's Azienda Seliano, where the garden produces so much butternut and hubbard squash that she has to come up with a sizable repertoire of squash dishes.

1 tablespoon extra-virgin olive oil

1 to 2 ounces pancetta, cut into small cubes (optional)

2 links sweet Italian pork sausage, preferably without fennel (about ½ pound), removed from their casings

½ cup finely minced onion (1 very small onion or ½ medium onion)

1 large garlic clove, coarsely chopped

1 tablespoon fresh rosemary leaves

¼ teaspoon red pepper flakes

2 pounds butternut squash or cheese pumpkin, cut into ½-inch cubes (4½ to 5 cups)

1 teaspoon salt

2 cups water

1 pound paccheri or rigatoni, zitoni, ziti, or penne

¼ cup finely cut parsley

Combine the olive oil, pancetta (if using), and sausage in a 3- to 4-quart saucepan over medium heat. With the side of a wooden spoon, break the sausage into small pieces as it cooks, and when it has lost its raw color, after 3 or 4 minutes, add the onion and garlic. Cook for another 4 or 5 minutes, until the onion has wilted.

Add the rosemary, red pepper flakes, squash, salt, and water. The water should barely cover the squash. Bring to a boil over high heat, then adjust the heat so the mixture simmers gently, uncovered, until the squash is tender enough to mash against the side of the pot with a wooden spoon, about 20 minutes. With a wooden spoon, smash the squash until you have a chunky puree with some cubes of squash—to your taste.

Cook the pasta in 4 to 5 quarts of boiling water with 2 heaping tablespoons of salt. Drain well. Add the pasta and parsley to the sauce and mix well.

Serve with grated Parmigiano, grana Padano, or pecorino cheese, to your taste.

Variation

Instead of using this sauce for pasta, use it to make risotto. Use vegetable broth as the majority of the liquid in the risotto, then add the sauce for the last 5 minutes of cooking. The sauce is also perfect for cavatelli, which is what Anna often serves it on.

Spaghetti alla Matarocco
Spaghetti with Garlic Pesto from Marsala

Marsala, Sicily   SERVES 6

In Marsala, the town where they make the fortified wine of the same name, the special local dish is this sauce of garlic, basil, parsley, tomato, pine nuts (sometimes), and olive oil. The name is that of a small town just outside the city of Marsala, but it is also sometimes called *pesto alla favignana*, referring to a beach-getaway island off the coast of Marsala, or more generically, *pesto siciliano*.

The traditional way of combining the ingredients is to pound everything together in a mortar with a pestle, forming a true pesto, albeit not a pretty one. Even with tomatoes, it turns out beige. But what it loses in looks it gains in a creamy quality that the other form of *matarocco* lacks. You can make a reasonable reproduction in a mini-processor. The more contemporary way to make *matarocco* is to dice the tomatoes, mince the garlic, and tear the basil by hand.

3 small heads of freshly dug garlic, or 2 small heads mature garlic, each clove peeled

1 loosely packed cup fresh basil

½ loosely packed cup flat-leaf parsley

A few celery leaves, if available

¼ cup pine nuts

¾ teaspoon salt

¼ teaspoon red pepper flakes, or a rounded ¼ teaspoon freshly ground black pepper

½ pound salad-type tomatoes, peeled, seeded, and juiced

6 tablespoons extra-virgin olive oil

1 pound spaghetti, or linguine

Combine all the ingredients, except the olive oil and pasta, in a large mortar. Grind and crush the ingredients until you have a rough sauce. Alternatively, put all the ingredients into a mini-processor and grind to a loose paste.

Add the olive oil and continue to work the ingredients, whether in a mortar or processor, to make them finer, the pesto creamier. Let stand for at least 3 hours before using.

Cook the pasta in 4 to 5 quarts boiling water with 2 heaping tablespoons of salt. Drain well, reserving a little pasta cooking water. Pour the pasta into a bowl with the pesto and toss well; add a few spoons of pasta cooking water, if desired, to thin the sauce. No cheese is required.

Variation

Besides using the pesto on pasta, it can be spread on hot *bruschetta*. It is also excellent on fish, hot or cold, of any kind. I particularly like it on cold shrimp. Or spread it on halved hard-cooked eggs. Or on halved new potatoes.

Reginette alla Matarocco di Barbara Rosolia
Curly Ribbons with Raw Sauce of Tuna, Garlic, Tomatoes, and Basil

Marsala, Sicily

At Villa Favorita, the sprawling hotel resort at the edge of Marsala, they serve elegant food for wedding receptions and business conferences, while at the front desk, associate manager Barbara Rosolia is eager to share local recipes and restaurant recommendations with her guests. This is her modern version of *matarocco*, the local garlic pesto (see page 121). Her creative addition is canned tuna, the protein that makes this dish a meal in a bowl—just what Americans and more and more young and busy Italians such as Barbara like. Barbara prefers to put the sauce on reginette, a ribbon pasta with a ruffled edge, but spaghetti or linguine is also excellent.

3 large garlic cloves, crushed with the side of a knife, then finely chopped

1 loosely packed cup fresh basil, torn into small pieces

1 cup grape tomatoes, diced

2 (5-ounce) cans light tuna packed in olive oil, drained of oil

¼ teaspoon red pepper flakes

½ teaspoon salt

½ cup condiment-quality extra-virgin olive oil

12 ounces to 1 pound reginette, ruffle-edged ribbons

Combine the garlic, basil, tomatoes, tuna, red pepper flakes, salt, and oil in a large pasta serving bowl. Let stand at room temperature for at least 4 hours before using it to dress pasta; the flavors will blend.

Cook the pasta in 4 to 5 quarts of boiling water with 2 heaping tablespoons of salt. Drain the pasta very well. Toss the pasta with the marinated ingredients.

Serve immediately or at room temperature.

Strascinati alla Crotone
Pasta Disks with Shrimp, Fennel Seed, and Arugula

Crotone, Calabria

SERVES 4

This is a contemporary, original recipe from a home cook, Rossana Zizza of Crotone, who I met in a restaurant in the Sila Grande Mountains of Calabria, about an hour's drive from her home by the sea. She and her husband and friends were at an adjoining table in a restaurant. One word led to another and we began swapping recipes. I have made it many times: it's fast, easy, and unusual. It features a favorite pasta of Calabria, strascinati, which are, in essence, large orecchiette (the perfect substitute). They are dressed with fennel seed, shrimp, arugula, and Calabria's famous cheese, pecorino Crotonese. Any mild, not salty pecorino can be substituted, such as Tuscan pecorino. Or leave out the cheese altogether. The dish has big flavors without it.

2 tablespoons extra-virgin olive oil

½ pound large shrimp (20 to 24 to the pound), cleaned, each cut into thirds

½ cup dry white wine

½ teaspoon fennel seeds

¾ cup diced fresh tomato

¼ teaspoon salt, or more to taste

Big pinch of red pepper flakes

2 cups loosely packed small-leaf arugula, or larger arugula cut into crosswise strips

8 ounces strascinati or orecchiette

Grated pecorino Crotonese cheese

Heat the oil in a 9- to 10-inch skillet or sauté pan over medium-high heat. Add the shrimp and sauté them until they turn pink—within seconds.

Add the wine and fennel seeds. Simmer for 1 minute. Add the tomato, salt, and red pepper flakes. Simmer for 5 minutes. Taste for salt and pepper and adjust as necessary. (Set aside if preparing ahead.)

Cook the pasta in at least 2 quarts of boiling water with 1 tablespoon of salt. Drain well.

Add the hot pasta to the pan with the shrimp and place over medium heat. Toss well. Add the arugula and continue to toss until the arugula wilts, about 30 seconds.

Serve immediately. Pass grated pecorino Crotonese or another mild pecorino cheese at the table.

Maccheroni alla Diavolo
Macaroni with Eggplant, Fresh Sausage, and Dried Hot Sausage

Stilo, Calabria   SERVES 4

You don't go to Stilo for food. The big attraction is the Catolico, a very small Byzantine-style church which was built on a mountain cliff for reclusive monks in the eleventh century, and still has discernable frescos and an aura of holiness.

But then you have to eat. In the town below is Da Mario, where Mario cooks in a tiny kitchen behind a tiny dining room served by his wife and two children. The fusilli-type macaroni, which Mario calls *maccheroni*, are fresh and handmade. I wouldn't doubt both the fresh and dried sausage are, too.

Olive oil for frying

1 (1-pound) eggplant (approximately), cut into about 20 3-inch long, ½-inch-thick strips

2 tablespoons extra-virgin olive oil

2 large garlic cloves, minced (about 2 teaspoons)

2 links Italian sweet sausage, casings removed

1 cup chopped canned plum tomatoes

1 to 1½ inches dried hot sausage (pepperoni), cut into ⅛-inch slices, each round cut in half rounds

Big pinch of red pepper flakes (optional)

Salt to taste

8 ounces macaroni

Grated pecorino, or shredded ricotta salata, or ricotta infornata

Heat about ¼ inch of olive oil in a 9- to 10-inch skillet over medium-high heat. When the oil is hot enough to make bubbles around the handle of a wooden spoon, add the eggplant strips and fry them until tender and beginning to brown on all sides, about 5 minutes. Remove with a slotted spoon and set aside in a bowl.

Discard the oil and reduce the heat to low. Add 2 tablespoon fresh extra-virgin olive oil and sauté the garlic until it is beginning to brown. Add the sausage meat, increase the heat to medium-high, and with the side of a wooden spatula or spoon, continue to break up the meat into little pieces as it browns. When the sausage has lost its raw color, add the tomatoes and the pieces of hot sausage. Let the meat simmer a couple of minutes, reducing the heat if necessary to maintain a slow, steady simmer. Taste and correct the seasoning with red pepper flakes and salt. The sauce should be at least slightly hot.

Add the eggplant strips, toss them with the meat and tomato, and continue to cook another minute. Remove from heat.

Cook the pasta in at least 2 quarts of water with 1 tablespoon of salt. Drain well.

Turn the pasta into the pan with the sauce. Toss the pasta in the sauce over medium heat until well mixed.

Divide the pasta and sauce among four pasta bowls, top with cheese, and serve.

SPAGHETTI ALLA CARRETTIERE

More basic than tomato sauce, garlic and olive oil could be the most beloved pasta dressing in all of Italy. In the eighteenth century, before the tomato was used with pasta, spaghetti was dressed with melted lard and garlic, and perhaps some black pepper. It was cooked and sold on the streets by vendors called *carrettiere,* "carters." Today, the word is used for myriad simple pasta seasonings, most likely some combination based on garlic and olive oil. Typical additions include oregano, or chopped olives, or basil, parsley, or mint, and/or chopped tomatoes. If the dressing is only garlic warmed or sautéed in olive oil, it's called *aglio olio.*

It's said that when you change one ingredient in an Italian recipe, you have a new dish. Here are some based on oil and garlic:

- **Aglio Olio:** Most people cook the garlic in the oil until it is tender, or even nutty brown, but I prefer it raw. Let it macerate for a few hours in the oil, or for as long as it takes to bring the water to a boil and cook the pasta. To either cooked or raw *aglio olio* you might add parsley and hot pepper, either fresh or dried.

- **Pasta cu muddica:** Sautéed garlic and oil with bread crumbs. *Muddica* is the dialect for *mollica,* which is the doughy interior of bread. *Pasta cu muddica* can be made in one of two ways. The first way: Cook chopped garlic in oil until soft but not colored, toss it on the pasta, then top with bread crumbs toasted separately in a dry pan. I much prefer the second way: Sauté the chopped garlic, and before it turns color, add the bread crumbs and fry them until browned.

- **Pasta al'Acciughe:** Add a few anchovy fillets to the hot garlic and oil and mash them with a fork until they dissolve in the oil.

- **Pasta con Bottarge:** After the pasta is dressed with oil and garlic, garnish each plate with *bottarga* (see page 41), either a spoonful of the granulated type or shavings from a cake.

In the heart of Naples, in the quarter called Spaccanapoli, stores display local products.

GENERAL RULES FOR COOKING DRY PASTA

The water must be boiling furiously, it should be copious, and it should be well salted. Those are the most important points about cooking dry pasta. The Italian rule of thumb is to use at least 1 quart of water for each 100 grams (3½ ounces) of pasta. That means that for 1 pound of pasta you need at least 4 quarts of water, but even more is better.

Bring the water to a rolling boil, then add salt. For 4 quarts of water, I use 2 heaping tablespoons of salt. If you are on a low-salt regimen, you can halve that amount, but it is much better to dramatically reduce the salt in your dressing or sauce than to cook pasta with no salt. Most of it doesn't get absorbed, but it does magnify the wheaten flavor of the pasta.

As soon as you add the pasta to the pot, stir it to prevent sticking. Stir a few more times in the course of boiling the pasta. Follow package directions for timing, although it is best to check for doneness a minute or two before the box instructs. The degree that the pasta is cooked is strictly personal—and regional. In Naples and Campania, for instance, they like pasta much firmer than in other places. For some dishes, for instance spaghetti or linguine with a seafood sauce, Southern Italians want their pasta firm to the bite—al dente—but they prefer it very well cooked for other dishes, such as pasta and beans, or pasta with a vegetable, such as pasta and potatoes. When making a baked pasta casserole, it's best to undercook the pasta slightly. The pasta will continue to cook in the oven.

Once cooked, drain the pasta, then sauce and serve it immediately.

Do not rinse pasta unless it is going to be used in a baked dish or dressed as a salad.

Cooks who find that their pasta water foams and boils over aren't using enough water or a big enough pot.

Do not add oil to the pasta cooking water. Besides that it will not prevent foaming, it will coat the pasta when the pasta is drained, preventing the sauce from adhering well.

Maccheroni con Pesce Spada alla Franca Miceli
Franca Miceli's Macaroni with Swordfish

Siracusa, Sicily

SERVES 6 TO 8

Franca Miceli is my former assistant Iris Carulli's ex-sister-in-law. We have a strange kitchen connection in that Iris learned many things from Franca's now-deceased mother that Iris, in turn, taught me. So Franca and I have some kitchen habits in common because they came from the same source. Franca is a working woman and a mighty modern cook who feeds a family of health-conscious young sons, their spouses, and their children. Her low-fat baked, not as-usual fried, caponata (see page 208) is in this book, too. I love this fish sauce because, besides its great flavor, it is one of the few fish dishes that improve when made early in the day and gently reheated for dinner.

3 tablespoons extra-virgin olive oil

1 medium onion, finely minced

2 garlic cloves, finely minced

1 small carrot, peeled and finely minced (about ½ cup)

1¼ to 1½ pounds swordfish, cut into ½-inch cubes

4 ripe plum tomatoes, peeled, seeded, and diced, or 1 (14-ounce) can peeled plum tomatoes, chopped

2 rounded tablespoons pine nuts

2 rounded tablespoons raisins or currants

1 pound ziti, penne, or rigatoni

Toasted bread crumbs (optional; see page 35)

Heat the oil in a 10-inch skillet over medium heat. Add the onion, garlic, and carrot. Sauté, stirring frequently, until the vegetables are tender but not browned, about 10 minutes.

Add the fish cubes, mix well, and cook for 10 minutes, tossing the fish a few times. Add the tomatoes, pine nuts, and raisins. Increase the heat to medium-high and simmer for 10 minutes. (The sauce can be made ahead and reheated gently before serving on the pasta.)

Cook the pasta in at least 4 quarts of boiling water with 2 tablespoons of salt. Drain well.

While the pasta is cooking, return the sauce to the boiling point.

Add the drained pasta to the sauce and heat together for a minute or so before serving.

Serve hot, with toasted bread crumbs, if you like.

Spaghetti con Ragù di Tonno e Marsala
Spaghetti with Tuna and Marsala Sauce

SERVES 4

Gazza Ladra, named after the Rossini opera *Thieving Magpie*, is a small wine bar and restaurant in Ortigia, the island that is the historic center of Siracusa. It is perhaps the most comfortable, unpretentious place on the island to settle in and enjoy wine and, say, a platter of vegetable antipasti, *salumi*, and cheese. But don't miss the cooked food. Every morning, owner Marcello Foti goes to the wonderful Siracusa market to pick the produce, fish, and meat, and in the open kitchen behind the cash register, he and his wife, Maria Grazia, prepare the same food as they'd make at home.

2 teaspoons salt

1¼ pounds fresh tuna, cut into ½-inch cubes

3 tablespoons extra-virgin olive oil

½ cup finely minced onion (about ½ medium onion)

½ cup finely minced carrot (about ½ medium carrot)

½ cup finely minced celery (about ½ large rib)

1 large garlic clove, slightly crushed, stuck with 1 whole clove

2 tablespoons tomato paste

1 cup dry Marsala wine

Pinch of grated nutmeg

1 small bay leaf

Salt and freshly ground pepper to taste

12 ounces spaghetti

In a large bowl, dissolve the salt in 3 cups of cold water. Add the tuna cubes and let them soak for about 30 minutes. Sicilians do this to make the fish taste milder—you can skip this step if you like.

Heat the oil in a deep 10-inch skillet or sauté pan over medium heat. Cook the onion, carrot, celery, and garlic until very tender but not browned, about 10 minutes.

Drain the tuna. Turn up the heat under the skillet, and when the vegetables start sizzling, add the tuna cubes. Sauté, tossing constantly, until the tuna has lost its raw color, about 2 minutes.

Mash and dissolve the tomato paste in some of the Marsala with a fork. Add it to the tuna along with the remaining Marsala, the nutmeg, and bay leaf. As soon as the sauce comes to a simmer, reduce the heat and simmer gently for 5 minutes. Add salt as needed, and freshly ground pepper to taste. (The sauce may be prepared ahead to this point.)

Cook the spaghetti in 4 quarts boiling water with 2 tablespoons of salt until almost done to taste.

While the spaghetti cooks, reheat the sauce, adding up to ¼ cup of the pasta cooking water, a tablespoon at a time, to make it more liquid.

Drain the spaghetti well and put it in the pan with the sauce. Toss for a minute over medium heat. Serve immediately.

Soufflé di Tagliarini al Limone
Lemony Egg Pasta Souffle

Battipaglia, Campania

SERVES 6

Elvira Jemma, Cecilia's mother, was born in Battipaglia, near Salerno and the Amalfi Coast, an area known for its lemons. But she spent the war years raising her family more safely in her husband's northern hometown, Parma, known for its rich egg pastas and Parmigiano-Reggiano cheese, not to mention Parma prosciutto. After the war, back home in Battipaglia, she fused the two culinary traditions in this recipe—not a true soufflé, but a spongy and lighter-than-usual baked pasta. It's a great first course for a dinner party, when it deserves a glass of spumante, and I love the leftovers reheated for lunch the next day.

½ cup (1 stick) butter

4 tablespoons flour

2 cups whole milk

2 teaspoons salt

⅛ teaspoon grated nutmeg

¾ cup grated Parmigiano cheese

⅛ teaspoon ground red pepper (cayenne or Italian paprika)

½ teaspoon freshly ground black pepper

Juice and finely grated zest of 2 lemons

4 large eggs, separated, plus 1 egg white

About ½ cup dried bread crumbs

1 (8.8-ounce) package dried tagliarini (very fine ribbon egg pasta)

Melt half the butter in a small saucepan over medium heat. With a wooden spoon, stir in the flour and cook for 2 minutes, stirring a few times. Remove the pan from the heat and let it stand until the mixture stops bubbling.

Pour the milk into the pan and stir well until the flour-butter mixture is fully dissolved. Place the pot back on medium-high heat and, stirring constantly and scraping the bottom of the pan with the spoon, cook until the mixture simmers and thickens, about 5 minutes. Season with salt and nutmeg. Stir in the Parmigiano, red and black peppers, lemon zest, and lemon juice. Then stir in the 4 egg yolks. Scrape the sauce into a large mixing bowl. Set aside.

Prepare an 8 by 8 by 2-inch glass baking dish. Butter it with about a tablespoon of butter. Coat it well with bread crumbs, pouring about ⅓ cup crumbs in the dish, tilting the dish and shifting the crumbs around so they stick to the buttered sides.

Place a rack in the center of the oven. Preheat the oven to 375° F.

Bring about 3 quarts of water to a rolling boil with 1 tablespoon of salt. Break the pasta into approximately 3-inch lengths. Boil it until only about half done, usually (not always) 1 minute and no longer than 2. The exact timing will depend on the pasta. Drain well in a colander.

Return the pasta to its pot and toss it with 2 tablespoons butter. Let the pasta cool slightly.

Stir the cooked pasta into the cooled sauce, mixing thoroughly. (The dish can be made about 2 hours ahead to this point. Place a piece of plastic over the surface of the pasta sauce and keep at room temperature.)

In a large bowl, beat the egg whites until they hold stiff peaks. Carefully incorporate the egg whites into the pasta mixture: Spoon half of the egg whites on top of the pasta, then with a two-tined meat fork, lift the pasta up and over the egg whites, while rotating the bowl. When most of the egg whites are incorporated, put the remaining whites on top and lift and turn again until well mixed. Pour the mixture into the prepared pan.

Sprinkle the remaining bread crumbs (about 3 tablespoons) on the top. Dot with the remaining butter.

Bake for 40 to 45 minutes, until the center is set and the edges are lightly browned.

Let cool 5 minutes, then serve immediately. Cut into six squares. Once fully cooled, the soufflé will deflate slightly but it will still be very delicious and much lighter than conventional baked pasta dishes.

Pasta al Forno alla Palermitana
Baked Pasta, Palermo Style

SERVES 8 TO 10

This is Palermo's comfort food—pasta rings embedded in a ground-meat ragù with peas and cubes of cheese, all baked in a crumb-lined casserole. It is scooped out at workingmen's cafeteria-style joints and molded into timbales at elegant cafes and refined restaurants. You can certainly substitute any small macaroni, such as elbows, for the rings, but the authentic pasta rings are what make the dish seem special. I find them in Italian markets, and they are available on the Internet.

⅓ cup fine dry bread crumbs

1 pound anelli (small rings, also called anelletti)

1 recipe (7 cups) Sicilian Ground Meat Ragù with Peas (page 93)

8 ounces tuma, scamorza, or mild provolone, cut into ¼- to ½-inch cubes

¼ cup grated well-aged caciocavallo Ragusano, pecorino, or other grating cheese

Place a rack in the top third of the oven. Preheat the oven to 375°F. Heavily butter a 3-quart casserole not more than about 3 inches deep (a lasagna pan is perfect), then coat it with bread crumbs. Reserve the excess crumbs for the top.

Cook the anelli in at least 4 quarts of boiling water with 2 tablespoons of salt until al dente. Follow the package directions; most brands take 12 to 13 minutes to cook to al dente.

Drain the pasta well, then stir in the meat sauce and the cubed cheese.

Pack the pasta into the baking dish, pushing the mixture to fill the dish well. Combine the remaining bread crumbs with the grated cheese and sprinkle over the top. With the palm of your hand, press the crumbs into the surface of the pasta. It will moisten them slightly. You can prepare the casserole several hours ahead, but it also reheats very well.

Bake the casserole for about 40 minutes, until thoroughly heated through. The crumbs on top will not thoroughly brown. Don't worry.

Let stand 10 minutes before serving.

Risotto con Lucaneca e Scamorza Affumicata
Risotto with Sausage and Smoked Cheese

This rich risotto is a showcase for several Lucanian flavors. The pork sausage of Basilicata (Lucania) is considered so special that the word for it, *lucaneca* (also spelled *luganega*), has become synonymous with Italian-style sausage in some parts of the world. In the United States, it is usually the coiled style of sausage that gets the name. Smoked scamorza, a low-moisture form of mozzarella, and grated sheep's milk cheese, pecorino, finish the dish. With all these, the risotto can easily serve as a meal in a bowl (add a salad) unless you serve it in very small portions.

5 cups vegetable broth

3 tablespoons extra-virgin olive oil

1 small onion, finely chopped (about ¾ cup)

1 tablespoon chopped fresh rosemary leaves

½ pound sweet or hot sausage (preferably without fennel), out of its casing

½ teaspoon red pepper flakes (optional)

2 cups arborio or carnaroli rice

½ cup dry white wine

4 ounces smoked scamorza, cut into ¼-inch dice

½ cup grated pecorino or Parmigiano cheese, plus more to pass at the table, if desired

Keep the broth hot in a small saucepan.

Heat the oil in a 3-quart saucepan or stovetop casserole over medium heat. Add the onion and sauté until it is tender, about 5 minutes. After 2 or 3 minutes, add the rosemary and the red pepper flakes. Crumble in the sausage and cook, breaking it up into small pieces with the side of a wooden spoon. When the sausage has lost its raw color, add the rice, increase the heat slightly, and stir well. Cook the rice, stirring frequently, for 2 minutes.

Add the wine and stir well. It should sizzle and evaporate nearly immediately. Add about 1½ cups of the hot broth, just enough to barely cover the rice. Stir well, then adjust the heat so the rice simmers briskly but not violently.

Continue to add broth a little at a time, and stir it in, keeping the rice barely covered. If you run out of broth before the rice is done to taste, add warm water a small amount at a time. The rice will cook for approximately 18 minutes from the time you add the first measure of broth.

Remove the rice from the heat. Stir in the scamorza and pecorino cheeses, let it rest for a minute or so, then stir again.

Serve immediately.

Risotto al Limone
Mamma Agata's Lemon Risotto

Agata Lima teaches cooking in her home in Ravello, in the beautiful, colorfully tiled kitchen that her daughter, Chiara, quite accurately calls "Mamma Agata's Heaven." High on an Amalfi Coast cliff, it seems to be at the point where the sky and the sea meet. Besides cooking lessons, Agata and Chiara prepare dinner for small groups on their expansive covered terrace, also overlooking the sea. Chiara's husband, Gennaro Petti, a professional sommelier and *affineur* (cheese finisher and expert), selects the wine. Papa Giovanni tends the terraces, where he grows the vegetables, fruits, rabbits, and chickens that Agata puts on the table. Naturally, there are Amalfi lemons the size of grapefruits, which Mamma uses in this risotto. Worthy of note here is the use of heavy cream, an Amalfi Coast hallmark. Until fairly recently, dairy cows grazed on the Sorrento Peninsula. Their milk was made into superb *fior di latte*, cow's milk mozzarella, which is why almost any dish called "alla Sorrentina" contains mozzarella. The cows also provided the tourists who have been flocking here since the eighteenth century, mainly the English, with the cream for their beloved desserts and the creamy sauces so familiar to them at home.

2 tablespoons butter

1 pound carnaroli rice (2¼ cups)

1 cup dry white wine

¾ cup fresh lemon juice (juice of about 6 lemons)

Grated zest of 6 lemons

2 teaspoons salt, or more to taste

¼ teaspoon freshly ground white pepper, or more to taste

½ to ⅔ cup heavy cream

Grated Parmigiano cheese

Melt the butter in a 3-quart saucepan or stovetop casserole over medium heat. Add the rice and stir over the heat for about 2 minutes. Add the white wine. It should sizzle instantly. Stir well and cook until the wine has nearly evaporated, usually less than 2 minutes. Add the lemon juice, half the lemon zest, about 1 cup of water, and the salt and pepper. Stir well, then let simmer until the liquid reduces to under the level of the rice.

Add approximately ¾ cup more water, just enough to cover the rice. Stir well again. Continue adding water, stirring and simmering for a total of 18 minutes from the time the wine was added. Just before the rice is done, stir in the remaining lemon zest. When done, the rice should be tender but still firm at the center.

Stir in ½ cup of the cream, and a tiny bit more water if necessary to make the mixture more creamy than starchy. Taste for salt and pepper and adjust as necessary. If the risotto is a little too lemoney to your taste, add a bit more cream.

Serve immediately, sprinkled with grated cheese.

Risotto alla Temptation
Shrimp and Pistachio Risotto

This is a re-creation of a signature dish from the very popular Temptation Trattoria on the main piazza of the seaside suburb of Sferracavallo in Sicily, just outside Palermo. Combining Sicily's highly prized pistachios with the tiny, sweet red shrimp for which the sea around Sicily is famous, plus a pinch of curry powder, it is, like so many Sicilian dishes, very exotic. Tiny sweet red shrimp are available in the United States only in winter. They come from Maine and Iceland. But I like the dish so well that I make it all year with larger shrimp, which I chop to give them greater distribution through the rice, and more the effect of the original dish. Believe it or not, the ground pistachios give the rice the creaminess that butter or cream does in other risotto recipes.

1 cup shelled raw pistachios

1 small carrot, peeled and cut into a few big pieces

1 small onion, peeled and cut into quarters

1 small celery rib, with a few leaves if possible

1½ teaspoons salt

¾ pound shrimp, any size

¼ cup flat-leaf parsley leaves

3 tablespoons extra-virgin olive oil

1 rounded teaspoon finely minced garlic (2 average cloves)

2 cups arborio or carnaroli rice

1 cup dry white wine

Scant ½ teaspoon curry powder

¼ teaspoon freshly ground black pepper

Salt and freshly ground pepper to taste

Place the pistachios on a baking sheet in a 350°F oven for 8 to 10 minutes. Set aside to cool.

Combine 5 cups of water with the carrot, onion, celery, and salt. Bring to a boil over high heat, cover, and lower the heat so the water simmers for 15 minutes.

Add the shrimp, in their shells, for the last 3 minutes that the broth boils. You can leave the cover off at this point.

With a slotted spoon or skimmer, remove all the solids from the broth and put them in a bowl. Measure the broth, and add enough water to make 5 cups of liquid. Return the liquid to the saucepan it cooked in. Keep warm over low heat.

Remove the shrimp from their shells, discarding the shells and the vegetables.

In the small bowl of a food processor, or in a mini-processor, chop the cooled, roasted pistachios until they are mostly a fine powder, but not pasty. Scrape the nuts into a small bowl and set them aside. In the same mini-processor bowl, pulse and coarsely chop the shrimp. Turn them out into a small bowl and set them aside. Again, in the same processor bowl, pulse and coarsely chop the parsley and set it aside.

To make the risotto, combine the oil and garlic in

a 3-quart saucepan or stovetop casserole over low heat. Cook the garlic until tender but still white. Add the rice, increase the heat to medium, and sauté the rice, stirring constantly, for 3 minutes.

Stir the wine into the rice. It should sizzle immediately. Keep stirring until the wine has almost evaporated, then stir in the pistachios. As soon as the rice and nuts are well mixed, add 1½ to 2 cups of the reserved, warm broth. Stir well and let simmer briskly until the liquid is absorbed and no longer covers the rice. Add more broth, stir well, then stir in the curry powder and black pepper. Continue to simmer and stir each time you add liquid. The total cooking time for the risotto, from the point of adding the wine, should be 18 minutes. If you do not have enough broth to finish the cooking, use warm water, adding it a few tablespoons at a time.

When the rice is tender, stir in the chopped shrimp and parsley.

Serve immediately.

Sartu
Filled Rice Timbales

The Neapolitan word *sartu* comes from the French word *surtout,* which means "overall." As one of the grand dishes created for the Borboni royal court by their French-trained chefs, the Monzu (itself a corruption of the French *Monsieur*), *sartu* is today held up as a symbol of the refinement that *la cucina napoletana* can reach. *Sartu* is not only still made today, often in slightly contemporized versions, like the following, but you can buy *sartu* in Naples' snack shops and elegant take-out shops for eating on the spot or to take home for a party.

Originally, *sartu* was made in a giant mold. This looks great when it arrives at the table, but becomes a mess as soon as you put a knife to it. To our twenty-first-century eyes, the following individual presentation is much more appealing. This is the recipe that Cecilia often serves at her own festive dinner parties. *Sartu* is also a popular item on Azienda Seliano's catering menu. Molded in disposable foil baking cups, in which it can be kept refrigerated for a day before baking, it is easy to produce in volume as a first course. That said, it's a good American brunch or luncheon dish.

FOR THE RISOTTO

5 cups light meat or chicken broth

2 tablespoons extra-virgin olive oil

½ medium onion, finely chopped (about ½ cup)

2¾ cups arborio or carnaroli rice

⅔ cup dry white wine

4 to 5 cups ragù made with beef (page 94): 2 cups for risotto, at least 2 cups for serving (see Note)

¾ cup grated Parmigiano cheese

2 large eggs, lightly beaten

Salt

¼ teaspoon freshly ground pepper, or more to taste

FOR THE MEATBALLS

½ pound ground beef chuck

1 egg

¼ cup coarsely chopped flat-leaf parsley

¼ cup fine dry bread crumbs, covered with water to moisten

¾ teaspoon salt

¼ teaspoon freshly ground black pepper

Oil for frying

FOR THE FILLING

1 tablespoon butter, plus more for dotting

1½ ounces prosciutto, diced or cut into 1-inch-long, very fine strips

1 (10-ounce) box frozen peas

About 6 tablespoons butter, for greasing the molds and to dot the top of each one

About 1 cup fine dry bread crumbs

3 large eggs, hard-boiled, trimmed of their ends, each cut into 4 slices

¼ pound mozzarella, drained in a colander overnight if fresh, cut into ¼-inch cubes

To make the risotto: Keep the broth hot over low heat.

Heat the oil in a 3-quart or larger saucepan or stovetop casserole over medium heat. Add the onion and sauté until transparent, about 5 minutes. Add the rice and stir constantly for 2 minutes.

Add the wine and cook until it has evaporated. Add enough hot broth to barely cover the rice. Stir well. Increase the heat as necessary so the liquid simmers briskly. As soon as the broth is below the level of the rice, add more broth, then stir again.

Continue adding broth, little by little, and stirring each time, until all the broth has been used. Start adding the ragù when you run out of broth. The rice should be tender in about 18 minutes from the time you add the wine. If not, add water by spoonfuls until rice is cooked.

When the rice is still slightly al dente, remove from the heat and stir in the cheese. Let the rice cool about 10 minutes, then stir in the beaten eggs. Correct the seasoning with salt—if the broth and ragù were well seasoned, it may not need any—and pepper to taste. Set aside.

To make the meatballs: In a mixing bowl, combine the beef with the egg, parsley, soaked bread crumbs, salt, and pepper. Use your hands to mix the ingredients thoroughly. Form into meatballs the size of a hazelnut and place them on a baking sheet. You should have about 100; 48 are for inside the *sartu*.

Heat enough oil to skim the bottom of a 10- to 12-inch skillet over medium-high heat. When hot enough, a meatball should sizzle the instant it hits the fat. Fry the tiny meatballs in two batches. When well browned, set aside on absorbent paper.

To prepare the filling and molds: Heat the butter in a large skillet over medium heat. When the butter starts foaming, add the prosciutto and stir just to coat it with fat. Add the still-frozen peas and sauté until cooked, about 5 minutes. Set aside.

Place a rack on the highest level of the oven. Preheat the oven to 350°F.

Brush butter on all sides and the bottoms of twelve 6-ounce baking cups—custard cups or foil cups—then coat them thoroughly with bread crumbs.

Line each mold with about ½ cup of the cooled rice, pressing it into place and leaving a cavity in the center for the filling. Into each cavity, put a slice of hard-boiled egg, then 4 meatballs, a few cubes of cheese, and some peas and prosciutto. Top each cup with about ¼ cup more rice—to fill the mold level to the top. Dot each mold with tiny pieces of butter. (*Sartu* can be made a day ahead and kept refrigerated. Return to room temperature before baking.)

Arrange the *sartu* molds on a baking sheet. Bake for about 20 minutes, until well heated through and slightly crusty on top. Meanwhile, reheat the remaining ragù with the remaining meatballs.

Let cool for 5 minutes, then turn out each mold onto an individual plate. Either surround with ragù and meatballs, or top with ragù, letting the sauce run down the sides, and garnishing with the additional meatballs.

Serve while still hot, within 5 minutes.

NOTE: The remainder of the meatballs should be heated in the sauce, just before serving, and served on or around the *sartu*.

Formaggio
e Uova
Cheese
and Eggs

Cheese and Eggs.

Cheese is so much a part of the Southern Italian diet, and always has been a major source of protein, that very often Southern Italians will eat only cheese for dinner or supper, with some vegetables or a salad. They consider cheese equivalent to meat. In fact, one of the great dishes of Southern Italy is Grilled Cheese (page 144)—in essence a firm form of mozzarella called scamorza that is cooked over high heat in a skillet or on a griddle until it forms a golden crust. It is often included in a mixed grill with sausage, lamb chops, and slices of beef, proving how meatlike Italians consider it.

Eggs also have traditionally been a main source of protein in the Southern Italian diet, which is one reason that chicken is not: you don't eat the chicken that lays your eggs. A *frittata*, the Italian word for an open-faced omelet, is still considered a fine main course for lunch or dinner, but never breakfast. And a frittata, cut into small servings, is a frequent antipasto.

The mystery of cheese is that the exact same processes applied to milk can produce very different cheeses in different places. Naturally, the milk can have different qualities because the animals eat different things or are of different breeds, but the micro-ecology of the place where it is made has enormous impact on the finished product. Therefore, with all else being equal, even changing the location of an aging room will change the character of a cheese. It's exactly like wine making and bread baking, or any pursuit that requires people to control nature. In the case of cheese making, the point is to harness microorganisms, humidity, and heat to make a product that can be preserved longer than fresh milk.

In Southern Italy, the process for almost all of the cow's milk cheeses is the same: make curd, then cut, heat, and stretch it to form the cheese. You end up with mozzarella, scamorza, provola, caciocavallo, provolone, burrino, and burrata. The south also produces many cheeses made from sheep's milk that are generically called pecorino (the word for sheep is *pecora*). They can be young and sweet and supple, good as table cheese, or aged and sharp and crumbly, good for grating. Water buffalo milk is used mainly for making mozzarella. The south has goat cheeses, too, but most are not made commercially. They are usually made by and consumed by the people who tend goats, although occasionally you will see them for sale at local farmers' markets.

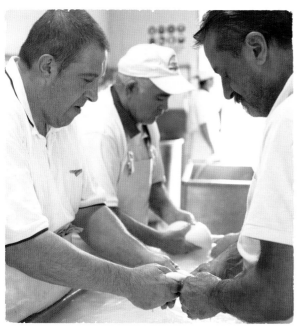

Left to right: Forming mozzarella di bufala; a young caciocavallo.

Scamorza alla Griglia
Grilled Cheese

All Regions, but mostly Campania

Grilled cheese—usually scamorza or provola, the smoked version of scamorza, itself a low-moisture version of mozzarella—can be a main course in Southern Italy. Sometimes it even appears on a mixed grill that includes sausage, beef, and maybe liver. Served alone, at the center of the plate, with a cooked vegetable or with a green or mixed salad, grilled cheese does seem like meat. In fact, cooking the cheese on a very hot griddle until it develops a brown crust on both sides—"caramelizing" the protein, so to speak—does give it a flavor related to grilled steak. I find a nonstick pan is essential for making the cheese. I've never mastered the skill necessary to successfully turn the cheese in any other pan, and no-stick makes it nearly no-fail.

By the way, the rubbery balls of mozzarella wrapped in plastic and found in U.S. supermarket dairy cases—the ones that don't give off any moisture when sliced—are actually scamorza and work well in this recipe.

Cut the cheese into ¼- to ½-inch-thick slices.

Heat a nonstick skillet until a drop of water will dance across the surface.

Place the cheese slices in the hot pan. When you see some browning on the bottom edge of the cheese, use a strong, wide spatula to flip the cheese over to its second side. Scrape along the bottom of the pan and under the cheese so as not to dislodge the crust.

Cook the second side as you did the first. The result should be a slice of cheese that is well crusted on both sides but not entirely melted, just soft and oozy.

Frittata di Cipolle
Onion Frittata

SERVES 4 AS A MAIN COURSE, MANY MORE AS AN ANTIPASTO

This is the most basic of frittatas, great for a main course, but also an excellent antipasto or finger food when cut into small squares. Using the technique that follows, employ your imagination and perhaps add some leftovers to create other flavors. See also the recipe for *Frittata di Spaghetti* (page 150).

3 tablespoons extra-virgin olive oil

3 medium onions, sliced

1 teaspoon salt

6 large eggs

¼ to ½ teaspoon freshly ground black pepper

⅓ cup freshly grated Parmigiano or grana Padano cheese

Combine the oil and onions in a 10-inch, nonstick skillet over medium-high heat and sauté, stirring to coat the onions with oil, for about 3 minutes. Season with salt, reduce the heat to medium-low, and cook for another 10 minutes, stirring and tossing the onions occasionally, until they are well wilted and translucent but not brown, about 10 minutes.

Meanwhile, beat the eggs, pepper, and cheese together in a bowl.

When the onions are cooked, add them to the egg mixture, leaving behind much of the oil. Mix well to combine.

Return the skillet to medium heat and when the oil starts sizzling, pour the egg and onion mixture into the pan. Using a fork (preferably wooden so it won't damage the nonstick surface), jiggle the eggs in the center of the pan so that the runny part runs to the bottom. Also push the cooked edge of the eggs very slightly toward the center so that some of the loose egg mixture runs to the sides. Do this only for the first 30 seconds or so of the cooking. Then allow the frittata to cook for 3 or 4 minutes.

When the bottom seems set, using a pot lid large enough to cover the pan, slide the frittata onto the cover, then flip it back into the pan for the uncooked side to cook. You may want to flip the frittata one or two more times, until the eggs are firmly set but neither side is overly browned.

Serve immediately, or let cool in the pan until warm or tepid. Serve cut into wedges or squares.

Fritelle di Ricotta
Ricotta Pancakes

MAKES NINE OR TEN 3½-INCH PANCAKES

This is one of many versions of fried ricotta, a delicate pancake with grated cheese and parsley, from I Bucanieri, a restaurant just down the road from the famous Florio Marsala wine cellars in Marsala. Other versions of fried ricotta usually count on the ricotta to be firm enough to slice, as most Italian ricotta is. This recipe works perfectly with looser American supermarket ricotta. Still, if you can get your hands on firmer ricotta, or sheep's milk ricotta, all the better. I like to serve these as an antipasto, with or without tomato sauce, in which case one or two a person is plenty. As a fine vegetarian second course, serve a larger portion.

1 (15-ounce) container whole milk ricotta (1¾ cups)

3 tablespoons all-purpose flour

1 heaping tablespoon finely shredded flat-leaf parsley

2 large eggs

⅓ cup grated pecorino, Parmigiano, or grana Padano cheese

1 teaspoon salt

½ teaspoon freshly ground black pepper

Vegetable oil for frying

Combine the ricotta, flour, parsley, eggs, cheese, salt, and pepper in a large bowl and mix well with a wooden spoon.

Heat enough oil to coat the bottom of a large skillet by ⅛ inch. Start frying when bubbles form around the handle of a wooden spoon.

Using a ¼-cup measure, drop the batter into the hot oil. It should sizzle immediately, but not frantically. Adjust the heat as necessary so the pancakes brown nicely on one side in 2½ to 3 minutes.

Using a metal spatula combined with a fork to hold the pancake in place on the spatula, carefully flip the pancakes and fry them about another 2 minutes, until the second side is nicely browned. Drain on paper towels.

Serve immediately or at room temperature.

Fritatta di Riso e Zucchini al Forno
Baked Rice and Zucchini Fritatta

SERVES 10 AS AN ANTIPASTO

Trattoria del Carmine, in Noto, is as simple as it gets, with plasticized paper tablecloths and kitschy fruit prints on the walls. Tour groups looking for a bargain come here, but so do locals who know the kitchen produces food that tastes homemade. This unique *frittata* is among as many as a dozen dishes that the restaurant might serve as their house antipasto. Rice is an unusual *frittata* ingredient, and this one is baked, not fried, as *frittatas* usually are. I find it's a great dish for parties, especially if you've invited a few vegetarians.

½ cup long-grain rice

1¼ teaspoons salt

2 pounds zucchini, washed, dried, and cut crosswise into 2-inch chunks

3 tablespoons extra-virgin olive oil

10 large eggs

⅔ cup grated Parmigiano or pecorino cheese, or a mixture of both

⅓ cup fine fresh bread crumbs (1 slice white bread)

¼ teaspoon freshly ground black pepper

Bring 1 cup of water to a rolling boil in a small saucepan. Add ¼ teaspoon of the salt, then the rice. Cover and simmer on low heat until all the water has been absorbed and the rice is tender, about 12 minutes. Let the rice cool, uncovered.

Pulse half the zucchini at a time in a food processor until it is finely chopped. Don't worry if there are a few larger pieces. Scrape the zucchini into a bowl.

Heat 2 tablespoons of the olive oil in a 12-inch skillet over medium-high heat. When the oil is hot enough to make a pinch of the zucchini sizzle, add all the zucchini, sprinkle with ½ teaspoon salt, and cook for 5 minutes, tossing constantly. Set aside to cool slightly.

Place a rack in the center of the oven. Preheat the oven to 375°F.

Beat the eggs until well blended in a large mixing bowl. Add the zucchini, rice, cheese, bread crumbs, remaining ½ teaspoon salt, and the pepper.

Pour the remaining 1 tablespoon of olive oil into a 9 by 13-inch Pyrex or ceramic baking dish. Tilt the dish to film the bottom and about 1 inch up the side of the pan.

Pour in the egg mixture. Bake for 25 minutes, until puffed and well set.

Let cool at least 15 minutes before serving. Serve warm or at room temperature. It reheats well.

Uova in Purgatorio Uova 'mpriatorio
Eggs in Purgatory Eggs Poached in Tomato Sauce

All Regions by Various Names   SERVES 2 OR 3

On nights when it seems like there's nothing in the house to eat, I can always count on eggs poached in tomato sauce. All it takes is a can of tomatoes, some seasonings, and eggs. They are all ingredients I always have on hand, and it is one of the easiest and most satisfying dishes imaginable—one of the standards of Southern Italian home cooking. I make it in one skillet, but when it's baked in a terracotta casserole, I've even seen it served in so-called fine dining establishments. As you drop the eggs into the simmering tomato sauce, they create their own pockets to cook in. The whites thicken the sauce around them. The yolks can be cooked firm or left runny. You end up with a mass of egg and tomato that looks beautiful on a slice of toasted rustic bread.

2 tablespoons extra-virgin olive oil

1 small onion, cut in half, then finely sliced or chopped

Pinch of red pepper flakes, or more to taste

2 cups canned crushed tomatoes, chopped tomatoes, or tomato puree (whatever is on hand)

½ teaspoon dried oregano

½ teaspoon salt, or more to taste

4 to 6 large eggs

4 to 6 slices toasted or fried crusty, dense bread (optional)

Grated cheese (optional)

Heat the oil in a 9- to 10-inch skillet over medium heat, and sauté the onion and red pepper flakes until the onion is lightly golden, 6 to 8 minutes.

Add the tomato, oregano, and salt. Stir well and simmer about 5 minutes, until the sauce has reduced a little. Taste and correct the salt and red pepper flakes as necessary, to taste.

Break the eggs into the gently bubbling sauce. Cover the pan and cook until the eggs are done to taste—about 10 minutes for firm yolks.

To serve, use a wide spatula to lift the eggs and the sauce that clings to them from the bottom of the pan. Place on a plate, with or without a slice of toasted or fried bread.

Serve with grated cheese, if desired.

Variation

Drop cubes of mozzarella or other cheese into the sauce between the eggs. Other possibilities are cubes of salami or ham, or small spoonfuls of ricotta.

Frittata di Spaghetti e Broccoli di Rapa
Spaghetti and Broccoli Rabe Frittata

Campania

SERVES 6 TO 8

Sometimes this is called *frittata di avanzi*, meaning "frittata with leftovers." Both the spaghetti and the broccoli rabe can be left over from the night before, and the spaghetti is all the better if it was previously dressed with tomato sauce or ragù. I love this *frittata* so much, however, that I often freshly cook the pasta and the vegetable specifically to make it. My Italian friends often eat this at room temperature, but it is lighter and more appealing soon after it is made, while it is still hot or warm.

1 pound broccoli rabe

3 tablespoons olive oil

1 large garlic clove, minced (about 1 teaspoon)

Salt and either black pepper or red pepper flakes to taste

5 large eggs

¼ cup grated pecorino, Parmigiano, or grana Padano cheese, or a combination

6 ounces spaghetti, cooked

3 to 4 ounces dried sausage or soppressata, diced into ¼-inch cubes (optional)

6 ounces mozzarella, diced into ¼-inch cubes (optional)

To prepare the broccoli rabe, cut off the heavy stems and discard, or if you have the patience, peel the stems before cooking them. Wash the tops very well; drain.

Bring a minimum of 4 quarts of water to a rolling boil and add a tablespoon of salt. Add the broccoli rabe and cook 5 minutes from the time the water returns to a rolling boil. Drain the broccoli.

Combine 2 tablespoons of the olive oil with the garlic in a 10-inch nonstick skillet over medium heat. When the garlic starts sizzling, add the broccoli rabe. Sauté for about 8 minutes, stirring and tossing the broccoli rabe frequently, until it is very tender. Season with salt and either black pepper or red pepper flakes.

Beat the eggs in a large bowl until well mixed. Add the grated cheese, broccoli rabe, spaghetti, and diced sausage, if using. Mix thoroughly. Season with about ¼ teaspoon salt.

Add the remaining tablespoon of olive oil to the pan and place over medium-low heat. Add half of the egg and pasta mixture and spread it out to the edges of the pan. Sprinkle the mozzarella, if using, evenly over the surface. Top with the remaining pasta and egg mixture.

Cook until the frittata is mostly set, jiggling it a bit in the center with a fork so some of the runny top goes to the bottom of the pan. When the bottom is well set, use a flexible, heat-resistant spatula to loosen the edges and bottom of the frittata, then slide the frittata onto a flat pot lid or plate the size of the pan. Flip it back into the pan for the uncooked side to cook. You may want to flip the frittata one or two more times, until the eggs are firmly set but neither side is overly browned.

Cut into wedges or squares to serve, preferably hot or warm.

Pesce e Frutti di Mare
Fish and Shellfish

Fish and Shellfish are the most prized foods of

Southern Italy. In these days of relative affluence, families who live inland will drive hours to the shore to enjoy a seafood feast at a special restaurant. Throughout history, however, Southern Italians, surrounded by the sea, have had access to an amazing number of the creatures that live in it. In Naples, even seaweed is eaten—in fritters. And in the mountains, salt cod and stock fish (both preserved by drying), salt-cured anchovies and sardines, mackerel and tuna, packed in cans in oil or sold out of a barrel, have been protein staples and seasoning ingredients for centuries; in the case of anchovies, millennia. Indeed, some Southern Italians' heavy consumption of "blue fish," *pesce azzurro*—so called for their dark, oily flesh—is often cited as a reason they live to be a hundred, or more.

Fresh tuna and swordfish have also always graced Southern Italian tables, especially in Calabria and Sicily, where schools of tuna run strong in May and June. In times past, bivalves were also affordable, while white-fleshed fish were eaten mainly by the aristocracy and other moneyed people. The taste for clams, cockles, and mussels continues, but today spaghetti or other pasta with all of the above would be considered a very luxurious plate; they are still plentiful but very expensive. Other shellfish, usually lumped together as *molluski di scoglio*, "mollusks gathered from the rocks," are also popular, not to mention many varieties of squid, *calamari*, from thumbnail-sized *calamaretti* to foot-long brown *totano*. Cuttlefish, *sepie*, are flatter, more tender, and more flavorful than calamari, and are the true source of the black ink used to color rice and pasta. *Spaghetti*

all'inchiostra di sepia, pasta blackened with "sepia ink," is a specialty of coastal Sicily and southern Calabria.

At fish markets all over, shrimp of all sizes squirm with life in plastic tubs of water. The tiniest are called *gamberetti*, the largest are *gamberone*, and there are relatives in between that go by unrelated names. The most prized are the red shrimp from Sicily, which are often eaten raw. When they are tiny, they may be tossed in an orange salad (see page 59) or cooked into a risotto (see page 136). If they are large, they may be eaten raw, too, just for their own sake, with merely a squeeze of lemon—perhaps.

The white-fleshed fish, delicately flavored as they are, are usually simply grilled, often basted with a sauce called Salamoriglio, which is nothing more than equal parts of lemon juice, olive oil, and water, seasoned with garlic, oregano, and perhaps fresh chopped parsley. This, without the water, is also used to dress otherwise unadorned, subtly flavored fish such as the Branzino and Orata that have become so popular in the United States now.

Sauté di Vongole o Cozze
Sauté of Clams or Mussels

This is the simplest, and I think the best, way to cook bivalves: nothing but high heat, great olive oil, garlic, parsley, and a bit of hot pepper, if you like. They're done when the shells have opened and their briny juices have been released. It takes only 3 minutes or so. With no further embellishment and in a smallish portion, a sauté of clams or mussels or mixed shellfish, *frutti di mare*, is a very popular antipasto throughout the south. Served with toasted bread to sop up the juices, it becomes *zuppa di frutti di mare* and possibly a first course. In a copious portion, the *zuppa* can be a main course. And when you pour these same sautéed clams and their juices over pasta, the dish becomes *Spaghetti* or *vermicelli* or *linguine alle vongole*. After spaghetti with tomato sauce, it is the second most popular pasta dish in Campania, and certainly on every Southern Italian's top-10 list.

3 tablespoons extra-virgin olive oil

2 large garlic cloves, thickly sliced

⅛ teaspoon crushed red pepper flakes, or a piece of fresh hot pepper, or more to taste

3 to 4 pounds clams or mussels, cleaned well

3 tablespoons finely shredded parsley

Combine the oil, garlic, and red pepper flakes in a deep 12- to 14-inch skillet or sauté pan or a wide, deep pot over medium-low heat. Cook the garlic on both sides until it is soft but still white, pressing it into the oil a few times.

Add the clams or mussels. Cover the pan, then shake it a few times. Shaking seems to speed the opening of the shellfish. Increase the heat to medium-high and cook, shaking the pan another time or two, until the bivalves open—usually no more than 2 minutes for mussels or Manila clams, and 3 to 4 minutes for littleneck clams. If using both, put the clams in the pan first, then after 2 minutes add the mussels.

When the shellfish have opened, stir in the parsley. Serve immediately.

Variation

In saffron-loving Sicily, the pasta for *spaghetti alle cozze* might be boiled in saffron-seasoned water. To save on the high cost of saffron, I cook the pasta in much less than the usual amount of water to ensure that the pasta takes on a light yellow color as well as the scent of the spice. Be sure to stir the pasta frequently, so it doesn't stick.

Cozze o Vongole Oreganata
Baked Mussels or Clams

In Italian-American restaurants, "baked clams" or "clams oreganata" are very popular. But in Southern Italy, clams are too small to stuff and bake. Instead, mussels are the usual receptacle for the olive oil, garlic, and oregano-flavored bread crumbs. Whether you use mussels or littleneck or cherrystone clams, these take a little time to prepare, but the work can all be done ahead.

2 pounds mussels, or littleneck or cherrystone clams (30 to 35 pieces), scrubbed; the mussels should be debearded, if necessary

FOR THE TOPPING

½ cup fine dry bread crumbs

3 tablespoons extra-virgin olive oil

1 to 2 tablespoons mussel or clam broth (from steaming)

3 large garlic cloves, finely minced (1 generous tablespoon)

½ teaspoon salt

½ teaspoon freshly ground black pepper

½ teaspoon dried oregano

Place the mussels or clams in a large pot over medium-high heat. Cover and steam the shellfish for 2 to 3 minutes, until their shells have opened.

Let the shellfish cool in the pot. If using mussels, remove them from their shells, reserving half the shells. Reserve the broth separately. If using clams, remove and discard the top shell, leaving the clam in the other half. Reserve the broth. Strain it if you think it is sandy.

Place 2, possibly 3 mussel meats in each shell half, depending on the size of the shell and the mussels. Arrange the mussels or clams in their shells in a single layer in a shallow baking pan that can go under the broiler.

In a small bowl, using a table fork, blend together the bread crumbs and other topping ingredients, using 1 or 2 tablespoons of the broth to moisten the crumbs slightly. Do not make them mushy.

Using a teaspoon, cover the mussels or clams with the topping, packing them slightly.

Arrange the shellfish on a baking sheet. (If preparing ahead, cover the sheet with plastic and refrigerate. Remove from the refrigerator about 30 minutes before broiling.)

Just before you are ready to serve the mussels or clams, place the baking sheet under the broiler, about 5 inches from the heat source. Broil until the tops have browned, 1 to 2 minutes. Watch carefully so the mussel topping does not burn.

Serve immediately.

Gamberi Oreganati
Shrimp Baked with Flavored Bread Crumbs

This is such an easy and such a delicious recipe that you will, as I do, make it for everyday meals all the time. It can also be an antipasto for a party. Be aware that not all the bread crumbs will stick to the shrimp. But an excess of delicious bread crumbs, to eat along with the shrimp on each forkful, isn't a bad thing.

⅓ cup fine dry bread crumbs

½ teaspoon salt

1 large garlic clove, very finely chopped (about 1 teaspoon)

1 teaspoon dried oregano

⅛ teaspoon hot paprika

1 tablespoon extra-virgin olive oil

1 pound cleaned large or jumbo shrimp (20 to 24 to the pound)

Lemon wedges

Place a rack on the top rung of the oven. Preheat the oven to 400°F.

Combine the bread crumbs, salt, garlic, oregano, paprika, and olive oil in a large mixing bowl. Stir well.

Add the shrimp to the bowl and toss until all the shrimp are coated with crumbs.

Arrange the shrimp in a single layer in a 10-inch baking pan or on a baking sheet. Sprinkle with the remaining crumbs.

Bake for 12 to 14 minutes, until the shrimp are cooked through.

Serve immediately with lemon wedges.

Spiedini di Gamberi e Cipolle
Grilled Shrimp and Onion on Skewers

When you have good shrimp, there's no need to do much to them. Southern Italians know this because they have many varieties of great shrimp, always fresh. You see them alive in all the fish markets, so you know they're not thawed frozen shrimp, as most shrimp sold in the United States are. These skewers are easy to assemble, and they cook in no time, whether on an outdoor grill, under the broiler, or on top of the stove in a skillet or on a flat griddle—my favorite way. "On a griddle," *alla pilastra*, they get a little charred, which, along with the olive oil and oregano, highlights the shrimp's sweetness.

1 small red onion, cut from root to
    stem end into 10 to 12 wedges

1 pound jumbo shrimp
    (24 to the pound), peeled
    but with tails left on

3 tablespoons extra-virgin olive oil

1 tablespoon dried oregano

Salt to taste

Freshly ground black pepper
    to taste

Lemon wedges (optional)

Pull apart the wedges of onion. Combine the onion segments with the shrimp in a large bowl. Add the oil and oregano. Toss well.

Thread an onion segment onto a skewer. Follow with a shrimp, threading the skewer through both the tail and the thick end of each shrimp. Add another onion segment, then another shrimp. End with an onion segment. Sprinkle both sides of all the skewers with salt and pepper.

Six shrimp makes a good single serving, but you can thread as many shrimp and onion segments as the skewer will hold. If cooking in a ridged grill or on a griddle, be sure to choose skewers that are not too long to fit into the pan. Bamboo skewers work (be sure to soak first), but flat metal skewers keep the shrimp and onion in place better.

If using an indoor broiler, place a rack as close as possible under the heat source. Place the broiler pan under the heat to preheat it. Alternatively, heat a ridged grill or griddle over high heat until it is so hot that a drop of water evaporates instantly. Or, have a hot charcoal fire ready.

Grill the skewers on the open fire or under the broiler for about 2 minutes per side, maybe slightly more. Shrimp cooked on top of the stove, *alla pilastra*, will take about 3 minutes a side, or slightly more.

Serve immediately. Lemon is not necessary, but you may want it anyway.

Pesce Spada a Ghiotta
Swordfish Gourmet Style

The term *a ghiotta* means "gourmet style," although some would tell you "gourmand." The word is not used much in conversation, as it is in English, but in Sicily it refers to a fish dish. It can be any fish, but it is usually swordfish simmered in a slightly liquid sauce of chopped vegetables. Recipes vary, but I like this one with celery, olives, capers, parsley, and very little tomato. *Alla ghiotta* is not supposed to be a kind of tomato sauce.

1 medium onion, cut in half from root to stem end, then thinly sliced in the same direction

1 celery rib, finely chopped with a few celery leaves (about ½ cup)

1 heaping tablespoon finely shredded flat-leaf parsley

3 tablespoons extra-virgin olive oil

1 (14-ounce) can peeled plum tomatoes, finely chopped

1 heaping tablespoon salted capers, rinsed and soaked in cold water for 15 minutes

¼ cup pitted and sliced green Sicilian olives

Salt and pepper to taste

4 (1-inch-thick, 2- to 2½-pound) swordfish steaks, skin removed

Combine the onion, celery, parsley, and olive oil in a 10- to 12-inch skillet over medium heat. Sauté, tossing occasionally, until the onion is tender and translucent, about 8 minutes.

Add the tomatoes, capers, and olives. Simmer gently for about 10 minutes, or until the sauce is very thick. Correct the seasoning with salt and pepper.

Salt and pepper the swordfish, then place the steaks in the skillet, spooning most of the sauce over the fish. Still over medium heat, cook the swordfish, uncovered, for about 6 minutes. Turn the steaks with a wide spatula, leaving the sauce on the bottom this time. Cook undisturbed for an additional 10 minutes. Add water by the tablespoon if the sauce reduces too much. There should be a small amount of liquid in the pan.

Serve immediately, or at room temperature.

Variation

"Change one ingredient in an Italian recipe and you have a new dish," I've heard said in Italy. So when you add thickly sliced or cubed potatoes, *alla ghiotta* becomes *alla messinese,* in the style of Messina, the city in the northeast corner of the island. Prepare the recipe as above, but **add the potatoes,** already cut and boiled, to the base sauce at the same time you add the **fish.**

Pesce Spada Impanata
Swordfish Breaded Palermo Style

I use this recipe regularly because it is so quick, simple, and appeals to almost everyone who likes fish. In Sicily, swordfish is the most popular fish baked with bread crumbs, but you can do the same with any firm-fleshed fish. The breading and method even makes bland flounder fillets and tilapia worth eating. I particularly like it on grouper, *cernia*, another popular fish in Southern Italy. Don't expect the crumbs to brown, as in fried fish—they'll be delicious, but relatively pale. Fish is not the only food that is breaded and baked this way; thin slices of beef are cooked *impanata*, usually smeared with rendered lard instead of olive oil

1 cup fine dry bread crumbs

1 teaspoon salt

1 teaspoon roughly ground
   fennel seed

3 large garlic cloves, finely chopped
   (about 1 tablespoon)

3 tablespoons coarsely chopped
   flat-leaf parsley

2 tablespoons extra-virgin olive oil

1 pound swordfish, cut into
   ¼-inch-thick cutlets

Salt and freshly ground black
   pepper to taste

Lemon wedges

Place a rack on the highest rung of the oven. Preheat the oven to 450° F.

Combine the bread crumbs, salt, fennel seed, garlic, parsley, and 1 tablespoon of the oil on a large plate. Mix until all the bread crumbs are moistened with oil.

Brush the fish slices lightly with the remaining tablespoon of oil and season lightly with salt and pepper.

Dredge each slice in the seasoned bread crumbs, pressing the crumbs into the fish so that each side is well coated. Arrange the fish slices on a baking sheet. (The fish can be prepared up to this point and refrigerated, uncovered, for up to 12 hours, until ready to bake.)

Bake the fish for 5 to 6 minutes.

Serve hot or at room temperature with lemon wedges.

Pesce Spada al Sale con Aglio e Menta
Salt-seared Swordfish with Garlic and Mint

You have to love salt and raw garlic to appreciate this dish, although you can make it with an herb other than dried mint. Finely chopped sage is my second choice, although mint is certainly the Sicilians' first. Large-crystal sea salt is essential because the salt isn't supposed to penetrate the fish and overseason it. It acts as a no-stick device and somehow keeps the fish juicy. Because the olive oil is eaten raw, not cooked, this is an opportunity to use your best extra-virgin oil to great advantage. Seasoned oil left on the platter can be recycled into a green salad the next day.

1 tablespoon dried mint

6 to 8 large garlic cloves, finely chopped

At least 6 tablespoons extra-virgin olive oil

1 tablespoon red wine vinegar

2 tablespoons large-crystal sea salt

2 (½-inch-thick) swordfish steaks, skin removed

With your fingertips, push the mint through a fine strainer onto a large platter. Add the garlic, olive oil, and vinegar. Blend with a fork.

Sprinkle the bottom of a heavy 9- to 10-inch skillet (I use black cast-iron) evenly with salt. Place over high heat. When the pan is so hot that you can't keep your palm 3 inches over it for more than 5 seconds, place the swordfish on top of the salt and cook for 3 minutes.

Turn the fish and cook another 2 to 3 minutes for medium-well, without a trace of pink in the center.

Lift the fish from the pan with tongs or a fork and brush off any large pieces of salt clinging to it. Place the fish on the platter and turn it to coat with the raw sauce, finally spooning some of the sauce on top.

Serve immediately.

Variation

In the United States, it is not usually possible to get swordfish sliced as thin as Southern Italians like it. But if you can, or have a fish market that will do it for you, cut it into ⅛- to ¼-inch-thick slices. These will cook in less than 1 minute per side.

Tonno Agro Dolce
Sweet and Sour Tuna

Sicily

SERVES 2 AS A MAIN COURSE, AT LEAST 6 AS AN ANTIPASTO

This is the perfect dish for those hot and humid summer days—a good part of the year in Sicily—when you can do a little cooking in the cool of the morning to prepare a meal that is best eaten cold or at room temperature. The tuna is lightly floured and seared, then topped with a seasoning sauce of sautéed onions made sweet and sour with sugar and vinegar. Let it sit at room temperature for a couple of hours, or even longer, and the tuna absorbs the flavors of the sauce, and develops a velvety texture.

2 (1½-inch-thick) tuna steaks, about 8 ounces each

Salt

½ cup all-purpose flour

2 tablespoons extra-virgin olive oil

3 medium onions, sliced (about 3 cups)

1 tablespoon sugar

¼ teaspoon salt

⅓ cup dry white wine

¼ cup white wine vinegar

Oil-cured olives

Chopped fresh parsley

Dry the tuna steaks with paper towels. Salt them well on both sides, then dredge them in flour and shake off the excess.

Heat the oil over medium heat in an 8- to 9-inch skillet. When the oil is so hot that it is rippling, sear the tuna steaks for 2 minutes on each side, and briefly on the edges. Transfer to a deep serving dish just large enough to hold the tuna and, eventually, the onions.

As soon as the tuna is out of the pan, add the onions and 3 tablespoons of water. Cook the onions for about 3 minutes, until the water evaporates. Sprinkle on the sugar and salt. Toss constantly until the onions begin to caramelize, about another 5 minutes.

Add the wine and scrape up any caramelized specks. Add the vinegar and simmer for 1 minute. Pour the onions and their juices over the tuna. Let stand until ready to serve, at least 1 hour. (Or let stand for an hour, then refrigerate the tuna—for up to 24 hours—until 15 minutes before you are ready to serve it.)

Serve garnished with oil-cured olives and chopped fresh parsley.

You can add some color to the dish by dissolving 1 tablespoon of tomato paste into the wine before adding it to the pan.

Matalotta alla Siracusan
Fish Soup from Siracusa

SERVES 4

My friend Ethel Puzzo recited this recipe to me as we sat together one day and gorged on other fish dishes at Al Ancora, which used to be a modest restaurant near the bus station in Siracusa, but is now one of the most stylish hot spots in town. Ethel (short for Concetella) is a native of Siracusa, and Matalotta—the local fish soup—is a part of every home cook's repertoire. Whole green or black olives and quite a few capers are one distinction of this soup-stew, which is meant to be a main course or, with broken spaghetti added to the broth and the fish eaten afterward, a first course *and* a second cooked in one pot.

The choice of fish is less important than having at least three different ones. In Siracusa, *cernia* (grouper) and swordfish are often among them. I like monkfish in almost any fish stew—it can be cooked longer than most fish, which gives the broth flavor without the fish falling apart. To these, add a dark-fleshed fish, such as tuna or mackerel, or East Coast bluefish.

¼ cup extra-virgin olive oil

3 large garlic cloves, thinly sliced

2 tablespoons coarsely chopped flat-leaf parsley

½ cup thinly sliced scallions (white and some light green)

¾ pound salad tomatoes, peeled, seeded, and diced (juice strained from the seeds and reserved), or ¾ cup well-drained and seeded canned plum tomatoes

2 round tablespoons salted capers, well rinsed

12 cracked green or black Sicilian olives (whole with pits)

4 or 5 large basil leaves, torn into large pieces

2 pounds mixed fish, such as 1 thick slice swordfish and/or grouper fillet; a fillet of dark fish, such as mackerel or East Coast bluefish; and one other firm fish, such as monkfish

Finely shredded flat-leaf parsley

Combine the oil, garlic, parsley, and scallions in a 10-inch sauté pan or stovetop casserole over medium-low heat. Cook very gently until the scallions are tender and the garlic is tender but still white, about 8 minutes.

Add the tomatoes, any tomato liquid strained from the seeds, the capers, olives, and basil. Simmer gently for 10 minutes, until the tomatoes have mostly fallen apart. Add 3 cups of water. Cover and bring to a simmer.

Cut each fish into 4 pieces. Add the fish to the simmering broth, first arranging the tougher fish, or the thicker pieces, then the quick-cooking fish. Lower the heat, cover, and let the soup simmer gently for 10 to 15 minutes from the time you add the first fish. Do not stir. The fish should be well cooked but not falling apart.

You can serve the fish and soup in the same bowl, but in Siracusa it is traditional to serve the broth as a first course with broken spaghetti (see page 81) or linguine, sprinkled with parsley, then serve the fish as a main course with some olives and capers from the soup.

Zuppa di Pesce o Frutti di Mare
Fish or Mussel Soup

Naples, Campania

SERVES 4

When you order *linguine frutti di mare* in an Italian-American restaurant, you will likely get something like this, an assortment of seafood cooked in tomato sauce seasoned with plenty of garlic, more or less a Neapolitan *zuppa*. If the American chef adds enough hot pepper to make the sauce sting, he may call it *al diavolo*, but a dish by that name does not exist in Italy.

In Italy, a seafood stew like this would most likely be served with *bruschetta*, toasted bread, or maybe fried bread. I like it with dried bread—*freselle* or other *pane biscottato* baked for the purpose of sopping up juices of all kinds. If using dried bread, put it in the bottom of the bowl and pour the stew/soup over it. If serving toast, tuck a slice into each bowl and/or pass it on a platter or in a basket.

4 tablespoons extra-virgin olive oil

3 large garlic cloves, thinly sliced

1 (28-ounce) can Italian peeled tomatoes or *pomodorini di collina* (Italian cherry tomatoes)

Big pinch of red pepper flakes, or ½ dried hot red pepper, crumbled

½ teaspoon salt

¼ cup finely shredded flat-leaf parsley, plus extra for garnish

1 pound monkfish fillets

3 pounds cleaned mussels and/or littleneck or Manila clams, or a combination of both

Grilled bread, rubbed or not with garlic

Freshly grated pecorino cheese (optional)

Combine the oil and garlic in a deep, 10-inch sauté pan or stovetop casserole over low heat. Cook the garlic until tender but still white.

Add the tomatoes, red pepper flakes, and salt. Increase the heat to medium and break up the peeled tomatoes with the side of a wooden spoon or smash the cherry tomatoes. Simmer briskly, uncovered, for 6 to 8 minutes, stirring frequently.

Stir in the parsley, then add the fish. Cover the pot and reduce the heat to low. Let the fish simmer gently for 10 to 15 minutes, or until fully cooked. It should be tender but holding together. For the last 4 minutes of cooking, add the mussels and/or clams. They should open in that time and release their juices into the soup. Discard any bivalves that do not open.

To serve, you can leave all the mussels in their shells, or remove some of them from their shells and return them to the soup, serving some mussels in their shell just for looks.

Serve immediately with grilled bread and, if desired, pass grated pecorino cheese at the table.

Carne e Pollo
Meat and Chicken

Carne e Pollo.

It is for good reason that Southern Italy is known for sausage and meatballs. Historically, meat has been scarce, overly lean, and tough in the Italian south. Grinding meat for sausage and meatballs allows you to make it juicy with added fat, extend it with bread, and make it more savory with seasoning ingredients. Even today, although Southern Italy now has excellent pork and lamb, beef is still tougher and less flavorful and juicy than American grain-fed beef, and white veal is as expensive as it is in the United States, and rarely as good.

The star of the Southern Italian butcher shop is certainly lamb because it is generally meat from sheep that graze on mountain herbs and grasses. To the dismay of American tourists, however, all but the most elegant restaurants serve boney pieces of lamb, often with more fat attached than American tastes tolerate. For good reason, these pieces, whether neat chops or unidentifiable cuts, are often called *scottaditto*, "burn finger." The name gives the eater permission to pick them up, hot off the grill, and nibble the meat (and flavorful fat if you wish) off of the bone. Goat is also a popular meat, and to the surprise of many Americans, most of whom are not familiar with goat, it is a white meat more delicate than lamb. In the mountainous areas of Calabria and Basilicata, and in the Cilento of Campania, goat was the most available meat until recent times. Nowadays, it is still a feast-day delicacy. Both lamb and goat are frequently roasted with potatoes, often with rosemary and garlic, leading to the joke name for potatoes cooked thusly, but without the lamb, as *patate al' agnello scapato*, "potatoes with escaped lamb."

All those veal scallopini dishes that are served in American Italian restaurants—*picatta, al limone, alla Marsala,* and *alla Francese,* to mention a few—are not really Southern Italian. They were created by Italian chefs working in the international resorts and hotels of the Amalfi Coast, Sorrento, and Capri, all near Naples; Taormina in Sicily; and from the thousands of chefs, waiters, and maîtres d' who fed millions of rich people crossing the ocean in style, during the heyday of the great ocean liners. These veal dishes are made in Italy today, but the meat itself is invariably disappointing to Americans accustomed to white, fork-tender veal. In fact, in Italy, the word *vitello,* meaning "veal," is also applied to yearling beef, which is not as red as full-grown beef, but not white and tender.

Only in the last twenty years has chicken become an everyday food in Southern Italy. One could say that, traditionally, rabbit is the chicken of Southern Italy. Rabbits multiply quickly, are inexpensive to feed, and are easily raised in cages. Because they don't give eggs, they're favored over chicken as meat. Boneless, skinless chicken cutlets are typical everyday family food in Italy today, just as they are in the United States, and a good free-range chicken, *pollo ruspante,* perhaps even organic, *biologico,* is an affordable treat, but so prized that it is usually prepared simply grilled or roasted.

Polpette
Meatballs

Along with pizza and spaghetti with tomato sauce, meatballs are one of the most internationally famous specialties of Southern Italy. Even if you don't have good meat or much meat, you can still make great meatballs. Seasonings vary, but the basics are usually chopped garlic, chopped parsley or mint, and grated cheese of one kind or another—whatever the local taste dictates. Egg holds it all together. Raisins and/or pine nuts are an old-fashioned Neapolitan and Sicilian addition that I happen to like. One great cook I know in Campania adds a splash of red wine vinegar and some red wine to her meatballs, a great touch. Extending the meat with old bread soaked in water makes meatballs light, crusty, and juicy.

Meatballs are usually served for their own sake, fried, with or without sauce, as a main course with a side dish. However, it's a fallacy that Italians never serve meatballs with pasta. In Puglia, Basilicata, and Calabria, tiny meatballs are often combined in the same bowl with pasta and sauce. This recipe can be formed into either full-size main course balls or marble-size balls that can be used with spaghetti or macaroni or in baked pastas and *Sartu* (page 138), the molded rice extravaganza. As anyone who was an Italian or Italian-American child will tell you, the most delicious meatballs are those stolen behind your mother's back as soon as they come from the frying pan.

About 2 cups dried crustless bread (*mollica;* see page 125) in 1-inch cubes

1¼ pounds ground beef (preferably 80% lean, not leaner)

2 eggs, beaten to mix well

2 large garlic cloves, finely minced

½ cup loosely packed grated pecorino cheese

¼ cup loosely packed finely shredded parsley

⅓ cup pine nuts

⅓ cup raisins

1 teaspoon salt

½ teaspoon freshly ground black pepper

¼ cup vegetable oil (approximately)

1 quart Tomato Sauce (page 86; optional)

Soak the bread in cold water until soft, a few minutes.

Meanwhile, combine the beef, eggs, garlic, pecorino, parsley, pine nuts, raisins, salt, and pepper in a large mixing bowl. Do not mix yet.

Squeeze the bread by fistfuls to drain it, then break it up with your fingers, adding it directly to the bowl. Mix the ingredients very well, squishing the mixture with your hands to make sure the bread blends with the meat. Do not worry about handling the meat too much.

Roll the mixture between your palms into 12 meatballs, each using about ⅓ cup of meat.

Heat about ⅛ inch of oil in a 9- to 10-inch skillet over medium-high heat.

When the oil is hot enough to create bubbles around the handle of a wooden spoon, gently place the meatballs in the pan. As soon as a crust

Recipe continues

develops on one side, using two utensils (I use a metal spatula and a wooden spoon), dislodge the meatballs and turn them to another side. Continue rotating the meatballs. After about 10 minutes the meatballs should be well browned but still slightly rare in the center.

If serving the meatballs without sauce, lower the heat slightly and continue to cook, rotating the meatballs regularly, for another 5 to 8 minutes. Serve immediately.

If serving the meatballs with sauce, place them in the sauce once they have browned and simmer gently for 15 minutes. They may be held, but are best when served immediately or within an hour.

Polpette alla Maria Talerico
Maria Talerico's Meat Cakes

Calabria

MAKES 8 OR 9 PATTIES; SERVES 4

Polpette is the Italian word for "meatballs," but it is also used for patties—what Americans might call burgers. I found these small, juicy patties on a mixed meat platter served at La Casella, a restaurant in Calabria where Maria Talerico prepares fantastic home-style food in her husband Giuseppe Guarascio's rustic, stone ancestral house. I ran into the kitchen as soon as I finished eating to find out what secret these burgers held. Naturally, Maria fries her patties, which gives them a crunchy exterior. Their juiciness comes from a mix of beef and pork, neither of which you could call lean.

½ cup fine dry bread crumbs

½ pound ground beef (no leaner than 80% lean)

½ pound ground pork

1 large egg

2 rounded tablespoons finely shredded parsley

1 rounded tablespoon grated Parmigiano cheese

¾ teaspoon salt

¼ teaspoon freshly ground black pepper

Vegetable oil for frying

Tomato Sauce (page 86; optional)

Cover ¼ cup of the bread crumbs with warm tap water. Reserve the other ¼ cup to coat the patties.

In a mixing bowl, combine the meats, and with your hand, roughly mix them. Add the egg, the moistened ¼ cup of bread crumbs, squeezing out excess moisture, and the parsley, cheese, salt, and pepper. Again with your hands, knead the mixture until smooth and tight.

Spread the ¼ cup dry bread crumbs on a plate.

Using a ¼ cup measure, make the meat patties, then coat each patty in crumbs.

In a medium skillet, over medium-high heat, heat about ¼ inch of vegetable oil until bubbles gather around the handle of a wooden spoon. When hot, fry the patties until well browned on both sides. As soon as the pan is full of patties, lower the heat slightly. The patties should take 2 to 3 minutes a side. Drain on absorbent paper.

Serve immediately, or at room temperature. No sauce is necessary, but you can dress them with tomato sauce, if desired.

Variation

If you don't want to fry, the patties are also good grilled over charcoal, or cooked under a kitchen broiler, or on a griddle on top of the stove. If you use one of those methods, cook about 3 minutes a side under or over the highest possible heat. They should be crusty outside, still slightly pink and juicy inside.

Polpettone al Sugo di Verdure
Meatloaf Baked in Vegetable Sauce

Azienda Seliano, Campania

At the end of the summer, there are so many zucchini in Azienda Seliano's garden that Anna d'Amato, the head cook, is always looking for ways to use them. Her *parmigiana* with zucchini is particularly good, whether made with tomato sauce, or *in bianco,* "white," with no tomatoes. And I love the Macaroni with Zucchini and Ricotta (page 119) that the kitchen makes. The plethora of zucchini is, I am sure, why she created this sauce. It's heavy on diced zucchini, which gives substance and textural interest to what would otherwise be a simple tomato sauce.

All the meat served to the *agriturismo* guests at Azienda Seliano is from water buffalo. Females give the precious milk used to make *mozzarella di bufala.* Males have no use other than for meat. Water buffalo meat is, like American bison meat (what we colloquially call buffalo), much leaner than beef and with much more moisture. A large portion of soaked dried bread makes Anna's meatloaves light and juicy even though the meat has very little fat—a good thing to know when dealing with very lean American beef.

4 cups dried crustless bread in 1-inch cubes

2 pounds lean ground beef

2 eggs, beaten to mix well

3 large garlic cloves, finely minced (about 1 tablespoon)

½ cup loosely packed grated Parmigiano cheese

¼ cup loosely packed, finely shredded flat-leaf parsley

1 tablespoon salt

½ to ¾ teaspoon freshly ground black pepper

3 egg whites

¾ cup fine dry bread crumbs

2 tablespoons vegetable oil for frying

2 tablespoons extra-virgin olive oil

1 medium zucchini, washed and cut into ¼-inch cubes

1 medium carrot, peeled and cut into ¼-inch dice

1 medium onion, peeled and cut into ¼-inch dice

1 pint grape tomatoes, each cut in half

2 cups canned peeled Italian plum tomatoes (1 14-ounce can)

Soak the bread in cold water until soft, a few minutes.

By fistfuls, squeeze the water out of the bread and crumble it directly into a large mixing bowl. Add the meat to the bowl. With your hands, begin mixing the bread into the meat, squeezing pieces of bread to blend them into the meat.

Push the meat to one side of the bowl, and on the other side combine the whole eggs, garlic, grated cheese, parsley, 2 teaspoons of the salt, and ½ teaspoon of the pepper. Mix with a fork, then using your hands, mix all the ingredients well.

Divide the meat mixture into 4 parts and make 4 small meatloaves, each an even cylinder. Roll them on your work surface and tamp the ends, then roll again.

Beat the egg whites in a shallow bowl until foamy. Roll each meatloaf in egg white, then in the bread crumbs, coating all over, including the ends. Refrigerate for at least 30 minutes before frying.

Place a rack in the center of the oven. Preheat the oven to 350°F.

Heat 2 tablespoons of vegetable oil in a 12- to 14-inch skillet over medium-high heat. When the oil is hot enough for a loaf to sizzle as soon as it hits the pan, brown all the loaves well on all sides, including the ends. Brown the sides first and only when they have browned, turn the cylinders on end to brown them. Handle the meat with a metal spatula/hamburger turner and a wooden spoon. Transfer to a roasting pan into which they fit, but not snugly.

Heat the olive oil in a 9- to 10-inch skillet over medium-high heat. Add the zucchini, carrot, and onion. Sauté until the onion is tender, about 5 minutes. Add the fresh and canned tomatoes. Season with the remaining salt and pepper. Bring to a simmer and cook, uncovered, for 10 minutes.

Pour the vegetable sauce over the meatloaves in the roasting pan.

Bake the meatloaves for 40 to 50 minutes, until the sauce is bubbling.

Let stand a few minutes before serving, but serve very hot.

To serve, cut each meatloaf in half crosswise and stand each half, browned side up, on individual plates. Top or surround with sauce.

Falsomagro
Stuffed Sicilian Beef Roll

The name of this dish means "false lean" because it looks like an innocent roast, while hidden inside are rich layers of prosciutto and/or mortadella and/or pancetta and/or salami or sopressata, plus a ground-meat stuffing traditionally studded with peas, but maybe also with cubes of one of the aforementioned *salumi* plus batons of well-aged cacciocavallo. Finally, at the center, is a core of hard-cooked eggs: a bright yellow and white bull's-eye among the rings of meat. It's no wonder *falsomagro* (or, in one of several dialectical spellings, *farsumagru*) is called the "king of Sicilian meat dishes." When the pinwheel slices of meat are set on a platter covered in the rich meat-flavored sauce—a true ragù—the dish is quite dramatic, a perfect party dish.

2½ pounds round steak, about 1½ inches thick, butterflied and pounded to no more than ⅓ inch thick

¼ pound prosciutto (with fat), sliced paper-thin

¼ pound mortadella, sliced paper-thin

½ pound sweet Italian sausage, casings removed

½ pound ground beef chuck

1 large egg

½ cup fine dry bread crumbs, moistened with warm water

2 rounded tablespoons coarsely shredded flat-leaf parsley

¼ cup grated pecorino or aged cacciocavallo Ragusano cheese

¾ teaspoon salt, or more to taste

¼ to ½ teaspoon freshly ground black pepper, or more to taste

2 rounded tablespoons frozen peas

4 to 6 ounces sharp provolone or aged cacciocavallo cheese, cut into strips

6 hard-cooked eggs

2 tablespoons extra-virgin olive oil

1 medium onion, finely minced

½ cup dry red wine

3 cups tomato puree

Arrange the steak on your work surface with the long side of the meat at the edge nearest you. It should be roughly a rectangle about 14 by 8 inches. Arrange the slices of prosciutto, then mortadella, over the surface of the meat.

To make the ground-meat filling, combine the sausage, ground beef, egg, bread crumbs, parsley, grated cheese, ¾ teaspoon salt, and ¼ to ½ teaspoon freshly ground black pepper. Knead the mixture well with your hands.

Spread the ground meat mixture evenly over the lower half of the layered meats. Scatter the peas over the meat. Then arrange strips of cheese over the meat, placing them horizontal to the long edge of the meat.

Cut the ends off the hard-cooked eggs so that the yolks are still intact but exposed. Arrange the eggs end to end down the center of the filling-covered portion of the meat. Holding the eggs in place, roll the meat from the bottom up, over the eggs and finally onto the bare portion of the beef. Tie up the roast, being careful to tuck in any loose filling.

Place an oven rack in the lower third of the oven. Preheat the oven to 300° F.

Heat the olive oil in a casserole (I use enameled cast-iron) over medium-high heat and brown the roast, turning it frequently. When it is well browned, add the onion to the pot. Cook another few minutes, until the onion has wilted.

Pour in the red wine and turn the roast in the liquid, scraping the brown film from the bottom of the pan. Cook the wine briskly until it has nearly evaporated. Add the tomato puree and 1 cup of water. Stir well. Turn the roast in the liquid. When the liquid begins to simmer, cover the pot and transfer it to the oven. Cook for 1½ hours, turning the roast and stirring the sauce two or three times.

Let the roast stand for 20 to 30 minutes before cutting off the strings and carving it into ½-inch-thick slices. Ladle the sauce onto a deep platter, then arrange the slices of meat on top of it. (The roast can be prepared ahead and reheated in the sauce in a 350°F oven, for about 40 minutes if it is started at room temperature.) Serve hot.

Variation

The roast is delicious at room temperature, served without the sauce or with the sauce reheated. The sauce itself is delicious on pasta as a first course, with the meat served as a main course.

Stigghiole di Pancetta
Grilled Pancetta or Pork on Spring Onions

Catania, Sicily

SERVES 6

This is a popular dish in Catania, where butcher's stalls in the Pescheria market sell meat-wrapped scallions on skewers, ready for the grill or broiler, along with other "value-added" meat preparations such as *ravioli di carne:* seasoned ground meat formed into two triangles pinched together, stuffed with cheese.

For these *stigghiole,* you can use thinly sliced pancetta, though I prefer the thinly sliced cut of pork that we call "country ribs," but without the bone. The Catanese have a near fetish for spring onions, which are fatter than our scallions (also called green onions in some parts of the United States), so look for especially large ones. I am able to buy the larger, more Catanese-size ones at my local farmers' market during a brief period in early spring, then again in fall.

1 pound thin (no more than ¼ inch thick) boneless rib-end pork chops or "country-style" pork ribs, or 1 pound flat pancetta (not rolled), sliced paper-thin

Salt

12 thick scallions, trimmed of roots and wilted greens

Using a meat pounder, pound the meat to no more than ⅛ inch thick, then season with salt. Wrap each slice of meat around a scallion, spiraling it up so that the meat covers all but the very top of the greens.

Arrange the rolls in two groups and push 2 skewers through each group of 4 rolls. One skewer should go through the bottom end of the meat, the other near the top end of the meat. Alternatively, you can form individual pieces, using the short metal skewers that are used for trussing poultry, or sturdy toothpicks or bamboo skewers soaked in water to make them less flammable. If grouping the skewers together, leave space between the scallion rolls so the sides can brown, too.

If using a kitchen broiler, preheat the broiler pan for 5 minutes, placing it about 3 inches from the heat source, whether gas or electric. You should be able to cook 2 skewers of 4 rolls each at one time. Broil them for 5 minutes on one side, then turn and broil on the second side for 2 to 3 minutes.

If cooking on an outdoor grill (preferably on charcoal), the skewers may need another minute or two on the second side.

Serve immediately.

Puntine di Maiale in Padella
Pork Ribs in a Skillet

Campania   SERVES 4

I learned this very simple technique for cooking pork ribs from Eugenia Tammaccaro, the night chef at Azienda Seliano, and my assistant when I teach classes there. Simple as the method is, the ribs do need careful tending, especially during their final browning. The result is superb, however; unadulterated tender and succulent pork.

2 pounds meaty pork ribs,
   cut into individual ribs

½ cup water or dry white wine

Salt and freshly ground pepper
   to taste

Arrange the ribs in one layer, if possible, in a 14-inch skillet. It doesn't matter if they are crowded. Add the water or wine. Season liberally with salt and pepper. Place over high heat and cook, covered, until the liquid has evaporated, which doesn't usually take more than 10 minutes.

Reduce the heat to low and continue to cook the ribs, covered, about 30 minutes longer, turning them regularly in their own fat until they are tender and browned. You can uncover them for the last few minutes of cooking to promote browning.

Serve hot. They reheat very well.

Involtini Crotonese
Pork Rolls from Crotone

Calabria   SERVES 4

Crotone, on the Ionian coast of Calabria, is famous for its superb sheep's milk cheese, pecorino Crotonese, which has recently become available in the United States. It is nothing like Romano, the pecorino with which Americans are most familiar. The Crotonese cheese has a big sheepy flavor, but not as much of a bite. And it's not salty, even when aged long enough to be a grating cheese.

If you can't find pecorino Crotonese, a well-aged Tuscan pecorino or well-aged provolone will do. These are such good little meat rolls, and when previously rolled, so quickly cooked, that they will probably become a regular in your repertoire whatever cheese you choose to use. I prefer them sautéed in olive oil until they are well browned but still pink inside. But they are also excellent on an outdoor grill. In either case, be careful not to overcook them. They get done a lot quicker than one expects, and there should still be a trace of pink in the center when they are cooked just so.

1 pound pork cutlets (about 8), pounded thin to about 3 x 6-inch scallopini

Salt and freshly ground black pepper to taste

4 ounces (approximately) pecorino Crotonese cheese

2 large garlic cloves, minced very finely (about 2 teaspoons)

24 to 30 whole leaves flat-leaf parsley

2 tablespoons extra-virgin olive oil

Arrange the pork slices lengthwise on your work surface. Season with salt and pepper.

Cut very thin shards of the pecorino and arrange them down the length of each slice of meat. Sprinkle each cutlet with a pinch or two of garlic, then arrange 3 or 4 whole leaves of parsley on top.

Roll up the meat and secure with toothpicks. Or thread the rolls closed with short metal trussing skewers. Or tie them up. If cooking on an outdoor grill, you may well want to put them on skewers, alternating with onion segments. Sprinkle with salt.

Heat the oil in a 12- to 14-inch skillet over medium-high heat. When the oil is hot enough to make a roll sizzle on contact, brown all the rolls well on all sides. They should be cooked inside by the time they are well browned, about 5 minutes. Let stand 5 minutes before serving.

Serve immediately or at room temperature, but never more than an hour or so after the meat has been cooked.

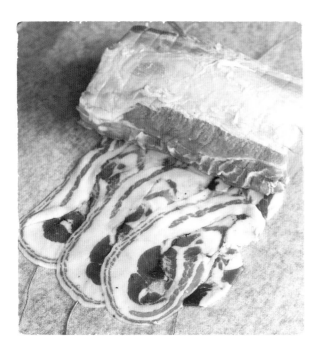

Lonza di Maiale alla Sorrentina
Pork Loin Roast, Sorrento Style

SERVES AT LEAST 8

This recipe must be making the rounds in middle-class Naples because I've been offered similar recipes from several cooks. This particular version is from Helene Tozzi, a native of South Africa who married a Neapolitan and has lived in Naples for nearly forty years. She in turn got it from the wonderful specialty food shop, La Tradizione, in Seiano, near Sorrento. La Tradizione sells both fresh and cured pork, but the shop also carries an impressive array of cheeses and many jarred and packaged products from the area, including Cecilia's Bella Baronessa brand of Figs in Wine Syrup (page 245).

It's no wonder Neapolitan home cooks have latched onto this roast: it is simple, delicious, and fool-proof. It's a great company roast, but it also tastes good at room temperature, sliced thin for sandwiches.

1 (2½- to 3-pound) boneless center-cut pork roast

Salt and freshly ground black pepper

¼ pound pancetta, sliced paper-thin

2 tablespoons extra-virgin olive oil

1½ cups orange juice (juice of 4 to 5 oranges)

2 bay leaves

1 tablespoon juniper berries, lightly crushed

Place a rack in the center of the oven. Preheat the oven to 450°F.

Season the meat generously with salt and pepper.

Wrap the pork roast with slices of pancetta, tying them with string. To do this most easily, lay a piece of waxed paper or parchment on a work surface. Cut pieces of string to a length that will generously wrap around the roast. Lay out 4 or 5 strings on the paper. Arrange the pancetta on top of the string, overlapping very slightly. Put the roast on the center of the arranged pancetta. Use the paper as an aid to gradually roll the roast with pancetta. Tie the pancetta onto the roast with the strings.

Pour the olive oil into the center of a roasting pan no smaller than 9 by 12 inches. Roll the meat in the oil and place the meat in the oven for 20 minutes.

Combine the orange juice, bay leaves, and juniper berries in a small bowl. Pour the juice and seasonings over the pork. Return the roast to the oven for another 25 to 30 minutes, until the center is done to the temperature of 140 to 145°F. By then the juices in the pan should be somewhat reduced and even caramelized.

Remove the roast from the oven and let it stand at least 15 minutes before carving.

To serve, cut into ¼-inch-thick (or thinner) slices and arrange on a platter. Strain the juices over the sliced meat, and discard the juniper berries and bits of bay leaf, which are attractive but not edible. The roast is delicious hot as well as at room temperature.

Cecilia tests her homemade pancetta.

SALUMI

Everywhere in Italy, every last bit of the pig is eaten; as we say in English, "everything but the oink." It is made into a nearly infinite variety of sausages and cured products, aside from having the tenderest muscles cut into cutlets, roasts and chops, to be eaten as fresh meat.

Ham—the thigh and upper leg—is the king of all pork cuts. *Prosciutto* is the word for "ham" in Italian, but Italians distinguish between *prosciutto cotto*, "cooked ham" like our sandwich meat, and *prosciutto crudo*, "raw ham," which is actually cured ham—what Americans think of when they hear the word *prosciutto*. (It is raw in the sense that it is never cooked by heat.) Almost every region of Italy also makes fresh pork sausage and an array of cured pork products called, generically, *salumi*, sold in a *salumeria*. In the Italian south, only the region of Puglia, because of its high humidity, does not produce many preserved pork products. A grand exception is the famous *capocollo* of Martina Franca, a small Baroque city that is high enough and dry enough to be a good place to age meat.

What we call salami, an Italian word used more in Northern Italy than in the south, is more usually called *salsiccia secca*, "dry sausage." *Sopressata* is the word used for a salami or dry sausage that is "surpressed," or flattened with a weight as it is aged and dried, although commercial sopressata often is not. Various types of excellent *salsicce secche* and *sopressate* are made all over Southern Italy, and there are many good ones made in the United States in the Southern Italian style. What Americans call pepperoni—the narrow, hot, dried sausage so popular on pizza—is a replica of a dried narrow Lucanian hot sausage. (*Peperoni* is the Italian word for sweet peppers; *peperoncino* is a hot pepper.) Sopressata, as well as other dried sausage, can also be seasoned with garlic, red wine, black peppercorns, and fennel seed. Like cheese, the taste of a sausage is determined by the ecosystem of the place where it is made.

Capocollo is a cured product like prosciutto, but made from the upper muscle of the shoulder (the word means "top of the neck"). It also comes in both sweet and hot forms. Italian Americans often call this "gabagool."

Culatello is the choicest muscle of the prosciutto, cured the same way as the whole ham.

Any or all of these meats are likely candidates for an antipasto course. In a restaurant, you can order *afettati*, simply "slices," and you will get an array of local offerings. Often, these meats don't travel out of their region, so the only place to try them is on the spot.

Salsicce al Forno con Patate
Sausage Baked with Potatoes

Fresh pork sausages are one of the most popular meats throughout Southern Italy, and there are many ways to cook them. In the Sila Grande Mountains of Calabria, there are roadside stands that tuck wood-grilled sausages into rolls, sometimes with sautéed onions and peppers, exactly as Italian sausages are served at American fairs. Sausages can be cooked in a skillet or grilled under the broiler (see page 190), but the easiest way is baked in a hot oven. I love to use one of my black cast-iron skillets for this, and sometimes I add sliced onion to the bed of wedged, cubed, or sliced potatoes that absorb some of the sausage's fat.

1½ pounds all-purpose potatoes, peeled and cut into 1-inch cubes, slim wedges, or ½-inch-thick slices

1 tablespoon extra-virgin olive oil

1 to 1½ pounds pork sausage, with fennel or other flavorings, hot or sweet, as desired

Preheat the oven to 450° F.

Put the potatoes in any kind of 10-inch pan. Drizzle with the olive oil, then toss to coat with oil. Spread the potatoes in a layer. Arrange the sausage on top of the potatoes.

Bake for 15 minutes. Toss the potatoes and turn the sausage. Use a metal spatula for the potatoes so you can scrape up and dislodge any that have begun to stick. Bake another 15 to 20 minutes, until the potatoes are tender and a bit browned, and the sausage is browned and cooked through. The only way to check for doneness is to slice a sausage. It's okay if the very center is slightly pink.

Variation

Slice a medium to large onion and toss it with the potatoes. You can also add a red bell pepper, cleaned and cut into ½-inch strips.

Salsicce con Broccoli di Rapa
Sausage with Broccoli Rabe

Pork sausage with broccoli rabe is true Southern Italian soul food. Everyone eats it, very often with orecchiette. The Pugliese like to claim it as their number-one most popular regional dish.

There are a lot of possibilities with the combination. You can cook the sausages separately any way you wish, then just put them on the same plate with the broccoli rabe. Or you can crumble the sausage and mix it with blanched broccoli rabe seasoned with garlic and hot pepper. Or you do as Eugenia Tammaccaro does at Azienda Seliano and cook them together in one pan, as in this recipe. The sausage fat enhances the broccoli rabe, the broccoli rabe the sausage. And it is excellent tossed with orecchiette and other pastas.

2 tablespoons extra-virgin olive oil

2 or 3 large garlic cloves, peeled and split in half lengthwise

3 bunches broccoli rabe, washed and heavy stems peeled

½ teaspoon salt, or more to taste

1½ pounds pork sausage, hot or sweet, or a combination (6 to 8 links), cut crosswise in half

Combine the oil and garlic in a 12- to 14-inch skillet over low heat and sauté until the garlic is tender but still white.

Add the moist broccoli rabe to the pan. Be careful—the fat will sputter. Sprinkle it with salt, then cover the pan. Increase the heat to medium. Cook the broccoli rabe for about 8 minutes, or until wilted.

Nestle the sausage halves in the broccoli rabe, cover the pan again, and continue cooking for about 15 minutes.

Uncover the pan. Toss the broccoli rabe. Turn the sausage. Some of the sausage pieces should be resting on the bottom of the pan now. Re-cover and continue to cook another 15 minutes, or until the sausages are cooked through (they will never brown, except in spots) and the broccoli rabe is soft, practically falling apart.

Serve hot, preferably immediately.

Salsicce in Padella
Sausage in a Skillet

This is another basic way to cook sausages in Southern Italy: put them in a skillet and cover with water. When the water evaporates, brown the links in the fat that has rendered from them. From there you can go almost anywhere. Good sausages are delicious as is, at the center of the plate with a potato and vegetable, particularly brocoli rabe.

1 pound Italian pork sausage of any kind

Cover the sausages with water in an 8- to 9-inch skillet over high heat. As soon as the water boils, reduce the heat so it gently simmers. Cook the sausages, uncovered, turning them several times once the water evaporates enough to expose the tops of the sausages.

When all the water has boiled away, after about 15 minutes, reduce the heat to very low, and turning the sausages frequently, brown them in the rendered fat in the pan. If you need a bit more fat, prick a couple of the sausages with the point of a knife.

Serve hot.

SALSICCE ALLA GRIGLIA

GRILLED SAUSAGE

Here's one more method of cooking sausage, especially for when you are in a hurry: split the sausages lengthwise down the middle, leaving the halves connected—in other words, butterfly the sausages.

Place the sausages, cut side up, under the broiler, close to the flame so they get slightly charred, or put them cut side down on a griddle or in a skillet. If cooking them on a flat surface, you can weight them down so they get more evenly browned.

Agnello con Le Olive
Lamb Chops with Black Olives

Although I got this particular recipe from the Hotel Barbieri in Altomonte, in northern Calabria, virtually the same dish can be found on other Southern Italian tables. The strong flavors of oregano, lemon, garlic, and oil-cured olives work especially well with shoulder lamb. I wouldn't try the recipe with loin or rib chops. That tender, more subtly flavored meat is best eaten simply grilled.

1 tablespoon extra-virgin olive oil

6 shoulder lamb chops about ½ inch thick (about 2 pounds)

Salt

¾ teaspoon dried oregano

¼ to ½ teaspoon red pepper flakes

Juice of 1 lemon (2 tablespoons)

1 garlic clove, minced (about 1 teaspoon)

¾ cup oil-cured black olives, pitted and very coarsely cut

Heat the olive oil in a 12- to 14-inch skillet or sauté pan over medium-high heat. When the oil is hot enough that a chop will sizzle immediately, add half the chops, season them with salt, and brown them on both sides. Remove to a platter and brown the remaining chops.

When all the chops are lightly browned, pour off and discard the rendered fat. Partially cover the skillet so the chops don't spill out, and tilt the pan to drain it. Return all the chops to the skillet.

Reduce the heat to low. Add the oregano, red pepper flakes, lemon juice, garlic, and olives. Turn the chops in the seasoning. Cover the pan and cook for 20 to 30 minutes, turning once or twice, until the chops are tender.

Serve the chops very hot, with a spoonful of the olives on top of each chop. There will be no sauce. If you want some sauce, add a bit of water to the pan. The olive mixture is so strongly flavored, it can be thinned somewhat and still make an excellent condiment.

Coscio di Pollo alla Grigila
Grilled Chicken Legs

Palermo, Sicily

SERVES 4

These chicken thighs and drumsticks, slashed and seasoned with rosemary and hot pepper, are one of the many embellished meat products—"value-added" meats, American butchers call them—you can find in Il Capo, the huge and colorful outdoor market of Palermo. Vucceria may be the more famous market, the one sought out by tourists, but Capo is "where the locals goes," as an Italian friend puts it in bad English. These are now a regular dish in my daily rapertoire.

4 chicken leg-thigh parts

2 teaspoons hot or sweet paprika or a blend of cayenne pepper and sweet paprika

8 to 12 small 3- to 4-inch rosemary sprigs

Salt

Place a rack on the top rung of the oven. Preheat the oven to 450°F or prepare a charcoal grill.

With a sharp knife, make two or three deep diagonal slashes down to the bone, across the skin side of each chicken section, one or two in the thigh, depending on their size, and one in the drumstick. Sprinkle the chicken on both sides with the red pepper or sweet paprika, concentrating it more in the slashes. Tuck a sprig of rosemary in each slash. Salt the chicken well on both sides.

Arrange the chicken, skin side up, on a baking sheet. (Keep refrigerated until ready to cook, for up to several hours.)

Bake 40 to 45 minutes, or if cooking on a charcoal grill, place chicken at a distance from white coals and cook slowly, turning several times.

Let stand 5 minutes before serving.

Verdure
Vegetables and Side Dishes

Verdure.

Long before the tomato was introduced by the Spanish (from Mexico) in the sixteenth century, and long before pasta became Southern Italy's staff of life in the seventeenth century, Southern Italians were known as the "leaf eaters." This was meant as an insult, but it was true. One Neapolitan eighteenth-century aristocrat and poet even called his beloved city "my broccoli."

Although life and food have changed south of Rome, as everywhere in the world, Southerners still dote on escarole, several varieties of broccoli, several varieties of chicory, several varieties of cabbage, cauliflower, and squash, many varieties of sweet and hot peppers, and—the queen of all vegetables—artichokes.

Vegetables appear in every course in the Southern Italian meal. They serve as antipasti—often several at once. They are the base for soups and salads. They dress pasta. And at least one if not two vegetables are usually served as side dishes, *contorni* in Italian, to main courses of meat, poultry, or fish. Vegetables can even find their way into dessert. In Sicily, green summer squash is candied and used in pastries, gelato, and cake fillings.

In the days of *cucina povera*, many greens were foraged from the countryside. Today, markets throughout the south overflow with cultivated vegetables from every southern region, and a few northern ones, too. If artichokes are not in season in Campania, there are artichokes from Puglia. In the middle of the winter, when it is too chilly to grow tomatoes in San Marzano, in Campania, Pacchino tomatoes from Sicily are in season.

The Southern Italian kitchen is largely based on pasta and vegetables, often in combination. Add some beans, lentils, or chickpeas, plus cheese and eggs, and, nutritionally speaking, you really don't need meat or fish.

Carciofini Siciliani
Baby Artichokes, Sicilian Style

The aromatics in this dish are the same as in Roman-style artichokes—mint and garlic—but the technique is different, and I think it epitomizes Sicilian intensity. When Romans cook artichokes they use a substantial amount of water. The result is delicious but more subtle. Sicilians use as little water as possible to achieve concentrated flavor.

1 lemon

1 pound baby artichokes (about 12)

3 tablespoons olive oil

2 large garlic cloves, finely minced (about 2 teaspoons)

¾ teaspoon salt

10 fresh spearmint leaves

Freshly ground black pepper to taste

Have ready a bowl of water with several ice cubes and the juice of 1 lemon. Save the spent lemon halves.

Break off the tough outer leaves of the artichokes, cut off about 1 inch of the top, and rub them with the reserved lemon halves. Add the artichokes to the ice water. (They can stay in the water for several hours, refrigerated. When you are ready to cook them, halve them and, as you do, put them back in the water to prevent darkening.)

Drain the artichokes, but don't dry them. Place them in one layer, cut side down, in a 10- to 12-inch skillet. Drizzle them with olive oil, then sprinkle with the minced garlic and salt. Tear the mint leaves into small pieces and scatter them over the top. Put just 2 or 3 tablespoons of water in the pan.

Cover the pan and place the artichokes over low heat. After about 5 minutes, check that they are cooking and the water hasn't totally cooked out. After about 10 minutes, turn them over and re-cover. You can hear when the water cooks out—the pan will start to sizzle. Keep the artichokes just barely moist. After 15 to 20 minutes, the artichokes will be thoroughly tender, the garlic still white, and there will be no liquid, just a bit of oil, on the bottom of the pan.

Add pepper, and serve hot or at room temperature.

Carciofi Arrostiti
Charcoal-Roasted Artichokes

One of the simplest and most popular ways to cook artichokes in Southern Italy is by nestling them in smoldering charcoal, although people don't usually do this at home. During artichoke season, which is March and April in Campania, later in Puglia, and during late winter in Sicily, vendors with portable charcoal brazieres post themselves along the roadsides and tend the artichokes. You jam on the brakes, pull over to the side of the road, no matter if there's another car two feet behind you, and you eat them unceremoniously out of hand with just a piece of paper to hold them. It's a messy, finger-licking, fabulous snack. The artichokes are seasoned with garlic and mint or parsley, olive oil, the smoky coals, and the hedonism of the moment. Hint: If you are traveling from Naples to Pompeii by car, there's usually an artichoke vendor right off the Autostrada exit at Gragnano.

FOR EACH SERVING

1 large artichoke, preferably with 1 inch or so of stem

1 garlic clove, finely minced

Several spearmint leaves, torn or coarsely chopped

2 tablespoons extra-virgin olive oil

Salt

Do not trim the artichokes. The outside leaves will definitely burn, but they will protect the inner leaves from burning. If the artichoke has some stem, cut it off at the base, peel it down to the lighter green, and mince it.

With your fingers, spread open the central leaves of the artichoke. Put pinches of chopped garlic, bits of mint, and the minced artichoke stem (if using) between some of the leaves. Drizzle oil over and into the leaves.

Place the artichokes, stem end down, in hot coals or briquettes. The artichokes should be about half buried. Roast until the inside leaves of the artichoke are tender, usually about 25 minutes.

Add salt to taste. Serve hot or warm.

Broccoli Saltati con Uova
Cauliflower Fried with Eggs and Cheese

Marsala, Sicily   SERVES 4 TO 6

I was feeling vegetable deprived when I arrived at Trattoria Pino in Marsala. In summer in western Sicily, eggplant and zucchini rule, and it is hard to find other vegetables in the restaurants. That's why I was so delighted to find that Pino's antipasto array was almost entirely vegetables. It was, of course, heavy on the eggplant and zucchini, but also with several mushroom preparations, several sweet pepper dishes, and this egg-coated cauliflower, which I still can't eat enough of. I prepare it with broccoli as well as with cauliflower now, and I serve it as a side dish.

1 small head cauliflower, cored
  and broken into florets, or
  1 bunch broccoli, florets only
  (reserve stems for another use)
  (about 4 cups)

3 large eggs

⅓ to ½ cup grated Parmigiano,
  grana Padano, or pecorino
  cheese, or a blend

¼ teaspoon freshly ground black
  pepper, or less to taste

2 tablespoons extra-virgin olive oil

Wash the cauliflower or broccoli.

Bring a large pot of well-salted water to a rolling boil over high heat and cook the cauliflower or broccoli until fully tender, usually 6 to 8 minutes from the time the water returns to a boil. Drain well. (You can cook the broccoli ahead and even refrigerate it for a day. Return to room temperature before proceeding.)

Beat the eggs, cheese, and pepper in a large mixing bowl.

Place the cauliflower or broccoli florets in the bowl and gently turn them in the egg, coating them as well as possible, letting egg seep into the crevices of the vegetable. All of it will not be absorbed.

Heat the oil over medium heat in a 10- to 12-inch nonstick skillet. When the pan is hot enough to cook a drop of the egg, give the cauliflower or broccoli a final toss in the egg, then lift it out of the bowl and place it in the hot oil. Once all of it is in the pan, drizzle the remainder of the egg mixture over the vegetable.

As soon as the egg begins to set, turn and cook on a second side. When the egg is lightly browned on all sides, remove the vegetable from the pan.

Serve hot or at room temperature.

Broccolo Affogato
Smothered Cauliflower

Catania, Sicily   SERVES 4 TO 6

In Catania, everyone seems to love this dish, and is proud of its strangeness—white cauliflower, gooey with melted cheese, and cooked with red wine and black olives, both of which stain it purple. In Sicily, I have eaten it only with white cauliflower, although Sicilians also have purple and pale green cauliflower. I have also read similar recipes in English-language books and on the Internet that call for broccoli. This is a misunderstanding. In Sicily, *broccolo* is a word for "cauliflower."

1 large head cauliflower

1 medium onion, very thinly sliced

2 tablespoons extra-virgin olive oil

1¼ teaspoons salt

¼ teaspoon freshly ground black pepper

10 oil-cured black olives, pitted and halved

2 anchovy fillets, cut into ½-inch pieces (optional)

¾ cup hearty dry red wine, such as Nero d'Avola

3 ounces diced young pepato cheese (see Note)

Cut off and discard the heavy leaf ribs of the cauliflower, if any. With a small sharp knife, cut out, then discard, the heavy white core. Cut the cauliflower into 2- to 3-inch florets, not too small. Wash well. Drain but don't dry. (In fact, rinse and moisten them again if you leave them standing in a colander for more than a few minutes.)

Heat the oil in a 3-quart saucepan over medium heat and sauté the onion until it is lightly golden, about 8 minutes. Remove from the heat. Scoop out about half the onion and reserve.

Arrange about half the cauliflower on the bottom of the pot. Season it with half the salt and a few grinds of the peppermill. Scatter about half the olives and half the anchovy fillets on the cauliflower.

Arrange another layer of cauliflower, season with the remaining salt and pepper, then scatter the remaining olives and anchovies on top of that layer. Top with the reserved sautéed onion. Pour on the red wine, making sure to stain all the cauliflower on the top layer.

Cover and cook over medium-low heat until the cauliflower is very tender and all the wine has evaporated, at least 20 minutes. After about 10 minutes, toss the cauliflower, moving the bottom pieces to the top. When the cauliflower is very tender, stir again, then scatter on the cubed cheese. Cover and let the cheese melt over all.

Serve hot or at room temperature.

NOTE: In Sicily, pepato comes in many stages of aging. It can sometimes be so *vecchio*, "old" (actually labeled *stravecchio*, "extra old"), that it is browned and crumbly, full of holes, and looking quite inedible. With this old cheese, you can, as Catanians do, put cubes of the cheese in the cauliflower from the beginning of cooking. With the usually very young and creamy pepato available in the United States, however, the cheese becomes stringy and exudes too much fat. That's why I add it only at the end of the cooking. If you can't find any pepato, of any age, you can substitute pecorino or well-aged caciocavallo Ragusano, or a young or sharp provolone.

Fave e Cicoria *'Ncapriata* (Pugliese dialect)
Fava Puree and Chicory

Hercules supposedly drew his strength from this combination of fava beans and chicory. It is one of the most beloved and famous dishes of Puglia, where the bean puree and boiled greens are eaten together in one bowl, and an olive oil cruet and a salt shaker are passed so everyone can dress his or her own to taste. The dried yellow fava beans used for this dish come already peeled. They are available in Italian and Greek food stores. And once they have been soaked and boiled, they fall apart when you smash them on the side of the pot and beat them vigorously with a wooden spoon. Perhaps the legend should be that Hercules gained his strength from the exercise of making this dish. As for the greens, although chicory is traditional, any boiled dark leafy green works.

1 pound dried skinned yellow fava beans

Boiled greens, preferably chicory or dandelions, but also broccoli rabe, escarole, mustard greens, or collards

Rinse the beans in a strainer under cold running water. Place them in a large bowl and cover with several inches of cold water. Let stand at least 8 hours. After soaking, remove any stray brown skins.

Pour the beans and their soaking water into a 2½- to 3-quart saucepan. If the water does not cover the beans by at least 2 inches, add more water. Bring to a boil, uncovered, over medium heat. Stir down the white foam. There is no need to skim it off.

Reduce the heat to medium-low and simmer the beans gently, stirring frequently with a wooden spoon, until they start to fall into a puree. After about 45 minutes, stir vigorously, mashing the beans with the back of the spoon. The end result should be a smooth puree. It may take as long as 90 minutes to get them very smooth. It will be necessary to add more water, but add no more than ¼ cup at a time, so the beans never stop simmering gently. In the end, you can adjust the puree's consistency with additional water, but it should be nearly as thick as mashed potatoes.

Serve the puree with hot boiled greens, either in separate bowls for everyone to help themselves, family style, or plate the fava and greens on the same plate or in a shallow pasta bowl. Pass oil and salt at the table.

The same fava puree, but made as thin as split pea soup with additional water, can be served as a soup with pasta. Season the hot puree with salt and pepper. Boil separately broken spaghetti or *pasta mista* (see page 81), or a small pasta shape, such as ditali or pennette, and stir the pasta into the fava puree. Serve very hot as a first course, or a meal in a bowl. Pass extra-virgin olive oil or *olio santo* (see page 73).

Melanzane o Zucchine alla Griglia
Grilled and Marinated Eggplant or Zucchini

All Regions

SERVES 4 TO 6

A ridged grill—a piece of cookware that has become very popular in the United States—is essential for preparing this very popular antipasto or buffet item. The eggplant or zucchini is sliced thin, grilled dry, then marinated with oil, which plumps it up. Usually eggplant and zucchini are marinated separately, but there's no reason you can't prepare and serve both together. They can take the same seasoning.

1 eggplant or 3 medium zucchini or more smaller ones (about 1 pound)

¼ cup extra-virgin olive oil, or more to taste

3 large garlic cloves, finely chopped (about 1 tablespoon)

½ teaspoon salt, or more to taste

⅓ cup loosely packed fresh mint, flat-leaf parsley, or basil leaves, torn

Wash the eggplant or zucchini. If it is round eggplant, cut it into ¼-inch-thick or slightly thinner crosswise slices. If it is a long eggplant, cut it into lengthwise slices. Cut the zucchini into slices no thicker than ¼ inch lengthwise. Discard the outside slices of eggplant, which are mostly skin.

Heat a ridged stovetop grill over high heat until a drop of water evaporates instantly.

Place a layer of vegetable on the grill. Lower the heat to medium-high. Press the slices with a spatula. After about 4 minutes, check to see if they are turning an uneven brown or getting dark marks from the grill. If they are not, adjust the heat accordingly. When the slices have dark grill marks, turn them and grill the second side for about another 3 minutes, checking to prevent burning. Again, adjust the heat if they start to color too much or not enough.

Arrange the cooked vegetable slices in one layer on a large platter. Drizzle with olive oil, then sprinkle with a few pinches of the minced garlic and a little salt. Scatter a few torn leaves of basil, mint, or parsley on the vegetable. (I prefer mint with zucchini and basil with eggplant, but anything goes. Dried oregano is also excellent and goes with either.) Continue cooking the remaining vegetable slices in batches.

Make layers of the vegetables, dressing each while still warm with another tablespoon or so of oil, more garlic, salt, and herb. Let stand for at least a few hours before serving. (The eggplant is even better if made in the morning to serve in the evening, or after marinating for 24 hours. Do not cover the platter with plastic wrap until the vegetables have cooled to room temperature. Once cooled, the vegetables can be kept refrigerated, tightly covered, for up to 1 week.)

Variation

To this seasoning, you may want to add a few drops of white wine vinegar to each layer, but only a very little bit.

Melanzane Impanata
Breaded Eggplant Slices

Eggplant cooked this way is sensationally delicious: the vegetable becomes creamy, doesn't absorb much oil, and is encased in a seriously crisp crust.

I like to make thick eggplant "steaks" that can be served like big slabs of meat in the middle of the plate with vegetables next to it. Or, as one sees so frequently on antipasto tables, these slices make a great base for any number of toppings. The most familiar would be a round of breaded eggplant topped with mozzarella, a sprinkling of grated cheese, and either tomatoes or tomato sauce, heated in the oven to melt the cheese. It's sort of an eggplant pizza or *finta parmigiana*—"fake parmigiana."

An eggplant "steak," served either hot out of the pan or at room temperature, is also a great appetizer with salad on top, like a *bruschetta* with chopped tomatoes, garlic, basil, and oil, or, say, with arugula tossed with oil and vinegar.

1 (2-pound) eggplant

2 tablespoons salt

2 eggs

½ cup all-purpose flour

¾ cup fine dry bread crumbs

Oil for frying

Wash and dry the eggplant. Do not peel. Cut the eggplant into crosswise slices about ½ inch thick. Salt the eggplant. Drain it and dry it well.

Break the eggs into a pie plate or shallow bowl and, with a table fork, beat until well mixed. Put the flour in another plate, the bread crumbs in a third.

Dredge the eggplant slices in the flour, shaking off the excess. Dip the slices in egg, covering both sides well. Finally, put the slices in the bread crumbs. Top with some of the bread crumbs. With your fingers, press the bread crumbs into both sides of the eggplant, flipping from side to side a few times, until the pieces are well coated.

As they are breaded, place the eggplant slices on a platter. When it is necessary to make another layer, put a sheet of parchment or waxed paper between the layers. When all the slices have been completed, place them in the refrigerator for at least 30 minutes, or up to several hours.

In a large skillet, pour about ¼ inch of oil. Place over high heat until the oil is hot enough to cause bubbles to gather around the handle of a wooden spoon. Add some eggplant slices. Soon after putting the slices in oil, the heat will probably need to be adjusted down to medium to medium-high. You don't want the bread crumbs to brown more quickly than the eggplant can be cooked. If the eggplant is ½ inch thick and the heat is correct, it will take about 3 minutes a side, then perhaps a final flip over to the first side for 1 more minute. The crumbs should be well browned, the eggplant very soft. When you can see tiny bubbles arise from under the bread-crumb crust, the eggplant is cooked.

Caponata al Forno
Baked Sweet and Sour Eggplant

MAKES ABOUT 7 CUPS

Think of the classic Sicilian *caponata* as a complex sweet and sour eggplant dish: fried eggplant cubes dressed with a tomato-based sauce containing celery, olives, capers, onions, and sometimes raisins and pine nuts or almonds. In the southeast corner of the island, they often add red peppers. And often, mainly in Palermo and the center of the island, cocoa is added, a legacy of the Spanish who first brought chocolate to southern Italy from Mexico. In Palmero, they might also add fried fish cubes or balls. However it is made, *caponata*, which is also called *caponatina*, is usually served as an antipasto, but it is also an excellent side dish when the main event is grilled meat or poultry.

Classic *caponata* can be very oily, what with the eggplant sponging up its frying oil and a sweet and sour sauce started with oil. The following contemporary baked version requires very little oil. It's the creation of my friend Franca Micelli in Siracusa.

1 large, preferably sweet onion, cut into ½-inch dice (about 1½ cups)

3 medium red and/or yellow bell peppers, cut into ½-inch dice (about 3 cups)

2 large celery ribs, cut into ½-inch dice (about 1 cup)

1 medium or 3 small eggplants (about 1½ pounds), not peeled, cut into 1-inch cubes (about 6 cups)

2 heaping tablespoons salted capers, well rinsed

3 large garlic cloves, coarsely chopped (about 1 tablespoon)

¼ cup extra-virgin olive oil

1 small (14 ounces) can peeled Italian tomatoes

2 tablespoons sugar

1 teaspoon salt, or slightly more to taste

2 tablespoons white wine or apple cider vinegar

⅓ cup cut-up, pitted Sicilian green olives

Preheat the oven to 400°F.

In an approximately 11 by 15-inch roasting pan, combine the onion, peppers, celery, eggplant, capers, and garlic. Toss to mix.

Drizzle the olive oil over all the ingredients. Toss well again. Crush the tomatoes in your hand, letting them fall into the vegetables with all their juice. Add the sugar, salt, and vinegar. Toss again.

Bake for 90 minutes, until all the vegetables are tender and the juices in the pan have reduced and thickened. If necessary, bake a little longer. Stir in the olives and let cool.

Serve warm or at room temperature. The flavor develops after a day in the refrigerator. The *caponata* can be kept, tightly covered in the refrigerator, for at least a week.

Funghi Gratinato
Crumb-Crusted Baked Mushrooms

SERVES 4 TO 6

I Bucanieri, a colorfully rustic but modern place just down the road from the Florio wine cellars in Marsala, is one of the best restaurants that I've eaten in in Sicily, and that's saying a lot. I am certainly not alone in my admiration. The local wine-business people flock here for lunch, and my new Marsalese friend and driver, Eugenio Lopez, practically insisted I eat here. At night, the restaurant is apparently a local social center.

Besides being a restaurant, it is also a butcher shop, and the meats are at a much higher level than you usually find in Southern Italy. And making them even tastier, they are cooked in the dining room on a spectacular and large hooded grill over a hardwood fire. That said, everything from the fish to the *arancini* are the absolute tops. Even something basic like these baked mushrooms are memorable. At the restaurant, they use a mix of local wild mushrooms, but even with cultivated white or cremini mushrooms, you'll be making this dish often.

3 tablespoons extra-virgin olive oil

1 pound white button, or cremini mushrooms, or mixed "exotic" mushrooms, cut into halves or quarters if large—all the pieces should be about the same size

¾ teaspoon salt

Few turns of the peppermill

2 rounded tablespoons grated pecorino cheese

2 rounded tablespoons bread crumbs

1 large garlic clove, finely minced

1 tablespoon finely chopped parsley

Place a rack in the top third of the oven. Preheat the oven to 400°F.

Select a 10-inch skillet (I like cast-iron here) or gratin dish, or an oven-safe ceramic or terracotta dish that you can put on the table.

Drizzle the bottom of the pan with 1 tablespoon of the oil. Spread the mushrooms in the pan, drizzle them with 1 tablespoon more oil, then season them with salt and pepper.

In a small bowl, mix the grated cheese, bread crumbs, garlic, parsley, and the last tablespoon of oil. Sprinkle the crumbs over the mushrooms.

Bake for 15 minutes.

These are best served immediately, while the top crumbs are still crunchy, but they are good at room temperature, too.

Finocchio coi Pomodori Secchi
Fennel Braised with Sun-Dried Tomatoes

Motta Sant' Anastasia, Sicily   SERVES 6 AS AN ANTIPASTO OR SIDE DISH

Since I got this recipe from Sara Romano I haven't stopped making it. I could eat a pan full myself, and nearly everyone I serve it to requests I make it again, or asks me for the recipe. Besides being nearly addictive, it is easy to put together and tastes even better when made ahead, making it perfect for entertaining. You can serve it either at room temperature or gently reheated. It can be part of an antipasto array or served as a side dish.

Sara was born in Motta Sant'Anastasia, a tiny town near Catania, where she lives now, and her fennel dish is seasoned with the typically strong flavors of Sicily—sun-dried tomatoes, oregano, onion, and fruity olive oil. In Northern Italy, licorice-tasting fennel is usually served with butter and Parmigiano, or béchamel and cheese. If you happen to find the very dense Sicilian sun-dried tomato paste, called *strattu* in dialect—it is occasionally available in the United States—use pinches of it instead of the sun-dried tomatoes in oil now available in every American supermarket.

3 large fennel bulbs, trimmed of stems and cut from stem to root end into ⅜-inch slices

1 tablespoon dried oregano

1 teaspoon salt

3 to 4 tablespoons finely chopped sun-dried tomatoes preserved under oil, or 2 to 3 tablespoons Sicilian sun-dried tomato paste

1 small onion, cut in half through the root end, then sliced as thin as possible

4 tablespoons extra-virgin olive oil

½ cup water

½ cup fine dry bread crumbs

Arrange a layer of fennel slices in a 10-inch sauté pan or deep skillet. Season with pinches of oregano—a scant teaspoon on each layer—and sprinkle with about ¼ teaspoon salt.

Sprinkle on about ⅓ of the chopped sun-dried tomatoes, or, alternatively, using a ¼-teaspoon measure, dot the fennel with 5 or 6 drops of tomato paste.

Spread about ⅓ of the sliced onion over the fennel, then drizzle with 1 tablespoon of olive oil. Continue layering the ingredients, making no more than four layers, dividing the ingredients more or less evenly, and using only 3 tablespoons of the oil.

Pour the water down the side of the pan, so as not to disturb the seasoning on the top layer. Cover the pan and bring to a boil over medium heat.

Lower the heat and very gently simmer for about 40 minutes, or until the fennel is very tender. Twice during the cooking, tip the pan and push a spoon into the vegetable layers so you can spoon some of the liquid from the bottom of the pan and drizzle it over the top of the fennel. If the liquid is evaporating, add a tablespoon or 2 of water.

If, after 40 minutes, the fennel is very tender but there is still liquid in the pan, not just oil, uncover the pan, increase the heat, and boil until no liquid remains on the bottom.

Combine and mix the bread crumbs with the remaining tablespoon of oil in a small bowl. Sprinkle the bread crumbs over the top of the fennel, covering evenly. Place the pan under the broiler, about 5 inches from the heat, and brown the crumbs. It takes just a minute or so.

Serve immediately, warm or at room temperature. It can be made hours ahead, but tastes best when never refrigerated.

Peperoni Saltate con Olive e Capperi
Sautéed Peppers with Olives and Capers

Sautéing peppers is easier and quicker than roasting them, and it also intensifies their flavor. Don't undercook them. They taste best when well wilted, even a little charred on the edges. Olives and capers are the seasoning ingredients here, but pine nuts and raisins, or just garlic and basil or parsley, are other possibilities.

3 medium red, yellow, or orange bell peppers (about 1 pound)

12 Gaeta olives or 6 to 8 large green Sicilian olives

2 tablespoons extra-virgin olive oil

¼ teaspoon salt, or more to taste

1 rounded tablespoon salted capers, rinsed well

⅓ cup loosely packed fresh basil or flat-leaf parsley leaves

Wash the peppers. Cut out the stem ends and the ribs. Discard the seeds. Cut them lengthwise into ¼- to ½-inch-wide strips.

With a paring knife, cut the flesh off the large green olives in large pieces, discarding the pits. Or pit the Gaeta olives (they are more or less freestone) and cut them in half. Set aside.

Heat the oil in a 9- to 10-inch skillet or sauté pan over medium-high heat. As soon as it is hot enough to make a pepper strip sizzle immediately, add all the peppers, season them with salt, and sauté, tossing regularly, for 5 to 8 minutes, until they are tender but not mushy. Add the olives and capers. Sauté another minute.

Tear the basil or parsley into the pan and toss again for another minute or so.

Serve hot, warm, or at room temperature.

Roasted Peppers

Roasting peppers concentrates their flavor and sweetness, adds a touch of smokiness if you roast them over an open flame, makes them easy to peel, and, last but certainly not least, cooks them.

Italians enjoy roasted peppers for their own sake—hot, cold, or at room temperature with nothing more than some olive oil, salt and pepper, and maybe a few torn leaves of basil or parsley. Dried oregano is good, too. They can be an antipasto or a side or the base of a more elaborate dish.

There are several ways to do the roasting. My least favorite is the one I see most frequently on the Internet and on TV cooking programs—cleaned, halved, and put under a broiler. That method makes the peppers dry and eliminates the possibility of collecting the deliciously sweet juices they exude when they are roasted whole and opened over a bowl. I much prefer turning the peppers over a flame on a gas burner or, even better, on a charcoal grill. It's a job for which you need patience, but it can be meditative.

Also very effective, and easy, is roasting the peppers in a hot oven. Put them directly on the rack of a preheated 450°F oven for about 20 minutes. At this point, the pepper skins should be slightly charred and either blown up or wrinkled.

Whichever method you use, as soon as the peppers are charred all over, place them immediately in either a covered pot or a paper bag. As they cool, they will continue to soften—they are steaming in their own heat—and become easier to peel.

Once cooled, split the peppers open over a bowl to catch any liquid inside. Reserve the liquid. Scrape out the seeds and ribs with a small sharp knife. Peel off the skins. I do this over a paper towel, so I can occasionally wipe pepper skins off the knife onto the towel.

As you peel the roasted peppers, arrange them in a shallow bowl or deep platter.

Dress with extra-virgin olive oil and, if desired, one or all of the following: chopped garlic, torn basil or parsley leaves, capers. Don't salt the peppers until serving time. Roasted peppers with oil, but without garlic, can be kept in the refrigerator for up to 1 week. Wrap the dish tightly in plastic.

Cut into strips, roasted peppers are delicious combined with cold boiled potatoes for a salad with garlic and basil to season it, or with warm boiled potatoes for a side dish. In either case, a generous amount of extra-virgin olive oil and only a splash or two of vinegar are called for.

Or toss roasted pepper strips with dried bread crumbs, dried oregano, minced garlic, olive oil, and, if desired, chopped anchovies, then bake until heated through.

Roasted and dressed sweet pepper strips are also an excellent topping for bruschetta, great tossed with pasta, and the perfect substitute for tomatoes to serve alongside slices of mozzarella.

Patate con Alloro e Vino Rosso
Potatoes with Bay Leaf and Red Wine

Catania, Sicily

SERVES 4 TO 6

Sara Romano's former husband was a vegetarian, and one night, she says, missing her meat flavors, she devised this potato dish with the seasonings she would use on lamb, if only the man would eat lamb. Black olives and red wine stain the white potatoes a purple hue, and although that's not a color Americans are accustomed to for their food, in Catania one of the most beloved dishes is cauliflower stained with the same ingredients (see page 200). For the sake of appearance, I sometimes put a crust of bread crumbs on top, which also adds some crunchy contrast to the soft and very well seasoned potatoes.

1½ to 2 pounds all-purpose potatoes, peeled and cut into ½-inch-thick slices

4 bay leaves

12 oil-cured black olives, pitted and halved

1 large garlic clove, thinly sliced

1 teaspoon salt

3 tablespoons extra-virgin olive oil

¾ cup water

½ cup hearty dry red wine

½ cup dry fine bread crumbs

Arrange a layer of potatoes in a 10- to 11-inch skillet, sauté pan, or casserole. Place 2 bay leaves on the potatoes, along with half the olives and half the garlic. Season with salt and drizzle with 1 tablespoon of oil.

Make another layer with the remaining potatoes, bay leaves, olives, garlic, salt, and 1 tablespoon oil. Pour the water over all.

Place the pan or casserole over medium heat, cover, and simmer until the potatoes are almost tender, about 12 minutes. Remove the cover. Add the wine. Increase the heat to medium-high and continue to simmer, uncovered, until all but a few tablespoons of the liquid has evaporated, about another 5 minutes.

Preheat the oven to 375°F.

In a small bowl, toss the bread crumbs with the last tablespoon of oil, then sprinkle over the potatoes. Bake until the bread crumbs are toasted, about 8 minutes.

Serve immediately.

Gattò alla Gena
Gena's Potato Cake with Broccoli Rabe, Sausage, and Smoked Cheese

Naples, Campania

Gattò is a variant of French *gateau*, meaning "cake," and it was likely so named by a Monzu chef, one of the cooks to the aristocracy who were trained in French cuisine. Whatever the name, it's a mashed potato casserole. The traditional version is dotted with ham, salami, and at least two cheeses, grated and cubed. This variation was created by chef Gena Iodice at her elegant, contemporary restaurant La Marchesella in Giugliano, at the edge of Naples. Besides this hearty casserole, Gena also makes a seafood *gattò* filled with asparagus, shrimp, and cod. As Gena is a friend of the Bellelli family, and we all love her version of *gattò*, Gattò alla Gena is now made at Azienda Seliano and gains rave reviews among the *agriturismo* guests.

4 pounds all-purpose potatoes, peeled and cut into large chunks

1 cup loosely packed grated Parmigiano cheese

¾ cup milk

2 eggs, beaten, plus 1 egg yolk

2 tablespoons extra-virgin olive oil

1 large garlic clove, finely chopped (about 1 teaspoon)

¼ teaspoon red pepper flakes

2 bunches broccoli rabe, stems removed, boiled and drained well (see page 150)

2½ teaspoons salt

1 pound sweet Italian sausage (with fennel, if desired), casings removed

4 tablespoons cold butter, cut into pea-sized pieces

12 ounces smoked mozzarella, scamorza, or other semi-firm smoked cheese, such as smoked Gouda, cut into ¼-inch cubes or shredded

4 slices white American cheese

Freshly ground black pepper

Put the potatoes in a large pot with enough cold water to cover them by a few inches. Salt the water well, bring to a boil over high heat, and cook the potatoes until tender. Drain well.

Rice the potatoes into a large mixing bowl, or put them through a food mill. Stir in the Parmigiano cheese, milk, and the 2 whole eggs beaten together. Refrigerate for 30 minutes to chill slightly.

Meanwhile, combine the olive oil, garlic, and red pepper flakes in a 10- to 12-inch skillet over low heat. When the garlic is tender but still white, add the broccoli rabe, season with about ½ teaspoon salt, toss the broccoli rabe in the oil, and continue cooking over slightly higher heat until the broccoli rabe is very well cooked, tossing it every few minutes. Coarsely chop the cooked broccoli rabe. Set aside.

In another skillet, sauté the crumbled sausage, continually breaking it up with the side of a wooden spoon, until it has lost all its raw color. Set aside.

When the potatoes have cooled, beat in the butter, leaving tiny pieces of butter in the potatoes.

Place a rack in the center of the oven. Preheat the oven to 375°F.

Butter a 9 by 13-inch baking pan, or one of equivalent volume.

Spoon about half the potatoes into the pan. Using a wet hand, gingerly press and smooth the potatoes into an even layer. Arrange a layer of sausage over the potatoes, then an even layer of broccoli rabe. Sprinkle with cubed or shredded cheese. Tear the American slices into pieces and scatter them on top. Season to taste with black pepper. Spoon the remaining potatoes over the top and, again using wet hands, spread and pat the potatoes into a smooth and even layer. Beat the remaining egg yolk with a fork and, with a pastry brush, paint the potatoes with egg.

Bake for about 40 minutes, until the top is golden.

Let stand for 15 to 20 minutes before cutting and serving in squares. *Gattò* reheats very well.

Patate e Verza
Potatoes and Cabbage

Potatoes and cabbage are a frequent theme in Southern Italy. It is poor-people food, *cucina povera* (think Irish, too!), and the south of Italy has always been poor. In small villages in Basilicata, historically the poorest of the poor, and in Calabria, which is also not exactly a land of luxury, the most typical village dish is often some version of potatoes and cabbage. It can be a soup, brothy or thick, or a dry dish like this, sweet from the vegetables but with a typically Lucanian kick of hot pepper. Serve it as a side dish, as part of an antipasto array, or as it was in its peasant past, a meal unto itself. Then it was a meal of necessity. Now we call it comfort food.

2 tablespoons extra-virgin olive oil

2 ounces pancetta, thinly sliced and cut into thin strips

¾ to 1 pound all-purpose white or yellow potatoes, peeled and cut into ½-inch-thick slices

1 teaspoon salt

1½ pounds green or Savoy cabbage (½ medium head), cut into ¾-inch squares

Big pinch of red pepper flakes, or more to taste

Several tablespoons water (optional)

Heat the oil and pancetta together in a 9- to 10-inch sauté pan over medium heat. Let the pancetta sizzle for a few minutes, rendering some of its fat, but not letting it brown.

Add the potatoes to the pan and cook them, turning them a few times, for about 2 minutes. Season with ½ teaspoon of salt and the pepper flakes. Arrange them in a layer, then put the cabbage on top of the potatoes. If it is not wet from being recently washed, add about 3 tablespoons of water. Sprinkle the remaining ½ teaspoon of salt on the cabbage. Cover the pan, lower the heat to medium-low, and cook for 10 minutes. Check after a few minutes. The liquid in the bottom of the pan should be simmering very gently. The cabbage should be wilting.

After another 10 minutes, turn the potatoes and cabbage together, scooping the potatoes up from the bottom of the pan with a spatula. Cover the pan again and cook until the potatoes are very tender, about another 10 minutes. Toss the mixture well. Inevitably, the potatoes will break into chunks.

Serve hot or at room temperature.

Zucca Gialla alla Griglia
Grilled and Marinated Butternut Squash

Campania

SERVES 8 TO 10 AS AN ANTIPASTO OR SIDE DISH

When Cecilia's crop of butternut squash and other pumpkins start maturing in August, squash becomes a star on the menus of Azienda Seliano, appearing in several guises, including paccheri with squash and sausage (see page 120), risotto with squash, and sweet and sour squash. Marinated slices of grilled squash or pumpkin may be the most popular, however. It is such a revelation that the guests have trouble identifying the thin grilled orange slices on their plates, but those plates are always wiped clean. It's good to make the squash in a large batch, not only because it is so delicious but also because it keeps very well in the refrigerator for as long as a week. I use the narrower, cylindrical top of a 4-pound squash, reserving the bulbous bottom half (with the seeds) for another use. This provides solid round slices to grill. Slice the squash as thin as possible, less than ⅛ inch thick, if possible. I use a meat slicing machine to make it very thin. A wide mandoline also works perfectly, as do good knife skills.

2 pounds butternut squash, peeled and sliced no thicker than ⅛ inch

1 teaspoon salt

3 tablespoons white wine vinegar

2 large garlic cloves, finely minced (about 2 teaspoons)

2 teaspoons dried oregano

¾ cup extra-virgin olive oil

Have a deep platter or 9 by 13-inch glass or stainless steel pan ready to receive the grilled squash.

Heat a ridged stovetop grill over high heat until a drop of water evaporates instantly.

Place slices of squash on the hot grill, and grill until the squash gets dark lines from the grill, about 4 minutes. Flip it over and grill the second side for 3 to 4 minutes.

As the slices are cooked, arrange them in layers in the pan, sprinkling each layer with salt, a few drops of vinegar, and pinches of garlic and oregano. Drizzle with olive oil. Continue to grill the squash, making seasoned layers in the pan.

Let stand at room temperature for at least 2 hours before serving. The squash is even better after marinating for a day. Keep refrigerated for long storage, up to a week.

Pomodorini Schiaciatti
Smashed Tomatoes

Puglia

SERVES 4 TO 8 AS AN ANTIPASTO OR SIDE DISH

In this traditional Pugliese recipe, slowly cooking the minced onion until it practically melts, but without coloring, underscores the sweetness of tiny grape tomatoes that are served either as a side dish, as part of an antipasto array, as a topping for *bruschetta*, or even to toss with macaroni. They are especially welcome in the winter when grape tomatoes are the only tomatoes that taste like tomatoes. As a side dish, they go with grilled or roasted meat, poultry, or fish, but also try them next to a slice or two of Grilled Cheese (page 144).

3 tablespoons extra-virgin olive oil

1 medium onion, very finely minced

½ teaspoon salt, or more to taste

1 pound (2 pints) grape tomatoes, washed but not dried

Freshly ground black pepper to taste

Combine the oil and onion in a 9- to 10-inch skillet over low heat. Cook very gently for about 30 minutes, until the onion is very soft and very slightly golden. Season with salt after a few minutes.

Increase the heat to medium-high and add the tomatoes, still with a bit of water clinging to them. Cook, covered, for about 5 minutes, until the tomatoes are heated through, then begin smashing them with the back of a wooden spoon.

Remove from the heat. Taste for salt and pepper, then adjust the seasonings to taste.

Serve hot or at room temperature.

Involtini di Zucchini Fritti
Fried Zucchini Rolls with Ham and Cheese

Campania

These were a big hit among my students when Alfonso Mattozzi brought them to our table to nibble while we waited for the main events at his now internationally famous, but very simple restaurant, Europeo di Mattozzi, in Naples. (See page 114 for Mattozzi's recipe for pasta and potatoes.) They are a great item to pass at a party, standing up, or at the table. Best of all, they can be made ahead, arranged on a baking sheet, and heated in the oven just before serving. Even though the zucchini are fried they are surprisingly light; the vegetable just gets a thin batter of flour and egg. If you don't want to fry, however, they are also delicious made with zucchini grilled over charcoal or on a ridged grill.

Vegetable oil for frying

½ cup all-purpose flour

2 large eggs

2 (7- to 8-inch-long) medium zucchini, cut lengthwise into ¼-inch-thick slices (about 12 slices)

3 thin slices cooked ham

About 4 ounces scamorza or mild provolone cheese

Heat ¼ inch of oil in a heavy skillet over high heat.

Put the flour on a plate. In a pie plate, beat the eggs with a table fork until well mixed.

When the oil is hot, dip each slice of zucchini into the flour. Shake off the excess, then drag the slice through the beaten egg. Fry several slices of zucchini at one time, but do not crowd the pan. The zucchini are done when the coating is lightly browned on both sides. The zucchini will be fully cooked and soft. Drain the zucchini slices on absorbent paper and let cool.

Cut the ham slices lengthwise so they are no wider than the strips of zucchini.

Cut the cheese into thin, small pieces.

Preheat the oven to 350°F. Place a rack in the center of the oven.

When the zucchini are cool enough to handle, arrange a strip of ham down the length of each, then a few thin pieces of cheese along the length. Roll the zucchini with the ham and cheese, then secure with a toothpick. (The rolls may be made ahead to this point. Refrigerate until ready to heat.)

Place the zucchini rolls on a baking sheet and bake for 10 minutes, until the cheese has become slightly melted. The exact timing will depend on the type of cheese. Serve immediately.

Delizie dal' Orto
Summer Vegetable Sauté

Cecilia's head cook, Anna D'Amato, makes this mixture often in the summer. It is a sautéed mix of the vegetables we most associate with "sunny Italy"—red peppers, zucchini, and eggplant—everything but tomatoes. With the vegetables cut as Anna does them, everything in strips, it makes a great filling for *Pizza Rustica* (page 48), or for little fried or baked turnovers using pizza dough—call them *calzoncini* or *panzarotti*. The vegetable strips are also a good dressing for big macaroni, such as paccheri. Or, dice the ingredients instead, and use the mixture to dress spaghetti or bucatini.

1 (approximately 1-pound) eggplant, wiped clean but not peeled, cut into ½-inch-wide, 3-inch-long strips

¼ cup extra-virgin olive oil

1 medium onion, halved and sliced ¼ inch thick

1 medium red bell pepper, seeded and cut into ¼-inch-wide strips

2 teaspoons salt

2 medium (about 12 ounces) zucchini, cut into ¼-inch-wide, 3-inch-long strips

Several twists of the peppermill

Several leaves fresh basil, torn

Salt the eggplant (see page 204). Dry well.

Heat the oil in a 12- to 14-inch skillet over medium heat, then sauté the onion until slightly wilted, about 2 minutes.

Add the red pepper, sprinkle with about ½ teaspoon of salt, and continue to toss and cook over medium heat another 2 minutes.

Add the eggplant. Toss it with the onion and red pepper, then add the zucchini and do the same. Sprinkle with the remaining salt. Add a little pepper. Toss again, and sauté all the vegetables together for about 12 minutes, until tender, tossing only occasionally. Toss in the basil, taste, and adjust the salt and pepper to taste.

Serve hot or at room temperature.

Dolci
Sweets

Dolci.

There's at least one good bakery in every Southern Italian town, not counting the cafés that sell pastry, cookies, and cakes. Southern Italians love their baked goods, sweet gelatins, Bavarian creams, ices, and ice cream. They eat them for breakfast, lunch, dinner, and in between meals.

The first meal of an Italian day is coffee or cappuccino with a *cornetto*, a crescent pastry similar to a croissant but glazed with sugar or filled with almond paste or marmalade. Brioche is another morning option: eggy, buttery bread to dunk into your coffee or to eat stuffed with gelato or with a bowl of gelato on the side, as they do in Sicily. In Naples, the morning pastry is *sfogliatella*, a clam-shaped, ricotta- and candied-fruit-filled treat, often with the scent of orange flower water. They come in two versions—with a crisp, layered pastry (*sfoglatella riccia*, the only one made in Italian-American bakeries) or a soft one (*sfogliatella frolla*) made with Italian short pastry, *pasta frolla*. Both are kept warm in a special glass box on every café's counter. In addition to these standard items, there are fried doughnuts everywhere, usually called *graffe*, from the German word *krapfen*, but sometimes called *zeppole* (see page 243).

It is no secret anywhere in Italy that southern bakers have made pastry into as high an art as the French, the Viennese, and the Hungarians, from whom they've borrowed, and also with strong influences from North Africa. For instance, in Puglia they make honey-dipped, rolled fried dough called *cartellate*, identical to the fried-dough confections of the Middle East. The honeyed balls of fried dough called *struffoli* in Naples and *pignolata* elsewhere are also equivalent to well-known North African pastries.

Wonderful, professional baked goods are so easy to purchase in Southern Italy that only dedicated home cooks and hobbyist bakers prepare their own. What follows are desserts that home cooks can accomplish fairly easily and well.

Pasta Frolla
Short Pastry

MAKES ENOUGH FOR A 9-INCH DOUBLE-CRUST
OR LATTICE-TOP TART

There are so many different recipes for *pasta frolla* that they could take up a book all to themselves. It is a generic term for what we might call short pastry, although it is also a cookie dough, a type of shortbread, or, in German, *Mürbeteig.* It can be flaky, especially when made with lard instead of butter, but it is usually denser than our thin, crisp flaky pie pastry.

In this book, this dough is used for *crostata* that are filled with marmalade or jam (see page 230), the Walnut Tart (page 228), and *Pastiera* (page 232), the Neapolitan Grain and Ricotta Pie.

1¼ cups confectioners' sugar

3 cups bleached all-purpose flour

½ teaspoon baking powder

¼ teaspoon salt

2 large eggs, lightly beaten together

½ teaspoon vanilla extract (optional)

1 cup (2 sticks) unsalted butter, cut into tablespoon-size pieces, at cool room temperature, not soft

Grated zest of 2 lemons or 1 large orange (optional)

Combine the confectioners' sugar, flour, baking powder, and salt in the bowl of a stand mixer fitted with the paddle attachment. Stir the ingredients together on low speed.

Beat the eggs and optional citrus zest together in a small bowl or cup with the vanilla, if using. Set aside.

Add the butter to the mixer bowl and, still on low speed, blend the butter into the dry ingredients until it looks like coarse meal. Add the eggs and mix again until the dough forms a ball.

Scrape the dough out of the bowl. There may be some dry portion that is not thoroughly blended in. Knead the dough a few times to make sure it is well blended. It will be slightly sticky, but should not require a floured surface to knead it just a few times.

For *crostate* and *torte*, divide the dough into two disks, one a third of the dough, the other two-thirds. Wrap each disk in plastic. Refrigerate for at least 30 minutes.

Torta di Noci
Walnut Tart

Sorrento, Campania

SERVES 8

Italians cook so seasonally that one day in September, when I wanted to make a dish with walnuts, Cecilia told me I couldn't because it was between seasons. Last year's walnuts, a crop for which Campania is famous, were gone or not fresh. This year's walnuts were not yet cured or even harvested. I'd have to wait a few weeks to buy this year's walnuts. In the supermarket, however, we found California walnuts in their shells packed in a cellophane bag. I thought they were just fine. Cecilia deemed them too old. They weren't rancid, so I used them anyway, and as I knew she would, she ate them anyway. Sorrento walnuts, actually a type of walnut grown all over Campania, but native to the Sorrento peninsula, are famous all over Italy. They are very plump, very flavorful, and very crunchy.

1 recipe *Pasta Frolla* (page 227)

1½ cups sugar

6 tablespoons water

2 tablespoons honey

¾ cup plus 2 tablespoons heavy
  cream, warmed

3 cups coarsely chopped walnuts

1 egg, lightly beaten, for egg wash

Place a rack in the center of the oven. Preheat the oven to 350°F.

Roll out the dough between sheets of waxed paper or parchment. Line a 9-inch cake pan with two-thirds of the *pasta frolla*, bringing the pastry up the sides of the pan just to the top edge. Save one-third of the pastry to make a lattice top.

Combine the sugar and 6 tablespoons of water in a minimum 3-quart saucepan over medium-high heat and simmer until the mixture turns medium amber, shaking the pan occasionally but not stirring. Be very careful not to burn the sugar. Stir in the honey.

Pour the warm cream about ¼ cup at a time into the simmering caramel, stirring constantly. Stir in all the walnuts. While still very hot, pour the mixture into the pastry-lined pan. Arrange a lattice pastry top.

Turn the edge of the bottom pastry over the edge of the lattice top. Brush the top of the pastry with the beaten egg.

Bake for 30 to 35 minutes, until lightly browned.

Cool thoroughly in the pan before serving. Turn out of the pan, by turning upside down on a plate, then reversing so the lattice is on top. Or, if you have large hands, turn out onto your hand with fingers spread open, then reverse on a serving plate.

Crostata di Marmellata alla Sorrentina
Sorrento-Style Jam Tart

Every bakery in Southern Italy features one kind of *crostata* or another—open-faced, lattice-topped, or double-crusted tarts filled with any kind of fruit jam or pastry cream and fruit. Only on the Sorrento Peninsula, however, have I found this wonderful way to top a jam tart, either with ground amaretti cookies and egg or, for similar effect, finely ground toasted almonds and sugar bound with an egg. The topping peaks through the lattice, covering the jam filling and making the flavor of the tart more complex and exceedingly delicious.

1 recipe *Pasta Frolla* (page 227)

1 (12-ounce) jar orange or other citrus marmalade or any flavor jam or preserves

2 large eggs

½ cup finely ground amaretti (about 3 ounces; the number depends on the brand)

Place a rack in the center of the oven. Preheat the oven to 375° F.

Roll out the dough between sheets of waxed paper or parchment. Line a 9-inch cake pan with two-thirds of the *pasta frolla*, bringing the pastry up the sides of the pan just to the top. Save the second disk of pastry to make a lattice top.

Spread the jam evenly on the pastry.

Beat one of the eggs in a small bowl until well blended, then add the amaretti crumbs and mix well. Spread this mixture evenly over the jam filling.

Roll out the remaining pastry. With a sharp knife or rolling pastry cutter, cut it into ½-inch-wide strips. Arrange the strips on top of the tart in a diamond-shaped lattice. Turn the edge of the bottom pastry over the edge of the lattice top.

Beat the remaining egg in a small bowl, then brush the pastry with it.

Bake the tart for 30 to 35 minutes, until nicely browned. Let cool in the pan for 10 minutes, then remove the tart from the pan and finish cooling it on a rack.

Variation

Sprinkle 2 tablespoons of finely chopped nuts—toasted almonds, hazelnuts, or walnuts—on the bottom pastry before pouring in the marmalade or jam.

At Masseria Astapiana, Villa Giusso in Vico Equense, near Sorrento, a magnificent fifteenth-century former monastery now operating as a bed and breakfast and party venue, they make a rather complex, but not difficult to accomplish, version of this tart (see photos). Instead of using 12 ounces of marmalade, use only 6 ounces. Then dip about 28 whole amaretti quickly into dry white vermouth. Arrange a layer of the cookies over the marmalade, packing them in closely and pushing them slightly into the marmalade. Now combine 2 beaten eggs with ¾ cup toasted and finely ground almonds. Pour this over the amaretti. There should be just enough to barely cover the cookies. Arrange a lattice pastry top. Bake as above.

Pastiera
Easter Pie Neapolitan Grain and Ricotta Pie

When I first started coming to Italy, nearly forty years ago, this pie was made strictly for Easter or, in any case, only in the spring. It is so delicious, however, and Neapolitans are so attached to it, that it is now made all year.

FOR THE GRAIN

½ cup hulled soft wheat berries (*grano*)

2½ cups water

Big pinch of salt

½ cup whole milk

Grated zest of ½ lemon

1 teaspoon unsalted butter

FOR THE FILLING

1⅔ cups whole milk ricotta (1 15-ounce container)

½ cup sugar

⅔ cup cooked whole wheat berries

Grated zest of 1 large orange

2 tablespoons minced glacé fruits (about 1 ounce; optional)

2 eggs, plus 2 egg yolks

1 recipe *Pasta Frolla* (page 227), separated into 2 pieces

To cook the wheat: Combine the wheat, water, and salt in a medium saucepan over medium heat. Bring to a brisk boil, stirring a few times. Reduce the heat slightly and boil for 45 minutes, stirring occasionally. Set aside to cool to room temperature, at least 30 minutes.

Stir the milk, lemon zest, and butter into the cooked grain and place the pan over medium-low heat. Bring to a gentle simmer and cook for 15 minutes, stirring occasionally. Remove from the heat and let stand until cooled to room temperature. (This makes enough grain to fill two pies. It can be refrigerated for up to a week, or frozen for future use.)

To make the filling: In a mixing bowl, stir together all the filling ingredients.

To form and bake the pie: Place a rack in the center of the oven. Preheat the oven to 375° F.

Roll out the larger piece of dough on a lightly floured surface to fit an 8-inch cake pan. Line the pan. Pour in the filling. There should be about ¼ inch of pastry above the level of the filling.

Roll out the second piece of dough to no thicker than ⅛ inch. Cut ½-inch-wide strips of dough—some short, some long—to make a lattice top on the pie. Pinch the lattice top to the edge of the pastry above the filling.

Bake for 50 minutes, until the filling is set and jiggles only in the very center. Let the pie cool on a rack to room temperature before unmolding it.

Run a sharp, thin knife around the edge. Turn it out onto a plate, then reverse onto another plate.

Serve at room temperature, or slightly chilled.

Torta di Frutta Secca di Zia Delia
Aunt Delia's Date-Nut Cake

Battipaglia, Campania

MAKES ONE 8-INCH PIE, SERVING 6 TO 8

Cecilia's aunt's cake is really more like candy, a rich and moist confection of walnuts and dates with very little flour. A mix of dates and dried figs can be used, too, and Cecilia often combines them because her farms in Paestum are at the foot of the Cilento, which is famous for white figs.

4 large eggs

1 teaspoon vanilla extract

1½ cups sugar

10 ounces pitted dried dates or 12 ounces dried dates with pits, pitted, cut into ½-inch pieces, or 2 cups mixed diced dates and diced dried figs, or 2 cups dates and chopped pitted prunes

3 cups (12 ounces) shelled walnuts, crushed in your fist into large pieces

5 tablespoons all-purpose flour

Cut a piece of parchment paper to fit, with much excess, an 8-inch square baking pan. Don't attempt to fit the paper inside it yet.

Place a rack in the center of the oven. Preheat the oven to 400°F.

Beat the eggs with the vanilla and sugar with a fork in a large mixing bowl. Add the dates and walnuts and mix well. Sprinkle the flour over the fruit and nut mixture and blend in very well.

Place the parchment paper over the pan and pour the batter into the pan. The weight of the batter will hold down the paper. As you spread the batter to fill the pan, the paper will give way and fit to the pan more snugly.

Bake for about 45 minutes, until the top is nicely browned and the cake feels solid to the touch.

Place the cake on a cake rack and let cool for 20 minutes. While the cake is still warm, unmold it, leaving the paper-lined side up, and let cool a little longer.

Carefully pull off the parchment paper while the cake is still warm. Finish cooling the cake with the sticky bottom up. Use a serrated-blade knife to cut the cake into approximately 1½-inch squares. Or cut into 1-inch by 2-inch bars or, truly, into any size you like.

The cake can be served warm, when it is particularly good with whipped cream or a scoop of ice cream. Or serve at room temperature. It improves with a few days of age.

Store at room temperature, in a tin or wrapped in aluminum foil, not plastic.

'Mpanatigghi
Chocolate and Beef Turnovers

It is always a big surprise to everyone who eats these little half-moon turnovers, a specialty of Modica, the chocolate capital of Sicily, that they have ground meat in their filling. In fact, the meat is meant to be indistinguishable. This is a pastry devised by nuns who, according to one theory, hid meat among the dark chocolate and crunchy toasted almonds during Lent, when meat was forbidden food. The name of the pastry is a variant on *empanada*, the Spanish word for "turnover," and the recipe has deep Spanish roots, dating from their four-hundred-year dominance over Southern Italy. Besides chocolate, which the Modicani still proudly process the way the Aztecs in Mexico did, grinding the cocoa beans between stones, the filling is flavored with vanilla, also originally from Mexico. It all goes inside a round of melt-in-the-mouth, flaky lard pastry.

FOR THE PASTRY

1¾ cups all-purpose flour

5 tablespoons sugar

¼ teaspoon salt

½ cup (4 ounces) lard, preferably leaf lard

3 large eggs, separated, plus 1 whole large egg

1 tablespoon water (approximately)

FOR THE FILLING

4 ounces ground beef or pork

½ cup sugar

1 ounce unsweetened chocolate, melted

½ cup toasted blanched almonds, finely chopped

½ teaspoon ground cinnamon

1 teaspoon vanilla extract

Several grinds of nutmeg

To make the pastry: Combine the flour, sugar, and salt in a mixing bowl. Add the lard to the bowl and with your fingertips or a pastry blender, cut in the lard until the mixture looks like coarse meal.

In a small bowl, with a table fork, beat the egg yolks together until well mixed, then blend them into the flour mixture. If the mixture is too dry to gather together into a ball, sprinkle with the water, adding a little at a time so as not to make the mixture too moist. Gather into a ball and refrigerate for about 30 minutes, or longer.

To make the filling: In a small skillet, sauté the beef without adding any fat. Cook until the meat has lost its raw color. Let the meat cool slightly.

In the bowl of a mini-processor, grind the meat and sugar together until the meat is very, very fine. Scrape the meat mixture into a bowl and stir in the melted chocolate, the almonds, cinnamon, vanilla, and nutmeg. Finally, work in the egg whites.

Place a rack in the middle of the oven. Preheat the oven to 375°F.

To shape and bake: Divide the dough into four parts. Set three parts aside, covered with a clean towel, while working on the first part.

On a very lightly floured board, roll out the pastry until it is about ⅛ inch thick. Using a 3-inch cookie cutter or the rim of a similarly sized glass, cut out pastry rounds. You should get 8 to 10 disks. Pastry trimmings can be gathered together and rerolled.

Put a generous teaspoonful of filling in the center of each disk. Brush the edge with the whole egg, beaten, then fold each disk into a half-moon, pressing to close. Then crimp with a fork. Brush the tops with egg, then, with the point of a knife, make a slit in the top of each pastry to let steam escape. The hole is also part of the look of the pastry. Continue making turnovers with the rest of the pastry.

Bake the pastries for 18 minutes. Let cool completely before serving. The pastries hold up well for several days, uncovered or covered in foil, not plastic.

Left: **Nonna Vincenza of Catania is famous for her almond paste sweets.**

Bavarese di Ricotta
Ricotta Bavarian

Cecilia often plays hostess to the National Italian-American Federation (NIAF), offering lunch at Seliano to many groups on tour with the organization. This is the dessert that she usually serves. So many NIAF members live in the New York metro area that, when I was on the radio, I started getting requests for this recipe. It became apparent I had to learn it. Now it is one of the most popular things we make in our Cook at Seliano classes. In Italy, however, cooks use sheet gelatin, which produces a more delicate gel than our powdered product. I've played with the proportions over the years, and the following formula makes a cake that cuts neatly. If you want a cake that is less firm, you can reduce the amount by ½ packet of gelatin. I make the crust with graham cracker crumbs, American style, but vanilla cookie wafers are what Cecilia and her staff use.

9 graham crackers, ground into fine crumbs in a food processor

1 stick (8 tablespoons) butter, melted

5 egg yolks

1 cup sugar

1 (15-ounce) container whole milk ricotta (1¾ cups)

1 cup blanched almonds, toasted for 8 to 10 minutes at 350°F, coarsely chopped

2 tablespoons orange liqueur (such as Grand Marnier, Cointreau, or Triple Sec)

1 cup heavy cream, whipped to soft peaks, plus ½ cup heavy cream

2½ (¼-ounce) packets unflavored gelatin

3 egg whites, whipped to stiff peaks

Combine the graham cracker crumbs and melted butter in a mixing bowl and mix thoroughly. Press the crust mixture evenly onto the bottom of a 10-inch springform pan.

Beat the egg yolks until thick and yellow on medium speed of a stand mixer with the whip attachment. Continue beating, adding the sugar ¼ cup at a time. Gradually beat in the ricotta, then the almonds, and finally the liqueur.

Pour ½ cup unwhipped heavy cream into a small saucepan. Sprinkle with the gelatin. Slowly bring up the heat and stir until the mixture is smooth, thick, and lump free. Gradually beat the gelatin mixture into the ricotta mixture.

Carefully fold in the whipped cream, then the egg whites. Pour into the prepared springform pan and refrigerate for at least 6 hours to set.

To unmold, draw a thin-bladed knife around the edge. Open the springform. Serve on the spring-form bottom, or from the kitchen on individual plates. The dessert is difficult to transfer from a springform base to a serving plate. If you want to attempt this, make sure the Bavarian is well chilled.

It is best served when out of the refrigerator for 15 minutes.

Amaretti di Nocciole
Hazelnut Crisps

Avellino, Campania

MAKES ABOUT 7 DOZEN 2-INCH COOKIES

According to the Espositos, the husband and wife owners of Sale e Pepe, a restaurant in Materdomini in the province of Avelliono, these small, domed cookies were originally Sicilian. They were brought to Avellino by the Sicilian laborers who, at the beginning of the twentieth century, built the aqueducts that continue to take Avellino's abundant water down to neighboring Puglia, where groundwater is scarce. It's a simple recipe, although it is a little time-consuming rubbing the hazelnuts in a towel to remove most of their brown skins, which would add a little bitterness to these sweet treats. They crunch then melt in your mouth.

1 pound hazelnuts (3 cups)

1⅓ cups granulated sugar, plus ½ cup granulated sugar to roll the dough in

¼ teaspoon fine salt

3 large eggs

Set a rack at the top of the oven. Preheat the oven to 325°F. Line a light-colored aluminum baking sheet—not dark metal, not nonstick—with parchment paper.

Spread the nuts in one layer on another baking sheet. Bake for 20 minutes, until some of the skins start to split.

Place the nuts—either hot or cooled—on a clean dish towel. Gather the towel together from the edges, then rub the nuts together to remove the skins. Open the towel and remove the nuts that are skinned. It's fine if they have a bit of skin still clinging to them. Repeat this several times, until all the nuts have been at least partly skinned.

If the nuts are not already cool, let them cool to room temperature. Pulse the nuts in a food processor until they are very finely chopped. Some of them will become powdery. Some should remain in visible but tiny pieces.

Combine the chopped nuts, 1⅓ cups of the sugar, and the salt in a mixing bowl. Mix well.

Beat the eggs together with a fork until well mixed. Pour the beaten eggs over the nuts and sugar mixture. Mix very well with a rubber spatula or wooden spoon.

Spread ½ cup of the sugar on a plate.

Using a teaspoon measure to approximate the

amount, scoop up the nut mixture and roll it between your palms into 1-inch balls. The dough will be sticky. Using the teaspoon measure, scrape the nut mixture off your palm every 6 or so balls to keep them clean. Keeping your hands wet helps prevent the dough from sticking. Roll the balls in the sugar—they will be less sticky now—and reroll them in your dry palms.

Arrange the balls about 2 inches apart on the parchment-lined baking sheet.

Bake for 20 minutes. Remove the cookies from the oven and let the baking sheet cool on a rack for at least 5 minutes. The cookies should release easily from the paper.

Kept in a tightly closed box or plastic bag, the cookies remain crisp and fresh for weeks— actually, until the nuts turn rancid, which could be months.

Torta di Mele
Apple Cake

This is the kind of homey cake that Southern Italians like to bake for their families, the kind of cake you can't buy from the neighborhood bakery. My friend Franca Miceli of Siracusa puts it in the oven just before she sits down to dinner and then serves it while it's still hot, when it has a pudding-like texture, its caramelized top still crisp, and its apple and buttery aroma as powerful as perfume. With all its apples, however, it is so moist that it holds for days, if you can resist devouring it immediately. I particularly love Franca's time-saving trick: she mixes the dry ingredients into the wet by using the turned-off beaters of her handheld mixer.

14 tablespoons butter (7 ounces or 1¾ sticks)

½ cup fine dry bread crumbs for bottom and sides of pan

2½ cups all-purpose flour

¼ teaspoon salt

1 tablespoon baking powder

¾ cup milk

3 eggs

1 cup sugar

1 tablespoon extra-virgin olive oil

Grated zest of 1 lemon

1 teaspoon vanilla extract

2 pounds McIntosh apples, peeled, cored, halved, and cut into thin slices (about 5 cups)

Place an oven rack in the middle of the oven. Preheat the oven to 375° F.

Put 2 tablespoons of the butter in a 12-inch cake pan or 13 by 9-inch Pyrex or other baking pan. Place in the oven and when the butter has melted, remove it from the oven and brush the butter around the bottom and sides of the pan.

Pour the bread crumbs into the pan. Shake the pan to spread the crumbs all over the sides and bottom. Shake out any excess. Set aside.

Combine the flour, salt, and baking powder in a large mixing bowl. Mix well and reserve.

In a small saucepan, combine 8 tablespoons of the butter (1 stick) with the milk. Heat until the butter has melted. Remove from the heat and let cool slightly.

Beat the eggs in a large bowl with a handheld electric mixer, then gradually beat in ¾ cup of the sugar. Continue to beat until the mixture is thick, foamy, and light yellow. Pour in the milk and butter mixture and beat until well incorporated. Beat in the tablespoon of olive oil, the grated lemon zest, and vanilla.

Add the dry ingredients to the wet ingredients and, with the electric mixer off, use the beaters to thoroughly stir in the dry ingredients.

Scrape the batter into the prepared pan. Evenly distribute the apples on top of the batter. Many of them will sink in. Sprinkle evenly with the remaining ¼ cup sugar.

Thinly slice the remaining 4 tablespoons of butter over the top of the cake.

Bake for about 30 minutes, until the batter has risen and the top has browned lightly. For a darker, more caramelized top, turn on the broiler for a few seconds. (If using a Pyrex pan, be careful not to overdo this as the pan can crack.)

Serve hot, warm, or at room temperature.

Zeppole di Patate di Barbara
Barbara's Potato Doughnuts

Salerno, Campania

MAKES ABOUT 5 DOZEN 4-INCH DOUGHNUTS

Barbara Di Maio, Cecilia's daughter-in-law, is the daughter of a pastry chef, Antonella Califano, and she has learned well from her mamma. These are the most sublime doughnuts I've ever eaten. In the cafes of Southern Italy, especially in Campania, they are called *graffe*, from the German/Austrian *krapfen*, revealing their origin. When made at home in the province of Salerno, however, they are usually called *zeppole*, although that word in the United States is usually reserved for fried balls of yeast dough that can be either sprinkled with sugar or with salt. In Southern Italy, those are mostly called *pettole* or simply *pasta cresciuta*, which merely means "risen dough." Mashed potatoes give this dough its delicate body without imparting noticeable flavor. It should go without saying that they are best when freshly fried. I'd plan a doughnut party around this recipe.

4 to 5 cups bleached all-purpose flour

1½ cups self-rising cake flour

½ teaspoon salt

1 cup sugar

Grated zest of 1 or 2 lemons

1 pound potatoes, boiled in their skins, mashed and cooled to room temperature

6 large eggs

1 (¼-ounce) packet active dry yeast

½ cup warm milk

1 cup (2 sticks) unsalted butter

Vegetable oil for frying

On a board or other work surface, make a mound of 4 cups of the all-purpose flour, all the self-rising flour, the salt, sugar, and lemon zest.

Make a well in the center of the mound and add the mashed potatoes. With your hands, start working the flour and potatoes together, then make another well and start adding the eggs, blending each one into the dough, at first with a table fork but eventually with your hands.

In a small bowl, dissolve the yeast in the warm milk, then stir in enough additional flour (about ½ cup) to form a batter.

Make yet another well in the center of the dough and pour in the yeast batter. Work it into the dough, kneading the mass together, adding a little more flour, a spoonful at a time, until you have a smooth and not terribly sticky dough. Keep scraping up the dough with a bench scraper and only add flour if the dough is very sticky. Once it gets only slightly sticky, more kneading is all you may need to do.

Recipe continues

Barbara's Potato Doughnuts continued . . .

Knead the butter into the dough until it has been completely absorbed. Set the dough aside to rise until doubled. You can leave it on the board with a clean dish towel to cover it.

When the dough has risen, break or cut off pieces about the size of a golf ball. Roll each piece of dough into a rope about 8 inches long and ½ to ¾ inch in diameter. Form into a ring. There's no need to pinch the ends together, but they should overlap very slightly.

Place the formed doughnuts on floured trays or baking sheets and let rise again until nearly doubled in size.

To fry, put about 1 inch of oil in a large frying pan. Heat to about 350°F, or until bubbles gather around the handle of a wooden spoon. Fry the doughnuts until nutty brown on both sides, turning only once. Drain on absorbent paper.

Serve immediately or when fully cooled. At both stages they have great, if different appeal. Covered loosely with foil, they hold up well for 1 day.

"La Bella Baronessa" Fichi al Sciropo di Vino
Figs in Wine Syrup

Paestum, Campania

MAKES 1 QUART, ABOUT 20 FIGS

The white (really green) figs of Cilento are famously sweet, fragrant, succulent, and thin-skinned. To market them outside the area, however, the Cilentani have developed various ways of preserving them, including drying them and turning them into confections—split and filled with an almond, coated or not with chocolate, compressed into a sausage-like roll called a "fig salami," and coating fig paste with cocoa to make bite-sized candies called *scugnizi*, the word also used for the dirty-faced street urchins of Naples. These treats are sold in American specialty food stores as well as on the Internet. The best are made by Antonio Longo in Ogliastro under the brand name Santomiele.

Baronessa Cecilia has another way of preserving figs, by cooking them in red wine syrup. These are sold under her Bella Baronessa label in select stores in Rome, Naples, and around Sorrento and the Amalfi Coast. Serve them with well-aged pecorino or caciocavallo cheese, or alongside a ball of vanilla ice cream, or on their own with a lagniappe of heavy cream.

1 pound purple Mission figs (about 20) (see Note)

20 whole cloves (same number as figs)

1¼ cups hearty dry red wine

2 cups sugar

1 or 2 (3-inch) cinnamon sticks, depending on strength

Rinse the figs. Stick a clove into each fig.

In a 2-quart saucepan, combine the red wine and sugar. Place over medium heat and, stirring frequently, bring the syrup to a boil. Add the cinnamon sticks.

Gently place the figs in the syrup. Watch the pot and adjust the heat so that the figs simmer, uncovered, very, very gently, the liquid barely bubbling, but steadily for about 3 hours. If the syrup reduces too much and it is getting too thick, add water by the spoonful to keep it liquid, but still thick.

Allow the figs to cool in the syrup. Pack into a jar, covered with syrup. If using a quart jar, you may have some excess syrup. I use it on vanilla or coffee ice cream or as a base for a soda—add seltzer or club soda. The figs and syrup should keep well in the refrigerator for up to a year. The skins soften up after a few weeks.

NOTE: This recipe works perfectly with other fig varieties. For larger figs, 20 figs will weigh between 1½ and 2 pounds, and although you will have to double the syrup, don't add extra cinnamon.

Semifreddo con Croccante
Almond Crunch Frozen Cream Dessert

Richer than even rich ice cream, this is a huge hit whenever I serve it. This particular version is shot through with crunchy nut brittle, but I also like it flavored with crumbled amaretti, with just coarsely chopped toasted almonds, with crumbled meringue, with chopped chocolate . . . use your imagination. Frozen in a loaf pan lined with plastic, it unmolds easily and looks nice decorated as a loaf or served in slices, especially with berries, or chocolate sauce, or caramel sauce.

8 egg yolks

¾ cup plus 2 tablespoons whole milk

¾ cup plus 2 tablespoons granulated sugar

Pinch of salt

1½ teaspoons vanilla extract

1 pint heavy cream

⅓ cup crushed or chopped store-bought nut brittle

Line a 9 by 5-inch loaf pan with a sheet of plastic wrap large enough to overhang the sides of the pan.

Combine the egg yolks, milk, sugar, and salt in a small saucepan. Whisk together, then place over medium-low heat and stir constantly with a wooden spoon. The custard will form before the mixture gets to the simmering point. Be careful: if you let it get too hot it will curdle. When the custard reaches its maximum thickness, the lighter colored surface foam will disappear and the sauce will be uniformly yellow, and will lightly coat the wooden spoon.

As soon as the custard has thickened, remove it from the heat and stir in the vanilla. Continue to stir another minute. Immediately push the custard through a fine sieve into a large mixing bowl. Let cool to room temperature, uncovered.

Beat the cream in a large mixing bowl until it holds medium-soft peaks. Gently fold half the whipped cream into the custard. When it is almost combined, fold in the remaining whipped cream.

Pour about a third of the mixture into the prepared loaf pan. Sprinkle about half the nut brittle over the cream mixture, then pour on another third of the cream mixture, then the remaining *croccante*, then the remaining cream mixture. Cover tightly with plastic and freeze for at least 6 hours.

To serve, unmold the semifreddo, then cut it into slices. Serve plain, or with caramel or chocolate sauce, or fresh berries.

Spuma di Ricotta con Grappa
Ricotta Mousse with Grappa

Naples, Campania

SERVES ABOUT 8

This is a recipe from innovative chef Peppone Russo, whose tiny restaurant is in Marcianise, just north of Naples, a town famous for Etruscan tombs and organized crime. Peppone's customer base is totally respectable, however, and people come from a long distance to eat his refined, contemporary cuisine based on strictly local products. This little give-away dessert, served in sparkling wine tulips with a long-handled spoon, has an *aperitivo* cousin that he serves the same way before the meal. Instead of flavoring the ricotta with sugar and grappa, he whips it with a puree of roasted red pepper, then tops the resulting fluff with diced, seasoned tomato. By the way, I have tried to make this dessert without the raw egg yolks, but the texture is not nearly as smooth and unctuous. They are necessary.

1¾ cups whole milk ricotta
  (1 15-ounce container)

1 cup confectioners' sugar

2 egg yolks

3 tablespoons grappa

1 cup heavy cream

Combine the ricotta, confectioners' sugar, egg yolks, and grappa in a food processor. Process the mixture until silky smooth.

Beat the cream in a large bowl until it holds stiff peaks. Carefully fold the whipped cream into the ricotta mixture.

Serve in tall or small glasses or bowls, garnished, if desired, with a wafer cookie. Or serve as a topping or base for fresh fruit, such as fresh berries, a mixed fruit salad, sliced pineapple, or peaches.

Gelo di Mellone
Watermelon Pudding

Sicilians love pudding and gelatin desserts. My friends Marcello Foti and his wife, Maria Grazie, at *oenotecca* Gaza Ladra in Sicily, always have several on their menu, made from carob, squash, prickly pear—whatever is seasonal. In the pastry shops, the most typical are jiggly lemon pudding and watermelon pudding, both of which can be set in decorative molds or in pastry shells. One conceit of the pastry shops that make watermelon pudding is to drop in chocolate bits in imitation of watermelon seeds. Chopped pistachios also sometime stud the pudding, but you can also just sprinkle the nuts on top.

10 pounds watermelon (approximately), preferably seedless

1¼ cups cornstarch

1 cup sugar

⅓ cup chocolate chips (optional)

⅓ cup raw pistachios (optional)

Cut the pulp off the watermelon rind. Remove the black seeds if it is not the seedless type. Don't bother removing the white seeds of a seedless variety. Discard the rinds. (Or use them to make candied or pickled watermelon rind, an American specialty, not Italian.) Cut the watermelon into large cubes. Puree about one-fourth of the pulp in a food processor fitted with the metal blade. Strain the pulp through a fine strainer, pressing with a wooden spoon to remove the remaining juice. Repeat with the rest of the melon. You should have 2 quarts of juice.

Whisk together the watermelon juice and cornstarch in a 3-quart saucepan until the cornstarch has fully dissolved. Stir in the sugar.

Place the pan over medium heat and bring to a boil, constantly stirring slowly with a wooden spoon, always scraping the bottom of the pot. This will take 15 minutes to 20 minutes. Stop stirring and let the mixture boil for 1 minute. Remove from the heat.

Immediately ladle the pudding into a 2-quart metal ring mold or other decorative mold that has been rinsed with cold water, but not dried. Just shake out the excess moisture. Or, divide the pudding among glass serving cups or stemware. Or divide among small metal molds or cups. Or pour into a prebaked shell of *Pasta Frolla* (page 227).

If using the chocolate and/or nuts, drop them into the pudding after it has been poured into the receptacles.

Refrigerate for at least 12 hours before serving.

To unmold, dampen a dish towel or paper towels with hot tap water and wrap around the mold for a few seconds. Turn out the pudding onto a platter.

A ring mold of the pudding is beautiful and delicious unmolded, and can be filled with fresh fruit salad, other melon, or fresh berries.

✳ Acknowledgments ✳

Without the generous friendship and encouragement of Cecilia Bellelli Baratta, whom I met fourteen years ago as a guest at her farm-inn, Azienda Agrituristico Seliano, I would never have wanted to or been able to write this book. As her late mother, Elvira Jemma, used to say, Cecilia is *sempre in giro,* always on the move, literally "always on tour," and I have been the fortunate beneficiary of her wanderlust, as well as her intelligence, curiosity, warmth, and care. Besides being the best, most thoughtful friend a man could have, she is the ideal travel companion—organized but flexible and spontaneous—although I have learned never to offer my opinion on driving directions. In her old Fiat Multipla, we have traveled everywhere south of Rome, to all six regions of Southern Italy. Much of the time my spouse, Bob Harned, an archaeologist, was along for the ride or actually planning our trips around visits to Southern Italy's abundance of Greek and Roman ruins. Cecilia kept the list of other obligatory sights, obscure museums, and local contacts. I figured out what we'd eat and where we'd eat it. Often, our dear friend Iris Carulli, an art historian and Rome city guide, was in the backseat, and we were also often joined by Nicolas Claes, our Belgian friend, an antiquarian who lives on Cecilia's farm-inn and acts as host there.

Cecilia's two adult sons, Ettore and Massimino, who these days run both the *agriturismo* and the family water buffalo farm, the largest south of Naples, honor and flatter me by saying I am like their brother (it's more like uncle). They, along with their wives, Veronica and Barbara, and Ettore's young sons, Gaetano and Luca, have made it possible for me to stay long stretches in the arms of an Italian family. Cecilia's larger family circle, including her four sisters, Enrica, also my good friend, Rosaria, Paula, and Laura; her brothers-in-law, Gerardo and Savj; and the many Baratta and Jemma cousins, nieces, and nephews, have all welcomed me and helped me discover what life and food are really like in Southern Italy.

I have, of course, learned much in Cecilia's Seliano kitchen, especially from her cooks, Anna D'Amato and Maria Ledda. Eugenia Tammarraco, the night cook at Seliano, is also my alter-ego in the kitchen when I conduct Cook at Seliano classes. After working together for eight years, four times a year, she thinks what I think before I think it. I have to say the same goes for Gerardina Costanza, another great cook with whom I am privileged to work at Seliano. Veliana Marsico is the chief waitress, kitchen assistant, and jack-of-all-housekeeping-trades, and she also cares for us.

Through Cecilia, I now have a circle of friends who not only nurture me, but have enthusiastically helped me find the best food sources, cooks, restaurants, wines, even pizza. Franco Rago has known Cecilia since they were in kindergarten together and it now seems like he has been my friend for life, too, and I often find myself sitting around the table with Susy Camera d'Afflitto of Salerno and Ravello, Camilla Aulisio of Naples and Giungano, Claus Schwargen, Ludovico Santoro and his nephew Franco Santoro of Giungano, Silvia Imperato of San Cipriano Picentino, and Luigi D'Avino of Casal Velino. In Naples, I am very grateful for the friendship of Mirella, Maurizio, and Chiara Barracco and the many members of the Mazzella family, particularly Domenico and his mother, Gabriella Rafone, who take care of me and my guests so well at their art-filled Donna Regina bed-and-breakfast—and Giovanna Rafone and her husband, Albert Coward. In Rome, my friend Giulia Borella takes great care of me and my Cook at Seliano students at her chic Caesar House Residenza.

Many other Italian friends, home cooks, and professional chefs have contributed to my understanding and knowledge of the regional cuisines of Southern Italy. They are acknowledged with the recipes I found through them or got from them.

Back in Brooklyn, New York, I got invaluable assistance from Michael Glosman, who took time out from being a boutique cookie baker (www.distinctivepalate.com) to help test recipes and, even more important, critically assess the results at lunch. Wil Crutchley is another young chef who came into my life at precisely the right moment for me to laugh with and cook all day.

* Index *

Note: *Italicized* page references indicate photographs.

A

Acquacotta, 74, 75
Aeolian Salad, 58
Agnello con Le Olive (Lamb Chops with Black Olives), 191
Almond(s)
    Chocolate and Beef Turnovers, 234–35
    Crunch Frozen Cream Dessert, 246
    Ricotta Bavarian, *236*, 237
Amaretti di Nocciole (Hazelnut Crisps), 238–39
Anchovies
    buying, 117
    colatura, about, 100
    Linguine with Walnuts and *Colatura*, *102*, 103
    salted, filleting and serving, 117
Antipasti, 20–21. *See also* Appetizers and snacks
Appetizers and snacks
    Bruschetta, 51
    Chickpea Fritters, 27–28
    Crostini di Bottarga, 41
    Eggplant, Red Pepper, and Onion Spread, 36, 37
    Eggplant Balls or Patties, 30–31, *31*
    Filled Potato "Pizza," 40–41
    Fried Olives, 22, *23*
    Pickled Cherry Peppers Stuffed with Tuna and *Giardiniera*, 38, *39*
    Pizza Napolitana, *42*, 43–44
    Pizza Rustica with Summer Vegetables, 49
    "The Pocket," Egg and Cheese Pie, 50
    Sausage Canapés, *32*, 33
    Savory Cheese Pie with Salami or Prosciutto, 48–49
    Sicilian Rice Balls Filled with Ragù, 24–25, *25*
    in Southern Italian cuisine, 20
Apple Cake, 240–41
Arancini Siciliani al Ragù (Sicilian Rice Balls Filled with Ragù), 24–25, *25*
Artichokes
    Baby, Sicilian Style, 197
    Charcoal-Roasted, 198
Arugula
    about, 55
    Shrimp, and Fennel Seed, Pasta Disks with, 123

B

Basil
    Spaghetti with Garlic Pesto from Marsala, 121

Tuna, Garlic, and Tomatoes, Raw Sauce of, with Curly Ribbons, 122
Bavarese di Ricotta (Ricotta Bavarian), *236*, 237
Bean(s)
    Chickpea Fritters, 27–28
    Ciceri e Trie, 104
    Fava Puree and Chicory, 202
    Flat Pasta and Chickpeas, 104, *105*
    and Greens Soup for the Feast of Saint Joseph, 77
    and Mushroom Soup, I Corti's, 76
    and Pasta, Baked, 106–7
Beef
    and Chocolate Turnovers, 234–35
    Filled Rice Timbales, 138–39
    Maria Talerico's Meat Cakes, 175
    Meatballs, 172–74, *173*
    Meatloaf Baked in Vegetable Sauce, 176–77
    Multi-Meat Ragù from Bari, Butcher's Ragù, 94
    Roll, Stuffed Sicilian, 178–79
    Sicilian Ground Meat Ragù with Peas, 93
Bottarga, about, 41
Bread(s)
    Acquacotta, 74, *75*
    bruschetta, about, 51
    cooking with, 34
    crumbs, cooking with, 34–35
    crumbs, toasting, 35
    hard, cooking with, 35
    Lamb Broth, 79
    Pancotto, 74
    in Southern Italian cuisine, 34–35
    and Tomato Salad, *60*, 61–62
Broccoli Rabe
    Orecchiette with, 111
    Sausage, and Smoked Cheese, Gena's Potato Cake with, 216–17, *217*
    and Sausage, Lentil Soup with, 78
    Sausage with, 188
    and Spaghetti Frittata, 150–51, *151*
Broccoli Saltati con Uova (Cauliflower Fried with Eggs and Cheese), 199, *199*
Broccolo Affogato (Smothered Cauliflower), 200–201
Brodo di Agnello o Cutturiddu (Lamb Broth), 79
Brodo di Aragosto con Spaghetti Ruoti (Lobster Broth with Broken Spaghetti), 80–81
Broth
    Lamb, 79
    Lobster, with Broken Spaghetti, 80–81
Bruschetta, about, 51

C

Cabbage, Potatoes and, 218
Cakes
    Apple, 240–41
    Date-Nut, Aunt Delia's, 233
Canapés, Sausage, *32*, 33
Capers
    Aeolian Salad, 58
    about, 63
    Fish Soup from Siracusa, 166
Caponata al Forno (Baked Sweet and Sour Eggplant), 208
Caponata Napoletana o Acquasale (Bread and Tomato Salad), *60*, 61–62
Carciofi Arrostiti (Charcoal-Roasted Artichokes), 198
Carciofini Siciliana (Baby Artichokes, Sicilian Style), 197
Carrot and Celery Root, Pickled, 64
Cauliflower
    Fried with Eggs and Cheese, 199, *199*
    Macaroni with, 116
    Smothered, 200–201
Celery Root and Carrot, Pickled, 64
Cheese. *See also* Ricotta
    Baked Pasta, Palermo Style, 132
    and Egg Pie, "The Pocket," 50
    and Eggs, Cauliflower Fried with, 199, *199*
    Enrica's Chicken Salad, 68, 69
    Grilled, 144, *144*
    and Ham, Fried Zucchini Rolls with, 222
    Lemony Egg Pasta Soufflé, 130–31
    Pie, Savory, with Salami or Prosciutto, 48–49
    Pizza Rustica with Summer Vegetables, 49
    Pork Rolls from Crotone, 183
    Smoked, and Sausage, Risotto with, 133
    Smoked, Broccoli Rabe, and Sausage, Gena's Potato Cake with, 216–17, *217*
    Smothered Cauliflower, 200–201
    in Southern Italian cuisine, 142–43
    Stuffed Sicilian Beef Roll, 178–79
Chicken
    Legs, Grilled, *192*, 193
    Salad, Enrica's, 68, 69
    in Southern Italian cuisine, 171
Chickpea(s)
    Ciceri e Trie, 104
    Flat Pasta and, 104, *105*
    Fritters, 27–28
Chicory and Fava Puree, 202
Chocolate
    and Beef Turnovers, 234–35
    Enna's Ground Pork Ragù with, 95
Ciceri e Trie, 104

Clams
  Neapolitan Seafood Salad, 66–67
  or Mussels, Baked, 158
  or Mussels, Sauté of, *156*, *157*
Colatura
  about, 100
  and Walnuts, Linguine with, *102*,
    103
Cookies. *See* Hazelnut Crisps
Coscio di Pollo alla Griglia (Grilled
  Chicken Legs), *192*, 193
Cozze o Vongole Oreganata (Baked
  Mussels or Clams), 158
Crostata di Marmellata alla Sorrentina
  (Sorrento-Style Jam Tart), 230–31,
    231
Crostini di Bottarga, 41
Crostini di Salsicce (Sausage Canapés),
    32, 33

D
Date-Nut Cake, Aunt Delia's, 233
Delizie dal' Orto (Summer Vegetable
  Sauté), 223
Desserts. *See* Sweets
Dolci. See also Sweets
  in Southern Italian cuisine, 226
Doughnuts, Potato, Barbara's, *242*,
    243–44

E
Easter Pie, 232
Eggplant
  Baked Sweet and Sour, 208
  Fresh Sausage, and Dried Hot
    Sausage, Macaroni with, 124
  or Zucchini, Grilled and Marinated,
    204–5, *205*
  Red Pepper, and Onion Spread,
    36, 37
  Slices, Breaded, 206–7
  Summer Vegetable Sauté, 223
Egg(s)
  Baked Rice and Zucchini Frittata,
    148
  and Cheese, Cauliflower Fried with,
    199, *199*
  and Cheese Pie, "The Pocket," 50
  Lemony Egg Pasta Soufflé, 130–31
  Onion Frittata, 145
  in Purgatory, 149
  in Southern Italian cuisine, 142–43
  Spaghetti and Broccoli Rabe
    Frittata, 150–51, *151*
  Stuffed Sicilian Beef Roll, 178–79

F
Falsomagro (Stuffed Sicilian Beef Roll),
    178–79
Fava Puree and Chicory, 202
Fave e Cicoria (Fava Puree and
  Chicory), 202
Fennel Braised with Sun-Dried
  Tomatoes, 210–11
Figs in Wine Syrup, 245
Finocchio coi Pomodori Secchi (Fennel
  Braised with Sun-Dried
  Tomatoes), 210–11

Fish. *See also* Anchovies; Shellfish;
    Swordfish; Tuna
  newborn, in Southern Italian
    cuisine, 25
  or Mussel Soup, 167
  Soup from Siracusa, 166
  in Southern Italian cuisine, 154–55
Fish roe (*bottarga*), about, 41
Focaccia di Patate (Filled Potato
  "Pizza"), 40–41
Focaccia toppings, 46–47
Fried foods, in Southern Italy, 21
Fritelle di Ricotta (Ricotta Pancakes),
    146, 147
Frittata di Cipolle (Onion Frittata), 145
Frittata di Riso e Zucchini al Forno
  (Baked Rice and Zucchini
  Frittata), 148
Frittata di Spaghetti e Broccoli di Rapa
  (Spaghetti and Broccoli Rabe
  Frittata), 150–51, *151*
Frittatas
  Onion, 145
  Rice and Zucchini, Baked, 148
  Spaghetti and Broccoli Rabe,
    150–51, *151*
Fritters, Chickpea, 27–28
Funghi Gratinati (Crumb-Crusted
  Baked Mushrooms), 209

G
Gamberi Oreganati (Shrimp Baked with
  Flavored Bread Crumbs), 159
Garbage Pail Thick Spaghetti, *112*, *113*
Garlic
  and Mint, Salt-seared Swordfish
    with, 164
  and olive oil pasta dishes, 125
  Pesto, Spaghetti with, from Marsala,
    121
  Spaghetti alla Carrettiere, 125
Gattò alla Gena (Gena's Potato Cake
  with Broccoli Rabe, Sausage, and
  Smoked Cheese), 216–17, *217*
Gelo di Melone (Watermelon Pudding),
    248–49
Giardiniera
  buying, 39
  and Tuna, Pickled Cherry Peppers
    Stuffed with, *38*, 39
Goat, in Southern Italian cuisine,
    170
Grains. *See* Rice; Wheat berries
Grappa, Ricotta Mousse with, 247
Greens
  arugula, about, 55
  and Bean Soup for the Feast of Saint
    Joseph, 77
  Fava Puree and Chicory, 202
  Pasta Disks with Shrimp, Fennel
    Seed, and Arugula, 123

H
Ham. *See also* Prosciutto
  and Cheese, Fried Zucchini Rolls
    with, 222
  Enrica's Chicken Salad, 68, 69
Hazelnut Crisps, 238–39

I
Insalata di Mare Napoletana
  (Neapolitan Seafood Salad),
    66–67
Insalata di Arance, Cipolle, e Olive
  (Orange and Onion Salad with
  Olives), 59
Insalata di Mare Trapanese (Seafood
  Salad, Trapani Style), 65
Insalata di Pollo alla Enrica (Enrica's
  Chicken Salad), 68, 69
Insalata di Pomodori (Tomato Salad),
    56, 57
Insalata Eoliana (Aeolian Salad), 58
Insalate, 55–56. *See also* Salads
Insalatina Sott'aceto (Pickled Carrot and
  Celery Root), 64
Involtini Crotonesi (Pork Rolls from
  Crotone), 183
Involtini di Zucchini Fritti (Fried
  Zucchini Rolls with Ham and
  Cheese), 222
Italy, Southern
  Basilicata, 16–17
  Calabria, 17
  Campania, 14
  cuisine of, 10–13
  history of, 8–10
  Molise, 14
  olive oil in, 11
  pasta and beans in, 12–13
  Puglia, 17
  Sicily, 14–16
  vegetables in, 12–13

J
Jam Tart, Sorrento-Style, 230–31,
    231

L
"*La Bella Baronessa*" *Fichi al Sciropo di
  Vino* (Figs in Wine Syrup), 245
Lagane e Ceci (Flat Pasta and
  Chickpeas), *104*, 105
Lamb
  Broth, 79
  Chops with Black Olives, 191
  Multi-Meat Ragù from Bari,
    Butcher's, 94
  in Southern Italian cuisine, 170
La Tasca ("The Pocket," Egg and
  Cheese Pie), 50
Lemon Risotto, Mamma Agata's, *134*,
    135
Lemony Egg Pasta Soufflé, 130–31
Lentil(s)
  and Pasta, Sicilian Style, *108*,
    109–10
  Soup with Sausage and Broccoli
    Rabe, 78
Linguine con Noce e Colatura (Linguine
  with Walnuts and *Colatura*), *102*,
    103
Lobster Broth with Broken Spaghetti,
    80–81
Lonza di Maiale alla Sorrentina (Pork
  Loin Roast, Sorrento Style),
    184–85, *185*

M

Maccheroni alla Diavolo (Macaroni with Eggplant, Fresh Sausage, and Dried Hot Sausage), 124

Maccheroni con Pesce Spada alla Franca Miceli (Franca Miceli's Macaroni with Swordfish), 127

Maccheroni con Zucchine e Ricotta (Macaroni with Zucchini and Ricotta), *118, 119*

Maccu di San Giuseppe (Bean and Greens Soup for the Feast of Saint Joseph), 77

Matalotta alla Siracusana (Fish Soup from Siracusa), 166

Meat. *See also* Beef; Lamb; Pork in Southern Italian cuisine, 170–71

Meatballs, 172–74, *173*

Meatloaf Baked in Vegetable Sauce, 176–77

Melanzane Impanata (Breaded Eggplant Slices), 206–7

Melanzane o Zucchine alla Griglia (Grilled and Marinated Eggplant or Zucchini), 204–5, *205*

Minestra e zuppa, 72–73. *See also* Soups

Mousse, Ricotta, with Grappa, 247

'Mpanatigghi (Chocolate and Beef Turnovers), 234–35

Mushroom(s)
Baked, Crumb-Crusted, 209
and Bean Soup, I Corti's, 76

Mussel(s)
Neapolitan Seafood Salad, 66–67
or Clams, Baked, 158
or Clams, Sauté of, *156,* 157
in Fish Soup, 167

N

'Ncapriata (Fava Puree and Chicory), 202

Neapolitan Seafood Salad, 66–67

Nuts
Almond Crunch Frozen Cream Dessert, 246
Aunt Delia's Date-Nut Cake, 233
Chocolate and Beef Turnovers, 234–35
Garbage Pail Thick Spaghetti, 112, *113*
Hazelnut Crisps, 238–39
Linguine with Walnuts and *Colatura, 102,* 103
Macaroni with Cauliflower, 116
Meatballs, 172–74, *173*
Ricotta Bavarian, *236,* 237
Shrimp and Pistachio Risotto, 136–37
Walnut Tart, 228

O

Oil
and garlic, pasta dishes with, 125
hot pepper, about, 73
Spaghetti alla Carrettiere, 125

Olive Fritte (Fried Olives), 22, *23*

Olive(s)
Baked Sweet and Sour Eggplant, 208
Black, Lamb Chops with, 191

and Capers, Sautéed Peppers with, 212
Eggplant Balls or Patties, 30–31, *31*
Filled Potato "Pizza," 40–41
Fish Soup from Siracusa, 166
Fried, 22, *23*
Garbage Pail Thick Spaghetti, 112, *113*
Orange and Onion Salad with, 59
Potatoes with Bay Leaf and Red Wine, *214,* 215
Smothered Cauliflower, 200–201
in Southern Italy, 29

Onion(s)
Frittata, 145
Spring, Grilled Pancetta or Pork on, 181
Sweet and Sour Tuna, 165

Orange and Onion Salad with Olives, 59

Orecchiette con Cime di Rapa (Orecchiette with Broccoli Rabe), 111

P

Paccheri con Zucca e Salsicce (Giant Pasta Tubes with Butternut Squash and Sausage), 120

Pancakes, Ricotta, *146,* 147

Pancetta or Pork, Grilled, on Spring Onions, 181

Panelle (Chickpea Fritters), 27–28

Pappucelle con Tonno e Giardiniera (Pickled Cherry Peppers Stuffed with Tuna and *Giardiniera),* 38, *39*

Pasta
Baked, Palermo Style, 132
and Beans, Baked, 106–7
broken spaghetti, about, 81
Ciceri e Trie, 104
cooked with garlic and olive oil, 125
Curly Ribbons with Raw Sauce of Tuna, Garlic, Tomatoes, and Basil, 122
Disks with Shrimp, Fennel Seed, and Arugula, 123
dried, cooking rules, 126
Egg, Soufflé, Lemony, 130–31
Flat, and Chickpeas, 104, *105*
Garbage Pail Thick Spaghetti, 112, *113*
Lamb Broth, 79
and Lentils, Sicilian Style, *108,* 109–10
Linguine with Walnuts and *Colatura, 102,* 103
Lobster Broth with Broken Spaghetti, 80–81
Macaroni with Cauliflower, 116
Macaroni with Eggplant, Fresh Sausage, and Dried Hot Sausage, 124
Macaroni with Swordfish, Franca Miceli's, 127
Macaroni with Zucchini and Ricotta, *118,* 119
Mista and Potatoes, Europeo di Mattozzi's, 114–15

Orecchiette with Broccoli Rabe, 111
with Ricotta, 101
in Southern Italian cuisine, 98–100
Spaghetti alla Carrettiere, 125
Spaghetti and Broccoli Rabe Frittata, 150–51, *151*
Spaghetti with Garlic Pesto from Marsala, 121
Spaghetti with Tuna and Marsala Sauce, 128, *129*
Tubes, Giant, with Butternut Squash and Sausage, 120

Pasta al Forno alla Palermitana (Baked Pasta, Palermo Style), 132

Pasta e Cavolfiore (Macaroni with Cauliflower), 116

Pasta e Fagioli al Forno (Baked Pasta and Beans), 106–7

Pasta e Lenticchie alla Siciliana (Pasta and Lentils, Sicilian Style), *108,* 109–10

Pasta e Patate all'Europeo di Mattozzi (Europeo di Mattozzi's Pasta Mista and Potatoes), 114–15

Pasta e Ricotta (Pasta with Ricotta), 101

Pasta Frolla (Short Pastry), 227

Pastiera (Easter Pie), 232

Pastry, Short, 227

Patate con Alloro e Vino Rosso (Potatoes with Bay Leaf and Red Wine), *214,* 215

Patate e Verza (Potatoes and Cabbage), 218

Peas, Sicilian Ground Meat Ragù with, 93

Peperoni Saltate con Olive e Capperi (Sautéed Peppers with Olives and Capers), 212

Pepper(s)
Baked Sweet and Sour Eggplant, 208
Cherry, Pickled, Stuffed with Tuna and *Giardiniera,* 38, *39*
hot, oil, about, 73
Red, Eggplant, and Onion Spread, *36, 37*
roasted, preparing, 213
roasted, serving ideas, 213
Sautéed, with Olives and Capers, 212
Summer Vegetable Sauté, 223

Pesce Spada a Ghiotta (Swordfish Gourmet Style), 161

Pesce Spada al Sale con Aglio e Menta (Salt-seared Swordfish with Garlic and Mint), 164

Pesto, Garlic, Spaghetti with, from Marsala, 121

Pickled Carrot and Celery Root, 64

Pies. *See also* Pizza
Easter, 232
Egg and Cheese, "The Pocket," 50
Savory Cheese, with Salami or Prosciutto, 48–49

Pine nuts
Macaroni with Cauliflower, 116
Meatballs, 172–74, *173*

Pistachio and Shrimp Risotto, 136–37

Pizza
Napoletano, *42,* 43–44

Rustica with Summer Vegetables, 49
Savory Cheese Pie with Salami or
  Prosciutto, 48–49
toppings, 46–47
"Pizza," Filled Potato, 40–41
Pizza Rustica dell'Orto (Pizza Rustica
  with Summer Vegetables), 49
Pizza Rustica (Savory Cheese Pie with
  Salami or Prosciutto), 48–49
Polpette alla Maria Talerico (Maria
  Talerico's Meat Cakes), 175
Polpette (Meatballs), 172–74, *173*
Polpette o Palle di Melanzane (Eggplant
  Balls or Patties), 30–31, *31*
Polpettone al Sugo di Verdure (Meatloaf
  Baked in Vegetable Sauce), 176–77
Pomodorini Schiaciatti (Smashed
  Tomatoes), *220, 221*
Pork. *See also* Ham; Sausage(s)
  cured, in Southern Italian cuisine,
    186
  Ground, Ragù with Chocolate,
    Enna's, 95
  Loin Roast, Sorrento Style, 184–85,
    185
  Maria Talerico's Meat Cakes, 175
  Multi-Meat Ragù from Bari,
    Butcher's Ragù, 94
  or Pancetta, Grilled, on Spring
    Onions, 181
  Ribs in a Skillet, 182
  Rolls from Crotone, 183
  Sauce or Ragù, 89
Potato(es)
  Aeolian Salad, 58
  with Bay Leaf and Red Wine, *214,*
    215
  and Cabbage, 218
  Cake, Gena's, with Broccoli Rabe,
    Sausage, and Smoked Cheese,
    216–17, *217*
  Doughnuts, Barbara's, *242,* 243–44
  Enrica's Chicken Salad, 68, 69
  and Pasta Mista, Europeo di
    Mattaozzi's, 114–15
  "Pizza," Filled, 40–41
  Sausage in Sauce with, 92
  Sausages Baked with, 187
Poultry. *See* Chicken
Prosciutto
  about, 186
  or Salami, Savory Cheese Pie with,
    48–49
  Stuffed Sicilian Beef Roll, 178–79
Pudding, Watermelon, 248–49
Pummarulo (Tomato Sauce), 86–88, *87*
Puntine di Maiale in Padella (Pork Ribs
  in a Skillet), 182

R

Ragù Barese, Ragù di Macelleria (Multi-
  Meat Ragù from Bari, Butcher's
  Ragù), 94
Ragù Ennese (Enna's Ground Pork Ragù
  with Chocolate), 95
Ragù Siciliano con Piselli (Sicilian
  Ground Meat Ragù with Peas),
  93

*Reginette alla Matarocco di Barbara
  Rosolia* (Curly Ribbons with Raw
  Sauce of Tuna, Garlic, Tomatoes,
  and Basil), 122
Rice
  Balls, Sicilian, Filled with Ragù,
    24–25, *25*
  Mamma Agata's Lemon Risotto,
    134, 135
  Risotto with Sausage and Smoked
    Cheese, 133
  Shrimp and Pistachio Risotto,
    136–37
  Timbales, Filled, 138–39
  and Zucchini Frittata, Baked, 148
Ricotta
  Bavarian, *236, 237*
  Easter Pie, 232
  Mousse with Grappa, 247
  Pancakes, *146, 147*
  Pasta with, 101
  and Zucchini, Macaroni with, *118,*
    119
Risotto
  Lemon, Mamma Agata's, *134, 135*
  with Sausage and Smoked Cheese,
    133
  Shrimp and Pistachio, 136–37
Risotto alla Temptation (Shrimp and
  Pistachio Risotto), 136–37
Risotto al Limone (Mamma Agata's
  Lemon Risotto), *134, 135*
*Risotto con Lucaneca e Scamorza
  Affumicata* (Risotto with Sausage
  and Smoked Cheese), 133

S

Salads
  Aeolian, 58
  Bread and Tomato, 60, *61*–62
  Chicken, Enrica's, 68, 69
  Orange and Onion, with Olives, 59
  Pickled Carrot and Celery Root, 64
  Seafood, Neapolitan, 66–67
  Seafood, Trapani Style, 65
  Tomato, 56, *57*
Salami or Prosciutto, Savory Cheese
  Pie with, 48–49
Salsicce al Forno con Patate (Sausage
  Baked with Potatoes), 187
Salsicce alla Griglia (Grilled Sausage),
  190, *190*
Salsicce al Ragù con Patate (Sausage in
  Sauce with Potatoes), 92
Salsicce con Broccoli di Rapa (Sausage
  with Broccoli Rabe), 188
Salsicce in Padella (Sausage in a Skillet),
  190
Salumi, 186
Sartu (Filled Rice Timbales), 138–39
Sauces. *See also* Pasta.
  Enna's Ground Pork Ragù with
    Chocolate, 95
  Multi-Meat Ragù from Bari,
    Butcher's Ragù, 94
  Pork, or Ragù, 89
  Sausage in Sauce with Potatoes,
    92

Sicilian Ground Meat Ragù with
    Peas, 93
  Tomato, 86–88, *87*
  Tomato, Baked, 91
Sausage(s)
  Baked with Potatoes, 187
  Broccoli Rabe, and Smoked Cheese,
    Gena's Potato Cake with, 216–17,
    217
  and Broccoli Rabe, Lentil Soup
    with, 78
  with Broccoli Rabe, 188
  and Butternut Squash, Giant Pasta
    Tubes with, 120
  Canapés, *32, 33*
  Fresh, Eggplant, and Dried Hot
    Sausage, Macaroni with, 124
  Grilled, 190, *190*
  Multi-Meat Ragù from Bari,
    Butcher's Ragù, 94
  in Sauce with Potatoes, 92
  Savory Cheese Pie with Salami or
    Prosciutto, 48–49
  in a Skillet, 190
  and Smoked Cheese, Risotto with,
    133
  in Southern Italian cuisine, 170, 186
  Stuffed Sicilian Beef Roll, 178–79
Sauté di Vongole o Cozze (Sauté of
  Clams or Mussels), *156, 157*
Scamorza alla Griglia (Grilled Cheese),
  144, *144*
Seafood. *See also* Fish; Shellfish
  Salad, Neapolitan, 66–67
  Salad, Trapani Style, 65
Semifreddo con Croccante (Almond
  Crunch Frozen Cream Dessert),
  246
Shellfish. *See also* Shrimp
  Baked Mussels or Clams, 158
  Fish or Mussel Soup, 167
  Lobster Broth with Broken
    Spaghetti, 80–81
  Neapolitan Seafood Salad, 66–67
  Pasta Disks with Shrimp, Fennel
    Seed, and Arugula, 123
  Sauté of Clams or Mussels, *156, 157*
  Seafood Salad, Trapani Style, 65
  in Southern Italian cuisine, 154–55
Shrimp
  Baked with Flavored Bread Crumbs,
    159
  Fennel Seed, and Arugula, Pasta
    Disks with, 123
  Neapolitan Seafood Salad, 66–67
  and Onion, Grilled, on Skewers, 160
  and Pistachio Risotto, 136–37
  Seafood Salad, Trapani Style, 65
  in Southern Italian cuisine, 155
Soufflé, Lemony Egg Pasta, 130–31
Soufflé di Tagliarini al Limone (Lemony
  Egg Pasta Soufflé), 130–31
Soups. *See also* Stews
  Acquacotta, 74, 75
  Bean and Greens, for the Feast of
    Saint Joseph, 77
  Bean and Mushroom, I Corti's, 76
  Lamb Broth, 79

Soups (*continued*)
  Lentil, with Sausage and Broccoli
    Rabe, 78
  Lobster Broth with Broken
    Spaghetti, 80–81
  Pancotto, 74
Spaghetti alla Carrettiere, 125
Spaghetti alla Matarocco (Spaghetti with
    Garlic Pesto from Marsala), 121
Spaghetti con Ragù di Tonno e Marsala
    (Spaghetti with Tuna and Marsala
    Sauce), 128, *129*
Spaghettoni all'Setaccio dell' Immondizia
    (Garbage Pail Thick Spaghetti),
    112, *113*
Spiedini di Gamberi e Cipolle (Grilled
    Shrimp and Onion on Skewers),
    160
Spread, Eggplant, Red Pepper, and
    Onion, 36, 37
Spuma di Ricotta con Grappa (Ricotta
    Mousse with Grappa), 247
Squash. *See also* Zucchini
  Butternut, and Sausage, Giant Pasta
    Tubes with, 120
  Butternut, Grilled and Marinated,
    219
Stews
  Fish or Mussel Soup, 167
  Fish Soup from Siracusa, 166
Stigghiole di Pancetta (Grilled Pancetta
    or Pork on Spring Onions), 181
Strascinati alla Crotone (Pasta Disks
    with Shrimp, Fennel Seed, and
    Arugula), 123
Stuzzico (Eggplant, Red Pepper, and
    Onion Spread), 36, 37
Sugo di Maiale (Pork Sauce or Ragù), 89
Sugo di Pomodoro (Tomato Sauce),
    86–88, *87*
Sugo Gratinato (Baked Tomato Sauce),
    91
Sweets
  Almond Crunch Frozen Cream
    Dessert, 246
  Apple Cake, 240–41
  Aunt Delia's Date-Nut Cake, 233
  Barbara's Potato Doughnuts, *242*,
    243–44
  Chocolate and Beef Turnovers,
    234–35
  Easter Pie, 232
  Figs in Wine Syrup, 245
  Hazelnut Crisps, 238–39
  Ricotta Bavarian, *236*, 237
  Ricotta Mousse with Grappa, 247
  Short Pastry, 227
  Sorrento-Style Jam Tart, 230–31, *231*

in Southern Italian cuisine, 226
Walnut Tart, 228
Watermelon Pudding, 248–49
Swordfish
  Breaded Palermo Style, 162, *163*
  Gourmet Style, 161
  Macaroni with, Franca Miceli's, 127
  Salt-seared, with Garlic and Mint,
    164

T
Tarts
  Jam, Sorrento-Style, 230–31, *231*
  Walnut, 228
Tomato(es)
  Acquacotta, 74, *75*
  Baked Sweet and Sour Eggplant, 208
  and Bread Salad, 60, *61*–62
  Eggs in Purgatory, 149
  Enna's Ground Pork Ragù with
    Chocolate, 95
  Filled Potato "Pizza," 40–41
  Fish or Mussel Soup, 167
  Italian canned, buying, 85
  Lobster Broth with Broken
    Spaghetti, 80–81
  Meatloaf Baked in Vegetable Sauce,
    176–77
  Pasta and Lentils, Sicilian Style, *108*,
    109–10
  paste, about, 88
  Pork Sauce or Ragù, 89
  Salad, 56, *57*
  Sauce, 86–88, *87*
  Sauce, Baked, 91
  sauce, in Southern Italian cuisine,
    84–85
  Sausage in Sauce with Potatoes, 92
  Sicilian Ground Meat Ragù with
    Peas, 93
  Smashed, *220*, 221
  Spaghetti with Garlic Pesto from
    Marsala, 121
  Sun-Dried, Fennel Braised with,
    210–11
  Tuna, Garlic, and Basil, Raw Sauce
    of, with Curly Ribbons, 122
Tonno Agro Dolce (Sweet and Sour
    Tuna), 165
Torta di Frutta Secca di Zia Delia (Aunt
    Delia's Date-Nut Cake), 233
Torta di Mele (Apple Cake), 240–41
Torta di Noci (Walnut Tart), 228
Tuna
  Aeolian Salad, 58
  Garlic, Tomatoes, and Basil, Raw
    Sauce of, with Curly Ribbons,
    122

and *Giardiniera*, Pickled Cherry
    Peppers Stuffed with, 38, 39
  and Marsala Sauce, Spaghetti with,
    128, *129*
  Sweet and Sour, 165
Turnovers, Chocolate and Beef, 234–35

U
Uova in Purgatorio (Eggs in Purgatory),
    149
Uova 'mpriatorio (Eggs in Purgatory),
    149

V
Veal, in Southern Italian cuisine, 171
Vegetable(s)
  giardiniera, buying, 39
  oil-preserved and pickled, 26
  Sauce, Meatloaf Baked in, 176–77
  in Southern Italian cuisine, 196
  Summer, Pizza Rustica with, 49
  Summer, Sauté, 223

W
Walnut(s)
  Aunt Delia's Date-Nut Cake, 233
  and *Colatura*, Linguine with, *102*,
    103
  Tart, 228
Watermelon Pudding, 248–49
Wheat berries
  Easter Pie, 232
Wine Syrup, Figs in, 245

Z
Zeppole di Patate di Barbara (Barbara's
    Potato Doughnuts), *242*, 243–44
Zucca Gialla alla Griglia (Grilled and
    Marinated Butternut Squash), 219
Zucchini
  Meatloaf Baked in Vegetable Sauce,
    176–77
  or Eggplant, Grilled and Marinated,
    204–5, *205*
  and Rice Frittata, Baked, 148
  and Ricotta, Macaroni with, *118*, 119
  Rolls, Fried, with Ham and Cheese,
    222
  Summer Vegetable Sauté, 223
Zuppa di Fagioli e Funghi alla I Corti
    (I Corti's Bean and Mushroom
    Soup), 76
*Zuppa di Lenticchie con Salsicce e
    Broccoli di Rapa* (Lentil Soup with
    Sausage and Broccoli Rabe), 78
Zuppa di Pesce o Frutti di Mare (Fish or
    Mussel Soup), 167

DATE			